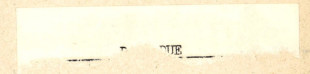

KEEPER OF THE KEYS

A LIFE OF POPE PIUS XII

Catherine Britt

San Mateo, Calif.

August Selection
1946

KEEPER of the KEYS

A LIFE OF
POPE PIUS XII

By Thomas McDermott

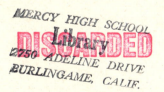

THE BRUCE PUBLISHING COMPANY
Milwaukee

Copyright, 1946
Thomas McDermott
Printed in the United States of America

To My Mother
Estella Busby McDermott
in Honor of
Her Seventieth Year
and in Gratitude for
Her Prayerful Life
of Sacrifice

CONTENTS

AUTHOR'S PREFACE

RICHELIEU once boasted: "If you give me six lines written by the hand of the most honest man, I will find something in them with which to hang him." While the practice of hanging authors is today outmoded, the hangman lives on in the disguise of censorious readers and captious critics. To defend to them KEEPER OF THE KEYS and to explain to everyone my reasons for writing it will be the objective of this preface.

KEEPER OF THE KEYS is not a definitive biography of Pius XII, because the restricted status of the biographical material and the happy fact that the story is not closed make such presently impossible. The lack of criticism and the paucity of praise which tend to make this work more a chronicle and less a biography have two sufficient reasons. First, praise and blame ought to be given a living person with scrupulous caution because the events of tomorrow and a fuller knowledge of yesterday may qualify the judgments of today. As a painting cannot be correctly valued until finished and framed, the life of Pius XII will be rightfully judged only after his death and in historical retrospect. Second, the biographer of a living person and leader ought to be delicately concerned lest he impede the mission and work of his subject by critical comment, which cannot be validated. Thus, while the pope is not divinely safeguarded from error in matters of international diplomacy, administration, and ecclesiastical appointments, the serious biographer will be cautious in criticizing *seeming* mistakes unless some good can come from the criticism.

Finally, I have shunned with scorn the psychoanalytic approach, which is the fetish of modern biographers. An individual is always a wall to himself. How can he be a window to another?

My reasons for writing KEEPER OF THE KEYS were many, but two are of determining importance. It is my hope that the life and the teaching of Pius XII will arouse Catholics and non-Catholics to remove from their personal lives the causes of war so that national and international life can lay the bases of peace. The individual, and not the nations and their leaders, is chiefly and ultimately responsible for peace or war, because the causes of war and the bases of peace are fundamentally of the moral, rather than the social, economic, or political, order. It is especially my hope that Catholics will learn from the life and the teaching of the Holy Father to grant every American and every man the justice and charity which is his right and our duty. No Catholic, without scorning the commands of Pius XII, may be anti-Negro, anti-Jew, anti-German, or anti-anyone. Anachronistic as it may seem to many, justice and charity are still the first and the absolute prerequisites of a peaceful tomorrow.

THOMAS McDERMOTT

KEEPER OF THE KEYS
A LIFE OF POPE PIUS XII

CHAPTER I

"WE HAVE A POPE"

A S THE gray twilight of March 1, 1939, cast Rome and Vatican City into changing patterns of lights and shadows, a muted bell rang thrice from the courtyard of St. Damasus in the palace of the popes. Past the murals of Raphael, the frescoes of Mantegna, and the tapestries of Ghent and Arras, hurried Swiss Guards calling *"Extra Omnes"* — All out. The heavy bronze gate of the courtyard, through which today's world and yesterday's centuries had come to the Vatican, clanged shut, and Prince Louis Chigi, grand master of the Knights of Malta and hereditary marshal of the Conclave, turned the keys in the gate's three outer locks. The papal flag at the top of the Royal Staircase, built by Bernini, was lowered, and the Chigi banner of crimson silk was raised into the silent air. Again, as at every papal election since 1721, the illustrious Roman family of the Chigis would guard the Conclave against the world's intrusion and interference.

Slim tapered hands with a diamond-encrusted sapphire on the right third finger gravely turned the keys in the gate's three inner locks. They are the hands of a tall spare man whose dark eyes glow with an inner fire of intense spirituality. The long sharp face, the firm square jaw, the thin taut lips, and the narrow, slightly curved nose cannot cloak with severity the gentle kindness that emanates from them. A red skullcap covers dark brown hair now graying with the time and troubles of nearly sixty-three years; and a violet cassock (the color of mourning worn by cardinals for a deceased pope) falls in stately folds from straight square shoulders. Today he is Eugenio Cardinal Pacelli, Camerlengo of the holy Roman Church, charged with the guidance and protection of Peter's Bark while the post of helmsman is vacant. Until February 10, the day that Pius XI died blessing him and the world, he had been Papal Secretary of State entrusted with the diplomatic affairs of the Holy See. Tomorrow he would be an elector of the Sacred College of Cardinals, burdened with the momentous task of choosing a successor to Pius XI.

Escorted by Swiss Guards in the black, red, and yellow uniforms which Michelangelo designed in the sixteenth century, Cardinal Pacelli crossed the courtyard and entered the City of the Conclave. It was truly a city, for an entire section of the Vatican Palace, three stories high and including the Sistine and Pauline Chapels, had been closed off with movable soundproof walls. At a cost of more than $100,000 carpenters, under the direction of Count Enrico Galeazzi, Vatican architect and representative of the Knights of Columbus in Rome, had divided this section into a series of apartments and servants' quarters. The apartments were then subdivided into three or four cells or small rooms, in each of which were placed a crucifix, a bed, a table, and a few chairs.

Within these apartments the cardinal-electors and their secretaries would live until a successor to Pius XI was chosen. The cells of the cardinals were lined with green cloth (at previous conclaves cloth of purple indicated the cells of the cardinals who had been appointed by the deceased pope) , and the doors to their cells were fashioned in the shape of a St. Andrew's cross. All the windows had been boarded up, and the glass panes in the doors had been blackened with paint. Telephone lines had been cut, and the entrances had been locked and sealed. Access to the Conclave (the word is from two Latin words: *cum,* meaning "with," and *clavis,* meaning a "key") would be through one door only, which would be locked from without by Marshal Chigi and from within by Cardinal Pacelli. Into this door had been inserted a turn-table pane, similar to that used in cloistered convents, through which food, urgent messages, and letters could be passed. Guarded every hour of the Conclave, the door would be opened only if one of the cardinals should arrive late or be obliged to leave because of illness.

Besides the cardinal-electors there would be present at the Conclave their conclavists, the secretary and valet allowed each cardinal, and Vatican guards, cooks, waiters, physicians, and other servants, in all, three hundred persons. The lives, characters, and political affiliations and interests of these persons had been minutely scrutinized by a committee of cardinals. World conditions and the intrigues of certain secular powers had made this necessary. On the preceding day, February 27, before the high altar of the Sistine Chapel Cardinal Pacelli had administered an oath of secrecy to the conclavists and the various servants and attendants. They were forbidden, under pain of solemn excommunication, to communicate or attempt to communicate with the outside world during the period of the Conclave. Under like penalty, they were prohibited from revealing later anything that they might have learned in the Conclave. At the close of the Conclave the conclavists would be honored with papal distinctions, and the servants and others would be rewarded with money.

Accompanied by Cardinal Di Belmonte, Dean of the Cardinal Bishops, Cardinal Caccia Dominioni, Dean of the Cardinal Deacons, and Cardinal O'Connell, Archbishop of Boston and Dean of the Cardinal Priests, Cardinal Pacelli, carrying a lighted torch, proceeded to a thorough search of the Conclave to make certain no unauthorized person was present. The three cardinal deans and the Camerlengo had governed the Church since the death of Pius XI. They had been assisted in their administration by a committee of three other cardinals, whose membership changed daily. The government of the Conclave also would be in the hands of these four cardinals, assisted by three others who would succeed one another in order of seniority every three days. After the search, Cardinal Pacelli locked and sealed the Conclave door, and retired to his cell.

Assembled in the City of the Conclave were sixty-two cardinals from fifteen nations. By ship from distant continents, by train from neighboring nations, by automobile from Rome and suburban cities, they had come to the Vatican. None had come by airplane, as Pius XI had predicted they would to Cardinal Ceretti: "You cardinals will probably fly to the next Conclave, while I wing my way by other means and in another direction." Cardinal O'Connell, vacationing in the Bahamas when Pius died, flew to Florida but there transferred to a fast coast steamer which brought him to New York in sufficient time to obtain passage on the *Saturnia*. From Naples he journeyed by special train to Rome, arriving in the early afternoon of March 1. Twice before Cardinal O'Connell had arrived too late to cast his vote in a papal election. When the cardinals assembled to select a successor to Benedict XV,

Cardinal O'Connell hastened across the Atlantic by the fastest liner, but he reached Rome just when the election of Pius XI was being announced to the people. In his first audience with the Pope, the Cardinal asked, and the new Holy Father ordered that the time for the assembling of cardinals for an election be extended from ten to eighteen days. Cardinal Mundelein of Chicago and Cardinal Dougherty of Philadelphia, sailing together from New York immediately upon the death of Pius, had arrived in Rome ten days before the Conclave.

At nine o'clock on the morning of March 1, the cardinal-electors had attended the Mass of the Holy Ghost, sung by Cardinal Di Belmonte in the Pauline Chapel, which is the traditional church of the papal household. Monsignor Antonio Bacci, Secretary of Letters to Rulers, preached a moving sermon on the responsibility of electing a new pope. Reminding the cardinals of their obligation quickly to give the Church her ablest son as ruler, he exhorted them to remember that the Vicar of Christ must be first and especially a man of prayer and good works. The world, he declared, would measure their choice in terms of knowledge and ability, but the Church would ask only if he was a saint.

On the chapel's walls are frescoes by Michelangelo of the conversion of St. Paul and the crucifixion of St. Peter. Peter had been the first pope, and Paul had been the first great convert to enter the newborn Church. These two princes of the Apostles had toiled, suffered, and died for their Master. The new Peter must be willing to do no less, if he would be worthy of them. The century is new, but the problems and the enemies from within and without are the same as when Paul rode horseback to Damascus and Peter died in Rome.

In the afternoon the cardinals had assembled in the Sistine Chapel to take the customary Conclave oath. They swore to obey the papal regulations governing the Conclave, to safeguard the Church's interests, and to vote as conscience dictated. Among the regulations is the excellent one forbidding the cardinals to discuss among themselves the papal succession during the pope's lifetime. By the same laws the cardinals are prohibited from imposing any conditions upon their choice for the papacy. The oath-taking completed, each cardinal was escorted from the chapel to his cell by a Noble Guard.

Of the cardinal-electors present thirty-four were Italian, eight short of the necessary two-thirds majority. There were three cardinals from the United States, one each from Canada, Brazil, and Argentina. Ireland, Portugal, Belgium, Poland, England, Czechoslovakia had each a cardinal-elector. From France, Germany, Austria, Hungary, Spain, and Iraq had come cardinals. In Rome there were a number of foreign cardinals at the head of religious orders and papal departments and bureaus. The non-Italian cardinals numbered twenty-eight. Therefore the curious wondered and the secular press speculated whether or not a non-Italian pope would be elected. The last one was the Hollander Adrian VI, elected in 1522.

The assembled cardinals, however, were not considering the two hundred and sixty-second successor of St. Peter in terms of his nationality. It was the year 1939, and historians would have to turn back to the year 1560, when the cardinals assembled to elect a pope to battle the rising tide of Protestantism, to find a more important and crucial Conclave. Blinded by sin and bewildered by falsehood, the world was stumbling toward war. Some nations and a few men wanted war, and all would be responsible for its coming. For twenty years God had sat in the corner, but He would remain there no longer. His commandments all men had broken, His teachings most men had scorned, and His Church many nations had persecuted. The hour of mercy was passing and justice was soon to come into her own.

The war would be a punishment for many sins. Private and public immorality had become the rule rather than the exception. Public morality in France was on the level of the "French" novel. Economic and political injustice manacled and defiled God's children. England ruled a quarter of the globe — her citizens by the millions decayed on the dole; and her subjects of India and other crown colonies were repressed and exploited. Brutal persecution and subtle opposition sought to crush and hobble the Church. Hitler's concentration camps, modern Golgothas, held thousands of the clergy and laity; Mussolini's organizations were paganizing the rising generation of Italy. Stalin had "removed" the clergy of Russia by firing squads and now worked to remove the God of Russia by atheistic propaganda. Errors and falsehoods were leading men everywhere into the bogs of idolatry and self-worship. American education was teaching youth how to live without grace; and American publications were polluting the wellsprings of tomorrow with materialism and gilded immorality.

What sort of man, then, was needed for this crucial point of the Church's history? Cardinal Faulhaber of Bavaria, whose episcopal mansion had been looted by Nazi thugs, asked himself: "Who among us has the knowledge to understand and the character to resist the new paganism of force and blood now engulfing the world?" The Prefect of the Propaganda of the Faith, Cardinal

Fumasoni Biondi, who had been Apostolic Delegate to the United States, besought God to enlighten him to vote for a truly Christlike shepherd. Cardinal Jean Verdier, Archbishop of Paris, knowing that Europe would soon shake to the tramp of marching hordes, realized that the new Peter must be as wise as the fox and as simple as the dove so that peace might be retained and, if lost, might be regained. Meditating on the moral hypocrisy of his countrymen, Cardinal Mundelein of Chicago sought in ceaseless prayer the name of the Holy Father who might remove the scales of their spiritual blindness.

In cell numbered thirteen knelt Eugenio Pacelli, to whom rumor pointed as the next pope. A quarter of a century ago in a German prison camp, a French soldier had expressed the hope that for the sake of humanity and religion the kindly Nuncio Pacelli, who had just visited and talked with him and his fellow prisoners, would one day be pope. On entering the Conclave, Cardinal Pacelli remarked to Cardinal Kaspar, Primate of Czechoslovakia, that he would vacation in the Alps as soon as the election was over. To which the Czech Cardinal knowingly replied, "Well, Your Eminence, we shall see what happens."

For varying reasons and from various motives the world without intently watched the Conclave. The faithful, confident in God and the cardinals, awaited only his name to cheer and revere the new Holy Father. Hitler, whose *Das Schwarze Corps,* news organ of the Gestapo, had blacklisted Cardinal Pacelli as anti-Nazi, wondered if the cardinals would elect a pope as ruthlessly opposed to Nazi paganism as had been Pius XI. Mussolini, who greeted the death of Pius airily with, "That old man is dead," knew and feared Cardinal Pacelli as the support of the late Pope in his attacks on Fascist racialism and other totalitarian doctrines. France, England, and the United States were confident that the cardinals would elect a pope who would continue to oppose the paganism of the forces seeking to enslave the world. Stalin, whose antihuman Communism had been a constant object of attack by Pius XI, showed little interest in the papal election.

At seven o'clock on the morning of March 2, servants awakened the cardinals with shouts of, "Arise, my lords, and pray." At previous Conclaves the cardinals had not been permitted to celebrate Mass, but assisted at the Mass of the dean of the Cardinal Bishops and from him received Holy Communion. Pius XI, however, abolished this rule; and all the cardinals who could celebrated Mass that morning at altars erected in the Sistine Chapel and the Sala Ducale.

Mass finished, the cardinals returned to their cells for breakfast. Then the rain, falling since early morning, broke into a glorious rainbow which painted with a thousand hues the palace roofs and spires. The shepherd-less flock huddled in the Square of St. Peter's quickly inter-preted the rainbow to mean that an angelic pastor would succeed to the throne of the popes. According to the prophecy of St. Malachy, the successor to Pius XI would be *Pastor Angelicus,* the Angelic Shepherd. When Cardinal Pacelli visited the Shrine of Lourdes in 1935, the devout pilgrims hailed him with reverent shouts of *"L'Ange! L'Ange!"* which in English would be "The Angel."

The prophecy of St. Malachy is interesting enough to justify a brief digression here. In 1139 St. Malachy came to Rome to report on the affairs of his Diocese of Armagh, Ireland, to Pope Innocent II. While at Rome he received a vision of the future wherein was unfolded a long list of illustrious popes who would govern the Church to the end of time. Malachy recorded his vision and gave the document to Pope Innocent to console him in the midst of his tribulations. For four hundred years the document remained unknown, gathering dust in the Vatican archives. By chance it was uncovered in 1590 and was immediately published.

One hundred and twelve short prophecies were written down by St. Malachy. They indicate some noticeable characteristic of certain popes from Celestine II, who succeeded Innocent in 1143, until the end of the world. The future popes are foretold by means of various symbols, such as their country, their name as pope, their insignia or coat of arms, the title of their cardinalate, the predominant note of their personality, or the most memorable achievement of their reign. The prophecy concerning Urban VIII, for instance, is the lily and the rose. He was a native of Florence on whose banner is the fleur-de-lis, and he had emblazoned on his own coat of arms three bees, and the bees gather honey from the lily and the rose. Leo XIII was termed "Burning Fire," and surely his zeal for the Church burned brighter than any flame. Pius XI was listed as the Pope of the Reconciliation, and he brought about the Lateran Treaty which reconciled Italy with the Church. The last pope will be Peter the Roman, who will feed his flock amid many trials and sorrows and will witness the destruction of the world. However, the Prophecy of St. Malachy does not limit the popes to one hundred and twelve from Celestine II to Peter the Roman. Between the last and his predecessor in the list, *Gloria Olivae* (Glory of the Olive Tree), room was left for many others not described.

Is the prophecy of St. Malachy true, or is it merely an

interesting fiction? The Church has never indicated her approval or disapproval of the saintly Irishman's prophecy, and in all likelihood never will. Prophecy or no, the Holy Ghost will always provide for Peter's Bark an able helmsman. There is, of course, no harm in believing the prophecy, and up to this time it seems to have been remarkably accurate. There is something more than coincidence in the designation given to Pius XI's successor, so many hundreds of years before his election.

At nine-thirty, the cardinals were summoned by the shout, *"Ad capellam, Reverendissimi Domini"* — To the chapel, Most Reverend Lords. Wearing their violet cassocks, hooded mozettas, and lace rochets, the cardinals took their places in the Sistine Chapel, where papal ceremonies and elections are usually held. They were accompanied by their secretaries bearing portfolios and writing materials.

The chapel, one hundred and thirty-three feet long and forty-six feet wide, was built between 1473 and 1481 by Giovanni de'Dolci during the pontificate of Sixtus IV, after whom it is named. Intricate marble grillwork separates the lower third of the chapel from the rest, and divides the space reserved for honored guests from that for the pope and the cardinals. A marble balustrade on the right, or Epistle, side encloses a box for the famous Sistine choir. The frescoes of Perugino, Botticelli, Di Cosimo, and other Umbrian and Florentine painters depict on the Gospel side scenes from the life of Christ. On the ceiling and the rear wall are the frescoes of Michelangelo which have made the Sistine Chapel the glory of the Vatican and the envy of the world. Creation, the fall, and the preparation for the coming of the Redeemer form the subject of the ceiling fresco. The history of sinful man as far as Noe is vividly recorded. The ancestors of Christ from Adam to Joseph are represented. The prophets of God and the soothsayers of paganism are immortalized in incomparable artistry.

The ceiling fresco silenced his carping critics, but the "Last Judgment" on the rear altar wall gained for Michelangelo the epitaph found on his monument in the Church of the Holy Apostles in Rome: "No praise is sufficient for so great a man." This painting covers the entire wall except for a small door on the right which leads to the sacristy. Christ, a huge towering figure, is depicted as the God of justice come to judge the sinful world for the last time. On each side of him are the saints and the blessed who have gained heaven by losing earth. Below him are the devils and the damned who have lost heaven by gaining earth. And among the damned is a figure upon which the cardinal-electors could gaze with fear — a cardinal in full prelatial robes who, though a prince of the Church and an elector of the pope, had failed to save his own soul and had lost all. Michelangelo used as his model a certain Roman cardinal for whom he had a great dislike. The angry cardinal, who was being twitted by all Rome on his sudden damnation, demanded that the pope order the artist to change the fresco. The amused pontiff replied: "My dear Cardinal, are you unaware of the Catholic doctrine that out of hell there is no redemption?"

Along the side walls temporary thrones had been erected, covered with canopies to indicate that the supreme rule of the Church was now in the hands of the cardinals. Before each throne stood a small writing desk draped in green. Six tall candles burned on the altar, upon which rested the gold paten and chalice to be used in the voting. After prayers said by the bishop sacristan, ballots were distributed and all except the cardinals withdrew. The doors were bolted from the inside. The election to select a successor to Pope Pius XI had begun.

Whom may the cardinals elect pope? Although since the election of Urban VI in 1378 nobody but a cardinal has been elected pope, no law of the Church reserves the right to the cardinals. Any male Catholic who has reached the age of reason and is not a heretic (one who denies some fundamental doctrine of faith or morals) nor a schismatic (one who accepts all doctrines of faith and morals but refuses to obey the pope in other matters) may be elected pope. Celestine V was a layman and Martin V was a cleric in minor orders at the time of their election. While there is no instance of such, except St. Peter, even a married man may be pope. Of course, a layman or a cleric not a bishop would have to be ordained and consecrated, because the pope must be the bishop of Rome.

By what procedure is a pope elected? During the early ages of the Church the bishopric of Peter was filled in the same manner as other bishoprics, that is, the election was made by the neighboring bishops and the clergy and the faithful. Usually a semiformal procedure was followed whereby the bishops and the clergy would vote in private and then submit their choice to the faithful for approval or rejection. At times the election of a new pope was spontaneous and inspired. When Pope Pelagius II died in 590, the people and the clergy of Rome as one rushed to the near-by Benedictine Abbey of St. Andrew to proclaim its saintly abbot Pope Gregory I. These methods were eminently successful for many centuries, as the long line of sainted and martyr popes attests. But later the Roman and, after them, the Frankish emperors and other kings and nobles began to interfere in papal elections, forcing the Roman clergy to vote for their favorites.

To end these abuses and to prevent the election of unworthy or incompetent popes, Pope Nicholas II in 1059 issued an epoch-making decree, according to which the cardinals were actually to elect the pope and were then to secure the approval of the Roman clergy and people. A simple majority of the votes cast by the cardinals elected. Alexander II, successor to Pope Nicholas, was the first to be elected in this manner. The Lateran Council of 1139 made it unnecessary for the cardinals to secure the consent of the Roman clergy and people. Alexander III in 1179 enacted the present rule that the pope is to be chosen by a two-thirds majority of the cardinals voting.*

Until 1274 the cardinals had not met in Conclave, but had elected the pope in the free and unrestricted manner of a national political convention. Pope Clement IV died in 1268, but two years and nine months later the cardinals were still balloting. Finally the mayor and the people of Viterbo, where the election was being held, rounded up the cardinals, locked them in the episcopal palace, and drastically limited their daily allowance of food. When the debating and balloting still continued, the people proceeded to take the roof off the palace. The cardinals quickly elected Gregory X. Appreciating the wisdom of the mayor and his people, the Second Council of Lyons in 1274 decreed that on the tenth day after the pope's death the cardinals should assemble in one house in the city where the pope died, and there hold an electoral meeting entirely cut off from all out-

---

*A new constitution on papal elections, issued early in 1946, provides that a majority of two thirds plus one is needed for election.

side influence. If they did not agree on a candidate by the third day, their food was to be lessened, with another reduction after a further delay of five days. Eventually their menu would be one of bread and water. This is the origin of the Conclave.

Many people wonder why the cardinals alone have the power to elect the pope. Though forbidden to do so by papal regulations, the pope could change these and appoint his successor. It is said, but not with convincing proof, that in past ages this was done. A council of all the bishops could be called to elect the new pope. The Council of Constance in 1414 elected Martin V. However, the history, the character, and the importance of the Sacred College of Cardinals have made its members the most worthy and competent electors of the pope.

In the early days of the Church a priest permanently attached to an important church was called a cardinal, in Latin *cardinalis*. The title is from the Latin *cardo*, meaning a hinge, which was a common ecclesiastical classification for an important church. In time the term *cardinalis* became the equivalent of the term *principalis*, which means excellent or superior. Eventually the term "cardinal" came to be limited to clergymen who, because of their position or work, were considered outstanding and important.

In early Christian days there were three groups of clergymen whose position and work made them worthy of the title "cardinal." The first of these included the pastors of various important churches in Rome and near-by cities. They were called cardinal priests. Early Christian Rome was divided into seven regions, each presided over by a deacon whose duty it was to feed the poor and to care for the orphaned and the homeless. They were called the cardinal deacons. In the immediate vicinity of Rome are six dioceses, Ostia, Porto, Sabina, Palestrina, Frascati, and Rufina. The early popes frequently called upon the bishops of these dioceses for advice on various problems and for assistance at ecclesiastical functions. They are called the cardinal bishops.

With the passage of centuries the cardinals formed themselves into a legal corporation known as the Sacred College of Cardinals. The three orders of cardinal priests, deacons, and bishops have been retained, but the maximum membership of each order has been changed many times. Today the number of cardinal priests is limited to fifty, of cardinal deacons to fourteen, and of cardinal bishops to six. The membership of the Sacred College of Cardinals is thus limited to seventy, in imitation of the seventy elders who advised Moses. If a pope is so inclined, he may increase or reduce the membership of the Sacred College, but the popes respect tradition, and the possibility of a change is slight.

The pope is free to elevate whomsoever he desires to the Sacred College of Cardinals. The heavy burdens and the distinguished privileges of a cardinal require he be a man of wisdom, learning, and sanctity. In addition, a cardinal must be at least thirty years of age and of legitimate birth. At one time a layman could be a cardinal. For example, Cardinal Antonelli, the brilliant Secretary of State during the long and difficult pontificate of Pius IX, was a layman and married. Even today a layman may be created cardinal, but he must within the year receive the order of diaconate. As a formality the pope requests for his choice the approval of the cardinals gathered in secret consistory. They indicate their assent by doffing their skullcaps, rising, and bowing.*

Every several months the pope and the cardinals in Rome meet to discuss the problems of the Church. In these consistories bishops are chosen, world and ecclesiastical conditions are analyzed, and policies are laid down. Frequently the pope uses these consistories to deliver important addresses on various subjects. The prefects of the twelve** congregations or departments which administer the affairs of the Church and Vatican City are generally cardinals. Other cardinals hold various positions of importance, for example, that of papal librarian.

To the many duties of the cardinals correspond important rights and privileges. They come immediately after the pope and precede in rank all other prelates. Theirs is the title of "Your Eminence," and they are considered the equals of the royal princes of Europe.

To each cardinal assembled in the Sistine Chapel had been given a ballot and a check list of the names of all the cardinals present at the Conclave. A conclave ballot is divided into three parts. On the top part are printed in Latin the words "I Cardinal," and here the cardinal who is voting will write his own name.*** He then folds the

* A month or more prior to this consistory *L'Osservatore Romano*, the Vatican's semiofficial newspaper, usually publishes the names and brief biographies of the churchmen to be elevated. The cardinals-designate are officially notified by the Papal Secretariate of State, and are requested to come to Rome for the ceremonies of elevation. A churchman actually becomes a cardinal at the moment of the consent of the older cardinals.

** The Code of Canon Law, which governs the Church, mentions only eleven congregations; but the *Annuario Pontificio*, the official yearbook of the Holy See, enumerates twelve. The latter adds the congregation of the "Fabric of St. Peter's" to those named by the Code.

*** The recent constitution, mentioned in the footnote on page 14 provides that the name and motto need no longer be attached to the ballots.

top and seals it with wax. On the middle part is printed "I elect Cardinal ———— as Sovereign Pontiff." The bottom is blank so that the cardinal may write thereon a scriptural text as a means of identification. This part is also folded and sealed. The top and bottom parts are then folded together, the bottom over the top, and sealed with wax. The conclave ballot is so divided to prevent the election of a pope by his own vote. For election a cardinal must secure two thirds of all votes cast exclusive of his own. When a particular cardinal has secured the necessary majority and no more, the top and bottom parts of his ballot will be opened. If he has elected himself, the election is invalid and balloting must begin again. However, there is no prohibition against a cardinal voting for himself.

The above method of electing a pope is called scrutiny. There are two other methods of election: acclamation and composition. When Cardinal Odaleschi entered the Sistine Chapel for the election of a successor to Clement X, all the cardinals surrounded him and, kissing his hands, acclaimed him Pope Innocent XI. This was election by acclamation. By the composition method the cardinals unanimously designate a certain number of their members to make a choice.

Shortly after the doors to the Sistine Chapel had been bolted, the balloting began. There would be two ballots in the morning and two in the afternoon until a decision had been reached. Since there were sixty-two cardinals in the Conclave, forty-two votes (exclusive of the candidate's own) would be needed for election. Using a quill pen, each cardinal wrote in his choice and individually walked to the altar. There he knelt and prayed. Rising he faced his brethern, and in a loud voice declared: "I call to witness the Lord Christ, who will be my judge, that I am electing the one whom according to God I think ought to be elected." Going up to the altar, he placed his ballot on the paten and tipped it into the chalice.

Presiding at the altar were the three cardinals known as the scrutineers. Theirs was the duty to inspect the ballots before they were cast and to guard against fraud in the balloting. Several of the cardinals were confined to their cells because of illness, and Cardinal Boggiani because of advanced age and failing eyesight. As provided by the laws governing papal elections, a committee of three cardinals was appointed to go to the cells of these cardinals and collect their votes. The committee brought the ballots in a sealed box to the senior scrutineer who placed them in the chalice.

After the balloting had been completed, a scrutineer holding the paten firmly down shook the chalice slowly. Then he drew the ballots singly from the chalice and placed them face up on the altar, counting aloud as he did so. Meanwhile another scrutineer made a count of the cardinal-electors present. The number of ballots cast tallied with the number of electors present. The ballots were then counted into a second chalice and carried to a table in the center of the chapel. The ballots were again drawn singly from the chalice by the first scrutineer, and handed to the second and then to the third scrutineer. As the last received each ballot, he broke the seal holding the top and bottom, and read aloud the name of the cardinal written on the middle part. The cardinals checked off the votes as they were read against the list of names which each had on his desk. The scrutineers tallied the score and announced the result of the first ballot. Thirty-five votes had been cast for Cardinal Pacelli.*

The chapel doors were unbolted and the cardinals returned to their cells. At eleven they were again summoned to the Sistine Chapel. On the second ballot forty votes were cast for Cardinal Pacelli, two short of election. The cardinals then recessed until the afternoon. The ballots mixed with wet straw were burned in a stove whose stack extended through a window of the chapel. The black smoke told the people in St. Peter's Square below that they were still without a shepherd.

The outcome of the second ballot spread through the City of the Conclave, and all looked upon Cardinal Pacelli as the man who within a few hours would wear the white cassock of the Holy Father. Visibly moved by the morning's events, he clearly showed his anxiety lest he be burdened with the responsibilities of the papacy. After lunch he walked nervously up and down one of the many frescoed halls of the Conclave. Descending a stairs he missed a step and fell down a flight to the second landing. Though shaken and bruised, he rose unaided and hurried to his cell.

At three-thirty that afternoon the cardinals returned to the Sistine Chapel to ballot for the third time. As the teller called his name for the forty-second time, Cardinal Pacelli put his face in his hands. Sixty-one ballots were cast for him; his own he cast for Cardinal Tedeschini. The chapel doors were opened, and papal notaries were admitted to record the subsequent proceedings.

* The results of the first and later ballots, as well as incidents of the Conclave, are not official, though they were obtained from good sources. Vatican servants have always succeeded in outwitting, without breaking, the Conclave regulations, and cardinals are not above (thank heaven) adding their bit to clerical "gossip."

Cardinal Di Belmonte, flanked by Cardinals Caccia Dominioni and O'Connell, approached the throne of Eugenio Pacelli, and inquired of him: "Do you accept your election as Sovereign Pontiff." In a breaking voice the new Pope replied: "I am not worthy of so august an office, but, since it is the will of God and of the Most Reverend Cardinals, I accept." Cardinal Di Belmonte then asked him: "By what name do you wish to be called in the future." The Holy Father reflected for a moment, and replied: "I wish to be called Pius XII because all my ecclesiastical life, all my career, has taken place under pontiffs of that name, and particularly because I have a debt of gratitude toward Pius XI who always caused me to be indebted to him for his affection to me." In changing his name from Eugenio to Pius, the new Pontiff followed a custom dating back to Pope John XII of the tenth century. Since that time each pope has taken a new name in memory of the first pope, whose name Christ changed from Simon to Peter.

It was five-thirty. White smoke from the burning of the ballots with dry straw announced to the joyful crowd in St. Peter's Square that a new pope had been chosen. The master of ceremonies lowered the canopies of all the cardinals except that of the Pope-Elect. He was no longer their equal but their sovereign. Pius XII walked to the altar, knelt, and prayed. Then, escorted by the master of ceremonies, he entered the sacristy adjoining the chapel. Three sets of papal robes, large, medium, and small, had been laid out to fit whoever might be elected. The new Holy Father was vested in a white skullcap and cassock, over which were placed a red mozetta, or short cape, edged in ermine, and a red stole embroidered in gold. On his feet were placed red slippers adorned with small crosses of gold. When he re-entered the chapel, his throne was ready for him before the altar on the Gospel side. He seated himself and received the first of the three obediences or homages of the cardinals. Each cardinal kissed the cross on the Pope's left slipper, then his knee, then his hand when in return he received the kiss of peace from the new Vicar of Christ.

The bells of Rome's more than four hundred churches had begun to sound the evening Angelus. *Il Campanone,* the eleven-ton master of the great bell tower of St. Peter's, was booming its call to prayer. It was six o'clock. The windows of the Hall of Benedictions overlooking the portico of St. Peter's suddenly lighted up. The doors leading to the balcony were thrown open, revealing the gilded columns and capitals inside and the marble friezes with large black inscriptions. Four papal guards in helmets that glittered in the soft twilight appeared on the balcony. From the marble balustrade they suspended an enormous cloth of white velvet, edged with a wide crimson border and emblazoned in the center with the papal arms of tiara and keys.

The countless thousands crowded into the square below fell silent. The only sound was that of the fountains to each side of the celebrated obelisk of Heliopolis. Preceded by a white surpliced acolyte carrying a golden cross, Cardinal Caccia Dominioni entered the balcony. In a sonorous voice, which twenty loud-speakers echoed through the Square, he half said and half sung the centuries-old formula: "I announce to you a great joy. We have a Pope. He is my most eminent and most reverend lord, the Lord Cardinal Eugenio . . . " Thunderous cheers drowned out Cardinal Dominioni. For the first time since Pope Innocent XII, who reigned from 1721 to 1724, the Romans had as pope a son and native of their own Eternal City. The cardinal signaled for silence and continued: "Cardinal Pacelli. He will take the name Pius."

The people spontaneously began to sing the *"Te Deum,"* that great hymn of exultation composed by St. Ambrose, Bishop of Milan, when the Church was still young. Italian grenadiers and carbineers, who had been standing at ease near the Square, cleared and occupied a space between the bottom of the steps leading to the Basilica and the point where the arms of the Bernini Colonnade begin their vast sweep toward Rome. HJV, the Vatican radio station, which Marconi built, began to broadcast in many tongues the happy tidings of a new pope. Reporters and correspondents hurried to the nearest telephone to "flash" the news to the waiting world. The news included the unusual item that March 2 was the new Pope's sixty-third birthday.

Meanwhile, a large group of cardinals from the Conclave took positions at the windows to the left of the balcony. The new Holy Father was about to appear. The singing softened and ceased. A sharp word of command brought the soldiers to attention. The sun had set and darkness was creeping over the Vatican, brushing away the shadows of twilight.

A tremendous shout arose. *"Viva il Papa. Viva il Papa."* — Long live the Pope. On the balcony was a white-cassocked figure with a gold and diamond cross gleaming on his breast. The soldiers presented arms and the people fell to their knees. The new servant of the servants of God, Pius XII, raised his right hand in blessing. A monsignor opened a book of pontifical prayers and blessings. The Holy Father intoned, "Blessed be the name of the Lord." The faithful replied, "From now and henceforth forever more." The Holy Father continued, "Our help is in the name of the Lord." The faithful answered, "Who made heaven and earth." The Holy Father then made the sign of the cross three times toward the city and toward the world, saying as he did so, "May the blessing of God Almighty, Father, Son, and Holy Ghost, descend upon you and remain there always." The faithful answered, "Amen." They blessed themselves and rose to their feet. Smiling and waving to his children below, the Pope remained on the balcony. Then suddenly he was gone. The windows in the Hall of Benedictions became dark. The crowd streamed slowly out of the square.

His Holiness returned to the Sistine Chapel for the second obedience of the cardinals and for the homage of the papal household. The chapel was crowded with prelates and Vatican dignitaries, Swiss, Palatine, and Noble guards, servants, and attendants. Among the latter was the anonymous person known as the secret sweeper, whose duty it will be to sweep and dust the new Pope's office before he arrives there in the morning. Having lived in the Vatican since 1930 as Papal Secretary of State, Pius XII could call by name all of the people who knelt to pay him homage. Among them were his nephews, Giulio and Marcantonio Pacelli, members of the Noble Guard.

The ceremony of homage and obedience over, His Holiness went to the apartments which he had occupied as Secretary of State. These beautiful rooms had been rebuilt during the pontificate of Pius X when Cardinal Merry del Val was Secretary of State. Originally the Borgia apartments, they were decorated by Pinturicchio with frescoes that are unrivaled by any in the Vatican for vividnesss of color and beauty of design. The apartments are on the floor below the papal apartments to which easy and quick access is had by means of a private elevator. The Pope summoned a secretary and dictated telegrams to the mayors of Desio and Milan, the birthplace and episcopal city respectively of his predecessor. In these telegrams he announced his succession to one whom they all so dearly loved, and conferred his blessing on the townspeople and flock of the great Pius XI.

Already the walls of the City of the Conclave were being torn down, and the paint was being removed from the door panes. The cardinal-electors were departing for their apartments and lodgings in the Vatican and Rome. Their choice of Cardinal Pacelli for the See of St. Peter was unusual and yet natural.

On the day following the election, Cardinal Verdier of Paris made this statement: "The value of Cardinal Pacelli was indisputable and his exceptional personality impressed all of us from the first moment we entered the Sistine Chapel for the balloting. The Sacred College — I may say this without violating the oath of secrecy which applies to the activities of the Conclave — could not hesitate to choose Pacelli for the papacy." Likewise, Cardinal Pacelli's election caused no great surprise in Vatican circles. In his last consistory Pius XI said: "We commend to Our brethren of the Sacred College of Cardinals the high esteem and lofty opinion We hold for the ability and high-mindedness of Our chief collaborator, Cardinal Pacelli, thrice worthy as Our successor in this Apostolic See." On the other hand, there is a strong tradition in the Church against the election of a Papal Secretary of State as pope. His identification with the policy of the deceased pontiff is usually considered a hindrance, and his responsible position inevitably makes for him many enemies within and without the Church. Cardinal Rampolla, Secretary of State for

Leo XIII, would have been pope, had not his policies antagonized the government of the Austro-Hungarian Empire. The last Papal Secretary of State to be elected pope was Gregory XI. And the Vatican has an old saw which says: "He who enters the Conclave a pope comes out a cardinal."

As the world had awaited so the world received the election of the new Pope with varied reactions. Guido Rocco, head of the Information Bureau of the Italian Ministry of Press and Propaganda, expressed the Fascist disapproval with, "It could have been worse." When informed of Cardinal Pacelli's election, Count Von Plessen, chancellor of the German Embassy in Rome, remarked: "A careful diplomat is undoubtedly better than a hot-tempered, impulsive old man like Pius XI." The Nazi newspapers were cool and sought to play down the election as inconsequential. For political reasons the Italian newspapers sought to imply that Pius XII would be pro-Italian.* The presidents of the United States and France and the king-emperor of Great Britain expressed their good wishes in messages of congratulation. The allied press voiced its undisguised satisfaction with the election of Cardinal Pacelli, for it knew him to be a fearless champion of human rights. And the allied press, likewise, sought to imply that the new Pope would be pro-French, pro-English, or pro-American. Because he is Christ's Vicar on earth, Pius XII would be the father of all men, regardless of race, color, creed, or nationality. To him there would be neither Axis nor United Nations, only children of God and brothers of Christ.

* "He (Mussolini) is satisfied with Pacelli. He promised to send the Pope some advice on how he can usefully govern the Church." — *Ciano Diaries*, Galeazzi Ciano (Doubleday and Company, New York, 1946), page 25, entry for March 3, 1939.

Late on the evening of the election Pius paid a visit to Cardinal Francesco Marchetti-Selvaggiani, an old friend and Vicar-General of Rome, who was confined to his bed. Surprised by the visit, the cardinal tried to rise.

"I beg pardon of Your Holiness," the cardinal said, "if I am unable to render due homage."

"Do not tire yourself," the Pope replied, "tonight let me still be your Eugenio to my Francesco."

"How well you look in that cassock," remarked the cardinal to his friend during the conversation that followed.

The eyes of the Holy Father saddened, and he gazed through the curtainless windows to the lights of Rome. "Perhaps," he answered, "I will never be able to travel again."

In a moon-shadowed olive grove the Master accepted the chalice of Calvary. In a magnificent chapel whose beauty is the world's glory the Vicar accepted the chalice of the papacy, whose sorrows and cares would end only with death. Presidents and dictators rule over the bodies of men which die and turn to clay. Popes rule over the souls of men which never die but return to God, their Creator and Judge. Greater responsibility no man can assume than did Eugenio Pacelli, when he spoke his "I accept." The Christ who gazed upon him from Michelangelo's "Last Judgment" will one day judge his stewardship.

CHAPTER II

A SHEEP DOG OF THE LORD

IN MIDSUMMER of 1819 Marcantonio Pacelli, eighteen or twenty years of age, received from his maternal uncle, Cardinal Caterini, a letter of advice and an invitation to leave his native village of Oriano and to come to the city of Rome. A few years before, Marcantonio had said good-by to his cousin, Dominic Barberi, as he was leaving Oriano for England. There Dominic would become an illustrious theologian and the founder of the English Passionists. He had urged Marcantonio to accompany him to England, but that country was too far away from the beautiful Pacelli farm with its sweet vineyard and fruitful fields. Rome, however, was only twenty to thirty miles off, so Marcantonio could accept his uncle's invitation and still make frequent visits home.

Rome was then the capital and principal city of the Papal States, which extended from the blue Mediterranean east to the still bluer Adriatic, and from Florence in the north to Naples. The States of the Church were historic at a time when the modern nations of Europe were unknown. In early centuries they had consisted solely of the Patrimony of St. Peter, that is, the private property and possessions of the Church of St. Peter in Rome. Later the emperors and wealthy nobles of Rome and Italy

presented the papacy with valuable and extensive possessions in Sicily, Ravenna, Genoa, the Duchy of Rome, and
elsewhere. Lands and forests, mines and quarries, villages
and cities, were given to the Holy See. By the sixth
century the pope was the chief landowner in central
Italy. The revenues from these possessions were employed
to relieve public and private want, hospitals, orphanages,
and homes for the destitute and the aged being erected
and maintained. The citizens of these possessions, though
subjects of the Roman emperors, began to look to the
pope not only for spiritual guidance but also for protection
against the barbarians who at frequent intervals swept
into Italy, as well as against the tyrannical emperors and
arrogant princes who oppressed them. When Attila, whose
Huns had made of Europe a charnel house, raged before
the walls of Rome, Pope Leo I alone had the courage to
withstand him. Attired in full pontifical robes and
preceded by a deacon carrying the cross, Christ's instrument of victory, the Holy Father went forth to meet
Attila. The awe-struck Hun, who proudly called himself
the Scourge of God, granted Leo's plea to spare Rome
and the lives of her citizens. When later taunted for his
submission, Attila rejoined: "I did not fear him, but the
threatening figure of heavenly brightness who hovered
over him."

More civilized than the Huns but no less oppressive
and hateful to the Romans and the Italians living in the
neighboring cities were the Lombards of northern Italy.
Their attempts to subjugate Rome and central Italy were
reaching success in 751, as Aistulf, the Lombard King,
captured the outlying cities and prepared to attack the
Eternal City itself. But on the throne of Peter sat the
indomitable Stephen II. In midwinter he crossed the Alps

into France to seek the aid of Pepin, King of the Franks. Heeding Stephen's plea the King marched with his knights and bowmen into Italy, and in a series of quick battles decisively routed Aistulf and the Lombards. Pepin then executed a deed to the recaptured lands and cities naming St. Peter as grantee. This he placed together with the keys of the cities on Peter's tomb in Rome. Thus were the States of the Church founded.

They were to endure for more than a thousand years. Conquerors, Christian and heathen, Catholic and heretic, would engulf them many times in blood and ruin. They would change hands frequently but would always come back to the pope. When Marcantonio was a boy of ten, Napoleon, Emperor of the French, confiscated the Papal States and imprisoned Pope Pius VII. The Congress of Vienna, where the brilliant Cardinal Ercole Consalvi, Papal Secretary of State, represented the Pope, re-established the States of the Church in 1815. Once again Marcantonio would witness the end of the pope's temporal power; but his grandsons would play an important role in its restoration.

To govern his several million subjects and to administer to their many needs, the Holy Father required the assistance of numerous lay officials — bankers, technicians, artisans, postmen, policemen, soldiers. The legal and judicial system was highly organized and served by a corps of skilled lawyers. Recognizing in his nephew the character and intellect which would make him a capable and praiseworthy lawyer, Cardinal Caterini advised Marcantonio to enroll as a student of canon and civil law at one of Rome's famed universities. An education in both the secular and the ecclesiastical systems of law would fit him for various positions in the papal service.

After completing his studies with distinction and honors in 1825, Marcantonio obtained, very likely through the influence of his cardinal uncle, an executive position in the Papal Department of the Interior. Government service in any nation has always been a fruitful subject for cartoonists and humorists. The papal service is no exception. Marcantonio, however, had real qualifications for the work, and as a consequence rose rapidly in the papal government. In 1851 he was named Undersecretary of the Interior by Pius IX. The Department of the Interior was responsible for the internal security and prosperity of the Papal States. The conditions of the times and the plans of the Church's enemies in Italy made this a difficult and, at last, an impossible task. Victor Emmanuel, King of Piedmont in northern Italy, and his prime minister, Cavour, were planning the annexation of the Papal States as the final step in the unification of the Italian people. Spies and troublemakers incited the riffraff of Rome and other papal cities to riot and revolution. In 1848 the Pope's prime minister, Rossi, was murdered by assassins on the steps of the Palace of the Cancellaria in Rome. The rebels seized the city, and Pius IX fled in disguise to Gaeta, Italy, which was then under the protection of the Austrians.

But the assassins masquerading as liberators soon fell to murdering one another. Law and order gave way to mob rule and rioting. Fearful that the lawlessness and anarchy would engulf all Italy and spread to their own countries, France and Austria sent armies to restore peace. Pius returned in 1850 to Rome, but security and stability did not return with him. The armies of Victor Emmanuel and the forces of Garibaldi plundered and looted the Papal States. Province after province, city after city, were taken from the Holy Father. Finally, on September 20, 1870, the Eternal City was stormed and captured. Pius IX became the prisoner of the Vatican.

With the end of the States of the Church there was no further need for the office of the Undersecretary of the Interior. Marcantonio, however, continued to work for the Holy See. In the troubled years prior to the seizure of Rome, he had founded and developed *L'Osservatore Romano,* the Vatican's semiofficial newspaper. Editorial and publishing duties occupied his time and talents until his death in 1906 at the age of 102.

Of Marcantonio's seven children, the third, Filippo, would make him the grandfather of another Pius. Filippo, through exceptional ability and unusual application, became the foremost lawyer of the Vatican in the pontificates of Leo XIII and Pius X. A brief explanation and description of the papal courts will enable the reader to understand Filippo's work and to appreciate his success.

As the Father of Christendom, the pope is obliged to dispense justice in thousands of cases involving hundreds of legal principles. Marriages must be declared valid or invalid, dispensations must be granted or denied, rights and duties must be determined and protected. To assist him in this vast task the pope has a series of courts to which are attached lawyers both lay and clerical. The complexity of the lawsuits before the papal courts requires of these lawyers widespread and exhaustive knowledge. Besides a thorough acquaintance with canon and civil law, they must be versed also in moral and dogmatic theology, in secular and sacred history, and in the various languages, modern and ancient, in which their lawbooks are written. They plead before the most learned judges, and can gain a favorable decision only by the superiority of their ability to bring out the truth. The papal courts, unlike civil courts, are not influenced by moving oratory, clever tactics, and technicalities. Their cases involve the welfare of souls, and truth is the prime object sought after. The most able of the ecclesiastical lawyers comprise the Consistorial College, whose membership is limited to twelve. Early in his legal career Filippo was elected to the Consistorial College and later became its dean, an office comparable to the presidency of the American Bar Association.

Filippo practiced also before the civil courts of the new Italian government, and became legal counsel for important industries and business establishments in Rome. As a director of the Unione Romana, a Catholic political association, he worked to better the Church's position in her relations with the Italian government. For many years as a councillor (alderman) of Rome's municipal government, he was considered the spokesman of the Blacks — the Romans who sided with the pope in opposition to the Whites, who were the adherents of the king.

Some years before the seizure of Rome, Filippo married Virginia Graziosi, the gracious and talented daughter of a well-to-do Roman family. They established their home on the third floor of a four-story brownstone building called Palazzo Pediconi, located on the quaint Via Monte Giordano in Ponte, one of the oldest quarters of Rome, across the Tiber from St. Peter's. There on March 2, 1876, a second son was born to them. On the same day the nurse carried the babe around the corner to the Church of SS. Celso e Giuliano, where his uncle, Monsignor Guiseppe Pacelli, baptized him Eugenio Maria Guiseppe Giovanni Pacelli. The godmother was Teresa Pacelli, a paternal aunt, and a maternal uncle, Filippo Graziosi, was the godfather. Besides Eugenio, Virginia Pacelli gave birth to another son, Francesco, the eldest of the family, and to two daughters, Guiseppina and Elizabetta.

Eugenio received his elementary education at a small school conducted by nuns, located a few blocks from the Pacelli residence. He early showed a decided liking for intellectual things and exhibited unusual talents of mind. At the same time he developed an interest in athletics and an intense love for religion. Riding, swimming, and other sports found him a skilled and eager participant. When later, for reasons of health, riding and swimming had to be discontinued, he turned to gymnastics. Today, when the burdensome duties of the papacy allow, he exercises in a small private gymnasium, which has been erected near the papal apartments. Recently he declared in a public audience to thousands of Italian athletes that sport based on fair play "elevates the spirit above small-mindedness, dishonesty, and trickery." At the same time he cautioned against participation to excess. Extolling sports as a means of developing will power and a Christian domination of the human body, he said: "What would be the use of physical courage and force of character, if Christians exploited them only for the worldly ends of winning a cup or giving themselves the airs of supermen."

The favorite exercise of the clergy is said to be walking. It was Cardinal Pietro Gasparri who once remarked to the then Monsignor Pacelli that a priest who speaks so much of heaven, is not harmed by feeling a bit of earth under his feet. Rome offered Eugenio many interesting and beautiful places for long walks. Northward he could follow the Tiber, and southward he could travel the famed Appian Way, which Rome's emperors had built so many centuries ago and which Rome's many conquerors, from the Vandals to the Yanks, have trodden in conquest. A favorite hike took him from St. Peter's to the Milvio Bridge and back on the east side, a distance of six miles. While vacationing at the family farm near Oriano, he walked and rode through the countryside, visiting religious shrines and ruins of history.

The class cartoonist prophetically portrayed Eugenio as kneeling in prayer. While engaged in sports and studies, the future Vicar of Christ would frequently break away to spend hours in prayer at Chiesa Nuova, which was built in the sixteenth century and despite its name "New Church" gives every evidence of age, or at Madonna della Strade, a small chapel in the neighborhood. In the company of his saintly mother and devout father he took part in the great religious feasts of the Church. On Corpus Christi they would attend services at Genzano, near the pope's summer residence at Castel Gandolfo. The Feast of St. Joseph was honored at Frascati, and that of the Divine Love at a shrine along the Appian Way some four or five miles from Rome.

The piety of Eugenio and the devotion of the Pacelli family were in sharp contrast to the anticlericalism and irreligion that degraded Rome in those days. When Eugenio was five, the procession bearing the corpse of Pius IX from its temporary resting place in the crypt of St. Peter's to the Church of San Lorenzo passed near his house. As the procession approached the church, a mob of anticlericals rushed forth from a side street. Shouting "Down with that lousy pope. Throw his —— body in the Tiber," they seized the coffin. A pitched battle ensued and dead and wounded stained the streets with their blood. Soldiers were rushed from their barracks to quell the rioting. Charging the mob with fixed bayonets, they succeeded in rescuing the coffin. The procession was dis-

banded, and the coffin was rushed to San Lorenzo's and
hurriedly entombed.

Filippo Pacelli desired Eugenio to become an attorney
in the state courts as well as a consistorial advocate. Therefore he sent him, following graduation from elementary
school, to the Ennio Quirino Visconti Lyceum, a govern-
ment-sponsored school corresponding to an American
preparatory school. The professor of history, anti-Catholic
and bigoted, one day assigned Eugenio's class an essay on
"The Greatest Heroes of History." All except one paper
treated of Napoleon, Caesar, Charlemagne, and other
well-known historical leaders. The odd paper chose St.
Augustine and St. Bernard of Clairvaux. The teacher, after
reading the paper to the class, contemptuously asked:
"Who was so stupid as to think that such men were
important in history?" Eugenio, rising from his desk, said:
"I was. I am ready to prove the validity of my choice."
An embarrassing silence followed. The class expected
Eugenio to be expelled; but the teacher flushed, said
nothing, and passed on to the next paper.

During the years at the Visconti Lyceum Eugenio laid
the foundations of his great proficiency in languages,
modern and ancient. Of the world's leaders Pius XII
speaks the most languages. In 1934, when Cardinal Secretary of State, he addressed the Catholic Press Convention
at Rome in Latin, Italian, French, Spanish, Portuguese,
German, and English (which he speaks very correctly but
with an accent). Had there been listeners to understand
he would have spoken also in Greek, Hebrew, and
Aramaic. In the early days of his pontificate Pius XII was
to receive in audience a group of pilgrims from Hungary.
Although he knew no Hungarian, he memorized the
sounds of every word of a speech in that language, and

to the amazement and joy of his visitors addressed them in their native tongue.

On graduating from the Lyceum in 1894, Eugenio told his father of his desire to become a priest rather than a lawyer. The question of his vocation had been the subject of earnest prayer and diligent thought for many years. Eugenio's indecision was ended by his mother's advice to become a priest, in which he heard God speaking to him. His father, by petition to Leo XIII, who had succeeded Pius IX in 1876, obtained for him admission into the Capranica College, founded by Cardinal Domenico Capranica in 1457. The oldest in Rome, because of which it is affectionately termed "Almo Collegio" (the foster-mother college), the Capranica is located in the very heart of the city near the present Italian parliament houses. It is a residence rather than a school, for the students take their courses at the Gregorian University conducted by the Jesuits.

Candidates for the priesthood usually begin their studies at the age of thirteen or fourteen. Immediately after primary school they enter a minor seminary, which prepares them for the study of theology and the sacred sciences. Having attended the Lyceum, Eugenio was several years behind in his ecclesiastical education, and therefore, long hours of the day and night were spent in making up time. Though he soon led his class, his health was seriously impaired. At the insistence of his parents and doctor he left the Capranica for the family farm near Oriano. There through the healthful air, long walks, horseback riding, and complete rest, he regained his health and strength.

He returned to Rome eager to resume seminary life. This the doctor forbade on the grounds that the strict rules and close confinement of the seminary would cause a relapse. Seemingly Eugenio's hopes for the priesthood would not be fulfilled. But the Church was not to be denied a future shepherd, and Pope Leo gave orders that Eugenio should continue his ecclesiastical studies as a day student. This extraordinary dispensation was early evidence of the esteem and confidence which the Vatican had for Eugenio Pacelli. It has been the law of the Church for many centuries that all seminarians spend their last six years of preparation for the priesthood together in community life. The reason for this rule is that community life promotes sanctity, and also enables the seminary authorities to become thoroughly acquainted with the seminarians so as to decide with full knowledge their worthiness for the priesthood.

His studies at the Capranica completed, Eugenio entered the Pontifical University of the Roman Seminary, which is the Church's most renowned school of theology. In addition to Pius XII the Roman Seminary has given to the Church Popes Gregory XV, Innocent XIII, Clement IX, and Clement XII. Again he excelled and received the degree of doctor both in philosophy and in theology. In the afternoon of commencement day, Pope Leo called Eugenio to the papal apartments and cordially congratulated him on his scholastic achievements.

On Holy Saturday, April 2, 1899, Eugenio received the Sacrament of Holy Orders from Archbishop Cassetta, Vicegerent of Rome and Patriarch of Antioch. On the next day, Easter Sunday, Father Pacelli offered his first holy Mass in the Borghese Chapel of the Basilica of St. Mary Major. Love of Rome and devotion to Mary moved the young priest to choose the Basilica of St. Mary Major rather than San Celso or Chiesa Nuova. The basilica is the mother church of Rome, for from her lofty site she has witnessed the joys and sorrows of Rome since 352. Above the jasper altar, upon which Father Pacelli consecrated bread and wine for the first time, hangs the Madonna of Rome, which legend claims was painted by St. Luke the Evangelist. This painting has made the Borghese Chapel Rome's favorite shrine to Mary. In centuries past it was carried through the streets whenever pestilence or enemies threatened the peace and happinsss of the Romans. During the pontificate of Pelagius II the Madonna of Rome is said to have stayed the cholera epidemic which was desolating the city.

During the two years following his ordination Father Pacelli assisted at the Chiesa Nuova, hearing confessions, teaching catechism to the children, and being in all ways an instrument of zeal and devotion to God's purposes. The wisdom and the holiness of their young shepherd drew the sorrow burdened to his study and the sin laden to his confessional, and none went away unrefreshed. The children loved him because he was gentle, kind, patient, and understanding with them and their problems. He had no desires or ambitions beyond the obscure and consoling life of a parish priest. His only outside activity was a postgraduate course in canon law at the Roman College of St. Appolinaris, from which Father Pacelli was graduated in 1902 with a doctorate *summa cum laude* in both canon and civil law.

While all priests are ordained for the service of God and His Church, they must serve not as they wish but as their superiors direct them. Some are pastors and missionaries whose main concern is attending to the spiritual needs of the faithful. Others serve God in less spiritual but equally holy and necessary ways. Being a world institution burdened with countless tasks, the Church must have diplomats and statesmen, financiers and administrators, instructors and teachers. These priests make a great sacrifice, because the consolations of the priesthood — the joy of administering the sacraments, the loving trust and confidence of a pastor's parishioners — are in great part denied them. They are no less Christlike than the more fortunate priests, for in obeying their superiors they do the will of God.

Although the Holy Father was no longer the Sovereign of the Papal States, he continued to maintain diplomatic relations with the Christian nations of the world. These nations, in turn, had ambassadors and ministers accredited to the Holy See. In many lands the path of the Church was difficult and thorny. Anti-Catholics and anticlericals in France and Italy plotted to destroy her. The social and economic upheavals caused by the industrial revolution of the previous century were bringing about tremendous changes and manifold problems. World peace and international harmony were being undermined by conflict and threat of war. The Church, therefore, had need of brilliant young priests in her diplomatic corps, who would be trained to succeed the papal nuncios and apostolic delegates abroad and the various officials of the Secretariate of State at the Vatican. Aware of Father Pacelli's talents and sanctity, Leo XIII gave instructions that he should be trained as a papal diplomat.

One evening in February, 1901, Father Pacelli's housekeeper answered the clamorous doorbell to find impatiently waiting there Monsignor Pietro Gasparri, Undersecretary of the Congregation for Extraordinary Ecclesiastical Affairs, the principal department of the Papal Secretariate of State. Ushered into the poorly furnished parlor, Monsignor Gasparri, without waiting to greet his host or to sit down, said: "I have come to ask you to join the Congregation's office. We need promising young priests there." Father Pacelli, whose lack of enthusiasm was evident, thanked the Monsignor, but replied that he preferred to remain a shepherd of souls. Monsignor Gasparri, not to be denied an able assistant, countered: "You wish to be a shepherd of souls. I'll train you to be a sheep dog who can chase away the wolves preying on the flock of the Lord." To his own arguments the Monsignor added the instructions of the Holy Father, and seeing in the latter the will of God, Father Pacelli obeyed.

Papal diplomacy, and also the modern system of sending and receiving diplomatic envoys, originated in the fifth century when Pope Leo I sent a legate to represent him at the capital of the Eastern Roman Empire, Constantinople. The legate kept the emperor informed of what was going on in Rome, and the Pope informed of what was going on in Constantinople. As papal relations with the Western Roman Empire, with the Franks, and with new political powers required, legates with the title of *nuntius* were sent to Ravenna, to Paris, and to other capitals. It was not until the pontificate of Alexander VI, however, that the papal legates became permanent representatives of the pope. Soon after his election in 1489 Alexander permanently assigned Angelo Leonini to the Republic of Venice with the title of *nuncio*.

There are two major classes of papal representatives, nuncios and apostolic delegates. To nations having diplomatic relations with the Holy See the pope sends a nuncio. He represents the pope in all civil and diplomatic relations with the government of the particular country and in all ecclesiastical matters with the bishops and clergy of that country. To nations maintaining diplomatic relations with the Holy See but unwilling to grant full diplomatic privileges to the papal representative, the pope sends an internuncio. An instance of this is Czecho-Slovakia, which declines to acknowledge the papal representative as dean of the Diplomatic Corps, a post held by all nuncios. Certain countries, for example England and China, maintain unilateral, as it were, diplomatic relations with the Holy See in that they have an official ambassador or minister at Vatican City but do not accept a nuncio or internuncio in return. Other nations, for example, the United States and Canada, do not have official diplomatic relations with the Holy See. To London and Washington the pope sends apostolic delegates, who have no diplomatic standing and are accredited not to the government but to the Church of these countries. However, an apostolic delegate is usually accorded diplomatic privileges, such as access to government officials, inviolability of dispatches, and for all practical purposes is accepted as the official representative of the pope and the authoritative spokesman of the Holy See. The Apostolic Delegate to the United States is, at the present time, His Excellency Archbishop Amleto Giovanni Cicognani, who has held the post since 1933.

Papal representatives are usually titular archbishops, so named because their dioceses exist only in history or are located in lands where heresy or schism have replaced the ancient faith. Nuncios and delegates to the major nations (the United States, prewar Germany, Italy, Spain, France) are customarily elevated to the Sacred College of Cardinals at the end of their mission.

The Papal Secretariate of State, or Office of the Secretary of State, as it is more exactly entitled, was founded by Pope Gregory I (590–604), when he established at Rome a correspondence office to handle all letters and documents to and from foreign rulers and papal representatives. Reorganized many times in the past fourteen hundred years, it now consists of three parts under the over-all direction of the Cardinal Secretary of State. The first section, presided over by the Secretary of the Sacred Congregation for Extraordinary Ecclesiastical Affairs, establishes or divides dioceses and promotes suitable candidates to vacant dioceses, whenever these matters must be negotiated with foreign governments. In addition, it looks after matters referred to it by the pope, especially those which involve civil laws and treaties with foreign countries. The second section, whose head is the Substitute Secretary of State, conducts routine relations of the Holy See with foreign countries, and also has charge of the papal decorations and honors which the pope bestows on persons who by their devotion and service to the Church and humanity merit public recognition. The third section, under the direction of the Chancellor of the Office of Apostolic Briefs, supervises the preparation and sending of papal letters to civil and ecclesiastical dignitaries. The Office of the Secretary of State, the Congregation for Extraordinary Ecclesiastical Affairs, and the Office of Apostolic Briefs are in themselves separate and distinct, but they function as a unit because of related work and common personnel. The Cardinal Secretary of State is usually both the head of his own Office and the Prefect (President) of the Congregation.

The Congregation was founded in 1793 by Pius VI to study conditions in war-torn France. In 1827 it was reconstituted to study the state of the Church in all countries and later was given the added duties just mentioned. If the Holy See could be said to have a bureau of secret police, this Congregation would be such. It keeps the Holy Father informed on ecclesiastical and civil matters throughout the world. The remarkable efficiency of the Congregation in gathering news is evident from the fact that the Holy Father knew by mid-August, 1939, that the order to attack Poland had already been given. As late as August 29 the American diplomats in Europe were cabling our State Department that there would be no war.

Father Pacelli began his training in papal diplomacy as an *apprendista* with duties similar to those of a junior clerk in a modern office. He wrote routine letters and memoranda, prepared digests of reports from papal diplomats abroad, and attended to the multitude of small details which underlie the efficient functioning of an organization whose activities reach into every nation of the world. The first step upward was promotion to the rank of *minutante* or private secretary. This was a position of considerable trust and importance because a *minutante* records the proceedings of important conferences and prepares confidential reports and documents. In addition he writes briefs on the canon and civil law involved in problems before the Secretariate of State and drafts the necessary legal papers. Through his work as *apprendista* and *minutante* Father Pacelli acquired an intimate knowledge of conditions, customs, and laws in many nations.

The understanding which Pius XII has of the nations and peoples of the world is due in great measure to personal observation and study as well as to the work just outlined. Father Pacelli early began to win his name as the

Church's most traveled pope. When Queen Victoria of England died in 1901, he journeyed to London with Monsignor Merry del Val to convey to the new king, Edward VII, the condolences of Leo XIII. This was his first trip abroad. In 1908 he returned to England as a monsignor in the entourage of the papal legate to the Eucharistic Congress being held in London. It was his first meeting with arrogant bigotry. The English government forbade the Catholics to carry the Blessed Sacrament in procession through the streets on the grounds that it was a "popish" superstition and an idolatrous practice. A youthful member of Parliament, Winston Churchill, protested such petty prejudice, but to no avail. Monsignor Pacelli was in England again in 1910 as a member of the papal mission representing the pope at the coronation of King George V and Queen Mary. Diplomatic affairs of the Holy See took him as well to France, Germany, and the many nations which made up the old Austro-Hungarian Empire. Through these trips abroad he came into contact and friendship with the leaders and future leaders of Europe. The skill and insight in dealing with secular rulers which would characterize his later achievements were now being developed.

Meanwhile, Monsignor Pacelli's success in his diplomatic career was being paralleled in his career as teacher and scholar. Shortly after entering the Secretariate of State, he accepted the position of substitute professor of canon law at the Roman College of St. Appolinaris. The fame of his lectures caused the Catholic University of America to offer him a professorship on its faculty of canon law, which offer he declined because of his work in the Congregation. Later he was chosen for another important teaching task, that of professor of Ecclesiastical

Diplomacy and International Law at the Academy of Noble Ecclesiastics. This institution, founded by Clement XI in 1701, trains promising clerics for the papal diplomatic service. The curriculum includes ecclesiastical diplomacy, diplomatic procedure, and modern languages. Eventually the burdens of diplomacy became so urgent that Monsignor Pacelli asked to be relieved of all teaching work.

It is not commonly known that Pius XII assisted in the preparation of an epochal law book. Impressed by his knowledge and studiousness, Pius X asked Monsignor Pacelli to collaborate with Monsignor Gasparri on his monumental codification of canon law. The Church and all her children are governed by the laws and regulations which through the centuries have been enacted by the popes and the ecumenical councils (meetings of the bishops of the Church under the authority of the pope to legislate for the faithful). From the earliest years these regulations had been scattered throughout many books and documents. There was no single book or series of books to which a bishop or priest seeking the law of the Church on a specific problem could turn for guidance. As a result there was much confusion and inefficiency, as well as an understandable ignorance of many of the laws of the Church. This antiquated and cumbersome legal system would have to be modernized and simplified, if the Church was to function effectively in the ever increasing complexity of the twentieth century. To Monsignor Gasparri, the foremost canon lawyer of his time, was given the task of modernization.

Monsignor Pacelli, aided by a staff of clerks and copyists, collected decisions, decrees, and laws from the centuries of ecclesiastical legislation. The Vatican library and archives were the chief source of information. Five thousand priests, bishops, and civil lawyers in all the nations of the world collaborated under an oath of secrecy. They furnished the particular ecclesiastical laws and customs of their own countries, and advised on national and racial problems. When this vast work of collecting was finished, Monsignors Gasparri and Pacelli undertook the task of codification. They divided the rules and regulations into separate classifications, e.g., those which governed persons as distinguished from places and things. The classifications were then subdivided into particular persons, e.g., priests, religious, and laity, and all pertinent rules and regulations were gathered within the respective subclassifications. The intricate work of classification done, Monsignors Gasparri and Pacelli proceeded to set forth in precise but complete form each rule. The stupendous work was completed in 1915, and the *Codex Canonicis Juris,* or *Code of Canon Law,* as it is officially known, was published in 1917.

It is difficult for a person unversed in law and unfamiliar with law books to grasp or to appreciate the scope and genius of the work of Monsignors Pacelli and Gasparri. A few comparisons with certain undertakings of law codification in the United States might prove useful. The cost of codifying the laws enacted by Congress since 1789 ran into millions of dollars. Monsignors Pacelli and Gasparri codified the laws which the Church has enacted since the death of Christ for the total sum of five thousand dollars. The laws which govern the state of Wisconsin and her three and a half million citizens are contained in a twelve by six-inch book of 3241 pages. The *Code of Canon Law* which governs more than 350,000,000 people and regulates the administrative organization of a universal institution is a six by four-inch book of less than four hundred pages, containing 2414 laws.

Amid the glamour and prestige of papal diplomacy, the future shepherd of Christendom never forgot that a priest is ordained primarily to save souls. Every week Monsignor Pacelli spent many hours in the confessional at Chiesa Nuova, absolving, consoling, and guiding the faithful. On Sundays he taught catechism to the boys and girls of one of Rome's poorest quarters. The clothes which many of his students wore were proof of their teacher's charity. Several evenings a month he gave spiritual conferences to the French Sisters of Namur, who conduct a high school and college for the daughters of the Roman aristocracy. Perhaps closest to Monsignor Pacelli's priestly heart was his work as the spiritual director of the House of St. Rose, a home for working girls. Here he came to learn and to experience the hardships and the problems of the working classes.

And laboring for the salvation of others, Monsignor Pacelli did not neglect his own. The many articles written about him since his election to the throne of Peter have stressed his character and experience as a diplomat. But much more than an able statesman and a foremost world leader — he is the Holy Father, a man of sanctity and deep spirituality. While an *apprendista* he began the practice of spending two hours of each day in communion with God before the Blessed Sacrament, and two weeks of each year in the silence and prayer of a retreat. In this remark to a group of seminarians Monsignor Pacelli revealed his own inner character and preoccupation with the spiritual life. "When I meet an ordinary man, I treat him with respect. He may be a saint. When I meet a priest, I see a man who ought to be a saint. But I wish to find out." The Church and the world soon saw the candle of holiness which humility as a bushel sought to hide.

Vatican circles nicknamed him *"Il Santo"* — the holy one.
A newspaper correspondent expressed the estimate of
many when he wrote: "Eugenio Pacelli has the sublime
greatness of a mortified, almost transparent body, which
seems to serve only as the cover of his soul."

Vacations were spent in travels through northern Italy
and Alpine Switzerland and in visits to the Pacelli country
home near Oriano. One afternoon while at the latter place
Monsignor Pacelli received a call from the Congregation
to return immediately to Rome, as an important conference had been summoned for that evening. Scalabreta, the
family coachman, was not at hand to drive the Monsignor;
and unwilling to wait he harnessed the horse and started
for the railroad station. Suddenly the horse turned off the
main highway, hurried down a side road, and stopped ex-
pectantly before a wineshop. Monsignor Pacelli shouted
the Italian equivalent of "Giddap," but the horse refused
to move. Perplexed at this strange behavior, the Monsignor inquired of the loafers in front of the shop what he
should do. They informed him that the horse was only
waiting for the pint of wine which the coachman always
gave him when he visited the wineshop. Not to be outdone
in generosity, Monsignor Pacelli said: "Bring the horse
two pints of wine. I wish him to feel his best and to travel
his fastest." The horse drank the two pints and started
off for the next hill at a furious gallop. Up to the crest,
and there the horse laid down "to sleep it off." Monsignor Pacelli continued on foot, missed the train, and was
late for the conference. A papal diplomat may know his
theology and his canon law, and have much to learn of
horses and wine.

These were formative years, and men as well as events
and experience aided in fashioning the character and the

talents of the future pope. Three popes and three cardinals greatly influenced the early life of Eugenio Pacelli. The popes were Leo XIII, Pius X, and Benedict XV; the cardinals, Mariano Rampolla, Merry del Val, and Pietro Gasparri. In a brief biographical sketch and character delineation of these men, one will find reflected the abilities and virtues so notable in Pius XII.

The long pontificate of Leo XIII, 1878 to 1903, regained for the Church world prestige and intellectual eminence. His astute diplomacy defeated Bismarck's campaign against the Church in Germany and won for the Holy See the admiration and respect of all nations. The dispute between Germany and Spain over the Caroline Islands in the South Pacific was referred to him for arbitration. His wise decision satisfied both nations and averted armed conflict. A brilliant student, Leo opened the Vatican library and archives to the scholars of the world, brought back the philosophy and theology of St. Thomas Aquinas to the seminaries and universities, and in the encyclical *Rerum Novarum* wrote a document for the ages. This encyclical is an eloquent cry to heaven against the oppressive injustice of unbridled capitalism. It details a masterful plan of economic and social reform which, had it been followed, would have prevented the tragic depressions of this century. Studying and working within the influence of this great mind necessarily inspired Eugenio Pacelli to intellectual achievements and inspired in him an enduring love of wisdom and knowledge.

The humility of Pius XII and his tender love of the poor have their inspiration in Pius X, Leo's successor. When Pius X was elected, he knelt before the cardinals and implored them tearfully to reconsider their choice. As Bishop of Mantua and later as Patriarch of Venice, he often pledged his episcopal ring and cross to buy food for the poor. Once a man came to him and said that his wife was sick and needed broth, but that he had no money with which to buy meat. The then Father Sarto said: "Come with me." Entering the kitchen he took the kettle of meat boiling for his own dinner and gave it to the man. So generous was he that when the Conclave was called, he was forced to pawn his watch to buy a railroad ticket to Rome. He bought a round-trip ticket, because it was two dollars cheaper, and he certainly expected to return home. Remembering the poor and their need of strength and consolation, Pius X introduced the practice of early and frequent Communion. The reform of sacred music, of religious ceremonies, and of liturgical books were among his achievements. It is possible that one day we will venerate him as St. Pius, because there are already reports of miracles worked through his intercession.

Benedict XV, who succeeded Pius X in September of 1914, was one of the finest diplomatic minds of the day. The tragedy of World War I overshadowed his great work for the world and for the Church. Had the nations of the world heeded his advice, World War I would have ended sooner, and World War II probably would never have begun. The policies of Pius XII on war and peace greatly reflect the influence and teaching of Benedict XV.

When Father Pacelli began as an *apprendista,* Cardinal Mariano Rampolla, a native of Sicily, was Secretary of State. He had come to the office when Italy and Germany were bent on destroying the Holy See as an international influence. But Cardinal Rampolla skillfully fought the Italians to a standstill, and gained the admiration and later the friendship of the German Chancellor Bismarck. The uncompromising courage and relentless zeal of Cardinal

Rampolla offered an inspiring example for the young *apprendista* to imitate.

Monsignor Merry del Val, the son of Spain's ambassador to the Vatican, attended, in the capacity of Prosecretary, the Conclave which elected Pius X. It was his duty to vest the new Pontiff in the papal robes. As Merry del Val placed the white skullcap on the new Pope, Pius X placed his own scarlet one on the head of the Prosecretary, indicating thereby that Merry del Val would be the first cardinal created by the new Pontiff. Retiring to the papal apartments when the Conclave ceremonies were over, Pius sent for Merry del Val and told him that he would be the new Secretary of State, and at the first consistory created him cardinal. Cardinal Merry del Val was then thirty-seven, the youngest Secretary of State in the history of the Church. He would be Eugenio Pacelli's superior for eleven years.

During these years Cardinal Merry del Val was confronted with bitter and hard problems. Chief among them was France whose hatred of the Church reached a climax when her premier, Combes, an apostate monk, declared in parliament that he proposed to tear the name of God from the sky. Combes died in 1921 in an insane asylum. The nuns and religious orders were expelled from France and education was completely secularized. But through his patience and wisdom Cardinal Merry del Val slowly won France back to the fold of Christ. He did not see the fruits of his efforts, but his able assistant, Eugenio Pacelli, would one day be welcomed to Paris by the president and cabinet of France.

Cardinal Pietro Gasparri became Papal Secretary of State with the election of Benedict XV, and occupied the post through his pontificate and that of Pius XI until 1930.

Filippo and Virginia Pacelli, parents of Pius XII.
— *International News Photo.*

Eugenio Pacelli as a schoolboy.
— *International News Photo.*

As a young student of law, Eugenio Pacelli shows the quiet serious-ness that marks him as Pope.

A group of curious Romans gaze up at the windows of the apartment where Pius XII was born in 1876. — *International News Photo.*

Pius XII in 1929 at the time of elevation to the cardinalate. — *Acme.*

Pius XII as he appeared in 1911 when in London for the coronation of King George VI. — *Acme.*

Left:
Cardinal Pacelli, Papal Legate at the Triduum in Lourdes, 1935.

Right:
Kneeling before the huge monstrance, Cardinal Pacelli takes part in the Procession closing the International Eucharistic Congress in Buenos Aires, 1934.

The supreme achievement of his diplomatic career was the Lateran Treaty (1929) with Italy. By it Vatican City was founded and the imprisonment of the popes was ended. To shrewd wisdom Cardinal Gasparri added a biting sense of humor. One day an American prelate was boasting to him of the magnificent prayer which he had composed for a national political convention. "And Your Eminence," the archbishop pompously said, "when I had finished working on it, the prayer was a masterpiece." "Indeed," replied Cardinal Gasparri, "and was it better than the Our Father?" When the bloody Calles was massacring the Catholics of Mexico, the cardinal taught his parrot to shriek in Latin: "They shall not prevail. They shall not prevail." Cardinal Gasparri trained Eugenio Pacelli in the art of diplomacy and set him an example of inflexible devotion to duty and principle — an oddity, perhaps, in today's view of a diplomat. Behind the diplomatic triumphs and the moral greatness of the pupil one can find the teaching and the influence of the tutor.

World War I, which would achieve nothing out of the death and suffering of millions, erupted July 28, 1914. Franz Joseph, Emperor of Austria, sent his ambassador to ask Pius X to bless the Austrian armies. In great anger the Vicar of the Prince of Peace rose from his throne. "Get out of my sight. Get out of my sight," he shouted, "Away. Away. I bless peace not war." The Holy Father, mortally struck, slumped back in his throne. He was put to bed, never to rise. On August 20 he died.

The new Pontiff, Benedict XV, named Cardinal Gasparri Secretary of State, and in 1915 appointed Monsignor Pacelli Secretary of the Congregation for Extraordinary Ecclesiastical Affairs. To Monsignor Pacelli's many duties was added that of distributing food and clothing to war prisoners and refugees, of exchanging internees and the wounded, and of obtaining information on those missing and captive. Through his efforts thirty thousand unfit prisoners of war were exchanged between France and Germany. In December of 1915 ten thousand wounded war prisoners from both sides were brought to Switzerland to recuperate.

Anxious about the spiritual welfare of the prisoners of war, Monsignor Pacelli sent Mass kits, rosaries, prayer books, and medals to the prison camps of both sides. In a letter to all the bishops of the belligerent nations, he ordered among other things: "The Most Reverend Ordinaries of the dioceses in which the prisoners are shall designate immediately one or more priests, possessing a sufficient knowledge of the prisoners' languages. These priests shall with all zeal seek the spiritual and material welfare of the prisoners, doing everything in their power to comfort and assist them in the various and often painful necessities in which they are. Especially, the priests shall ascertain whether the prisoners entrusted to their care have written or in some way sent news of themselves to their families, and if not shall persuade them to do so at once, at least by post card. When prisoners are unable, either through illiteracy or sickness, or for any other reason, to correspond in this way with their families, the priests themselves shall charitably undertake to do so for them in their name, and at the same time, do what they can to ensure safe delivery of the correspondence."

One April afternoon of 1917, Pope Benedict summoned Monsignor Pacelli to his private library. When he entered, the Holy Father greeted him with: "Archbishop Aversa, our nuncio to Bavaria, is dead. We are sending you to take his place."

CHAPTER III

A SOWER AMID RUINS

To MARK the importance of Monsignor Pacelli's appointment as nuncio to the Kingdom of Bavaria, and to give proof of his own esteem for him, Pope Benedict, on May 13, 1917, himself consecrated Monsignor Pacelli Titular Archbishop of Sardis. This is an ancient and now abandoned diocese in Asia Minor, of which tradition says: "He who gets Sardis goes higher."

At the close of the long and beautiful rite His Holiness received the new Archbishop and the Pacelli family in private audience. It was a meeting of friends, for the Pope had known the family over many years and had been Archbishop Pacelli's immediate superior in the Papal Secretariate of State. The new Archbishop received from the Holy Father a beautifully bound and illuminated Canon. This is the liturgical book used by the celebrant during a pontifical Mass and contains the Canon of the Mass, that is, the part beginning with the Consecration and ending with the Communion. The ring which Archbishop Pacelli now wore on his right third finger was his mother's gift, fashioned from her own jewels and family heirlooms.

The glory and the triumph of the day were hidden from the new Archbishop by his deep humility and profound spirituality. The robes of royal purple recalled the scarlet cloak with which the Roman soldiers clothed Christ.

The jeweled cross and the costly crozier, the sparkling ring and the precious miter, meant obligation and responsibility, not rank and honor. The future Vicar of Christ found in his elevation to the hierarchy, as he would in every personal achievement, greater cause to glory not in himself but in his God.

The days of May following the consecration were given to preparations for the journey to Munich, and to conferences with the Holy Father and Vatican officials. Archbishop Pacelli had personal belongings to pack and many farewells to take. Northern Italy, through which he would travel to Bavaria, was a theater of war, and special permits to pass through the Austrian and Italian lines and guarantees of safety from the various belligerent powers had to be obtained. These were readily furnished in accordance with international law and custom which grants full immunity and freedom of travel to the diplomats of neutral nations in time of war. There was much still to be done at the Secretariate of State. The new Secretary of the Congregation for Extraordinary Ecclesiastical Affairs had to be informed on tasks unfinished and on matters highly confidential.

The final farewells taken, Nuncio Pacelli began the journey to Munich. Spring was changing into summer and the country northward from Rome was young again with green fields and blossoming orchards. Sheep and cattle grazed drowsily on hilly meadows, geese and ducks fed noisily along shallow streams. Boys and girls skipping down dusty lanes waved gaily at the passing train. Peace had on display her countless blessings. But once the river Po had been passed, the Nuncio saw a horribly different land. The winter of war lay heavily on the countryside. Crater-pocked fields were dotted with decaying corpses and rusting machines. The dull boom of artillery broke through the noise of the train. War had on display his tragic horrors.

From Italy Archbishop Pacelli crossed into neutral Switzerland. This is a land of forested mountains and fairylike valleys, whose strategic position has saved it from the blighting hand of two world wars. Yet there were many things to remind the Nuncio of the urgency of his mission. Internment camps held escaped prisoners of war, and exchange trains were bringing to and from the borders the thousands of wounded and maimed soldiers for whom war had no further use. Crossing the German border Archbishop Pacelli entered the Kingdom of Bavaria.

Though only the size of Maine, Bavaria has played a major role in European life and history for more than fifteen hundred years. Consisting of Bavaria proper and the Palatinate of the Rhine, which are separated by Baden and Hesse, it mainly belongs to the basin of the Danube. Magnificent mountains and crystalline lakes form but a part of its natural wealth. There are extensive forests, bountiful fields, rich quarries and mines, and mineral springs famed for their curative properties. Before the destruction of the recent war, heavy and light industries flourished at Munich, the capital, Furth, and Aschaffenburg.

The early centuries of Bavaria's history were dominated by the Romans and later by the Franks. During the twelfth century, with the rise of the powerful Wittelsbach dynasty, Bavaria became an independent duchy. It was a precarious independence, threatened from without by Austrian domination and from within by civil and religious wars. In 1805 Elector Maximillian purchased the title of king by marrying his daughter to Napoleon's stepson. When the German Empire was proclaimed in 1870, the Kingdom of

Bavaria became an integral part of it, but retained a separate diplomatic service, military administration, postal system, and legislature. In 1917 Ludwig III was on the throne of Bavaria. To him Nuncio Pacelli presented his credentials on May 28.

The first missionary to Bavaria was Rupert, Bishop of Worms, who came in 691. St. Corbinian followed him a decade later and founded the Diocese of Freising, which in 1818 became the Archdiocese of Munich-Freising. The centuries since St. Corbinian have seen both ages of faith and periods of persecution, the most recent having been the Hitler regime. But faith prevailed, and today Bavaria is 70 per cent Catholic. When Bavaria is denounced as the birthplace of Nazism, it should also be remembered as the home of the Oberammergau Passion Players and of Theresa Neumann the stigmatist. It was in Munich that Hitler found his most courageous opponent, Cardinal Michael Faulhaber, who fearlessly denounced the Nazi crimes and evils. Father Rupert Meyer, the legless martyr who suffered ten years of the Dachau concentration camp, is also of Bavaria.

The papal nunciature was established at Munich in 1786, following a long period of anticlericalism. At the time of Archbishop Pacelli's appointment, it was the sole diplomatic link between the Holy See and Germany. Prussia was too belligerently non-Catholic to accept a papal nuncio at the Court of Berlin. The anti-Catholicism of the Nazis had an historical as well as an ideological basis. Since the time of Bismarck, German government circles contained a bigoted group whose primary objective was the subordination and destruction of the Catholic Church in Germany. Had Germany won World War I, German Catholics would, very probably, have been relegated to a

second-class citizenship and might eventually have been
destroyed as a religious unit. The anti-Catholics saw in
Nazism a means to their objective.

Munich of 1917 was a city of quaint charm and mellow
beauty. The name attests the city's Catholic origin for a
free translation is "City of the Monks." Its towering twin
spires with copper cupolas make the Frauenkirche the
most imposing of Munich's many churches, but the Hof-
kirche and the Church of St. Peter's are more beautiful.
Unhappily these and the other churches of Munich had in
1917 almost as many empty pews as worshipers, for irreligion and indifference were destroying the faith of countless
Catholics. Had the people of Munich and of all Germany
been more zealous, the efforts of the new Nuncio to obtain
peace might not have failed. They had little heeded the
exhortation of Pope Benedict: "In time of war more than
ever there is need of insistent and incessant prayer to move
divine Compassion that we may be given a truce in the
terrible course of avenging justice."

Spring of 1917 found the Allies and the Central Powers
in a bloody deadlock. Russia and Rumania had been
crushed, and Germany was in position to throw her full
might against the western Allies. But the allied blockade
was strangling Germany and Austria into economic collapse, and Turkey, the third member of the Central Powers, was in peril following the loss of Baghdad and Palestine to the British in 1916. Since America's weight was still
an unknown factor, there seemed little chance of victory
being achieved by either side. Therefore Pope Benedict
judged the moment favorable for renewed efforts to end the
horrible slaughter and to negotiate a just peace. Though
his frequent and moving appeals for peace had so far
fallen on unheeding ears, he would try again. The task

of presenting the papal peace plan to Germany was entrusted to Archbishop Pacelli, who had collaborated on it
with the Holy Father and Cardinal Gasparri.

A few days after his arrival in Munich, Archbishop
Pacelli went to Berlin. There he had a meeting with Von
Bethmann-Hollweg, the Imperial Chancellor, who was an
able statesman and sincerely desirous of peace. In a series
of conferences with the Chancellor and high government
officials, Archbishop Pacelli learned the war aims of Germany, which he transmitted to the Pope and the Cardinal
Secretary of State. Germany was prepared to restore Belgium and favored an all-round limitation of armaments.
The restoration of Belgium being a preliminary condition
to the acceptance of any peace plan by the Allies, the situation appeared hopeful.

The meeting of Archbishop Pacelli with Kaiser Wilhelm II took place July 29 in the imperial headquarters at
Kreuznach, Baden. Wearing the full-dress uniform of a
Prussian field marshal and carrying his sword and helmet,
the Kaiser received the Nuncio in his gilded throne room.
By the end of the conference Archbishop Pacelli must have
thought that he was participating in a comic opera. He
presented His Majesty an autographed letter of the Pope,
asking his help in the promotion of peace. The Kaiser read
the letter and then arrogantly remarked that he had made
a peace offer the previous December. It had been rejected.
Therefore his enemies and not he desired war.

The Nuncio tactfully suggested that more detailed and
specific proposals might be made. The Kaiser replied
with a harangue on how the Pope should conduct his
foreign affairs. His Holiness should command Italy and
France to make peace — of course, they would readily do
so. Then the war lord of the Prussians lectured his visitor

on how the Pope could defend the Vatican from armed assault. A pillbox here and a machine-gun emplacement there, and the Vatican would be a veritable fortress, impregnable against all attacks. Perhaps the Nuncio thought of Pius IX who, when informed that Garibaldi was marching on Rome, pointed to the crucifix above his desk and said: "That will be my artillery." The lecture in strategy over, the Kaiser invited his guest to lunch. Before leaving, Archbishop Pacelli obtained the Kaiser's promise to halt the wholesale deportation of Belgian civilians. In his memoirs Kaiser Wilhelm wrote of Nuncio Pacelli: "He has a distinguished likeable appearance, he is of a high intelligence, and has impeccable manners, the perfect pattern of a Roman prelate." It would be interesting to learn what his guest thought of the Kaiser!

An Inter-Allied conference was to open in London, August 7. Though the Kaiser's attitude had been pointless, Cardinal Gasparri instructed Archbishop Pacelli to press matters with the German government. The German foreign office advised the Nuncio that an official declaration on the papal peace plan would be forthcoming. Anxious lest the continued delay lead to complete failure, Benedict on August 1 ordered the papal representatives in all belligerent nations to deliver his peace note to the respective governments.

Since the beginning of Our Pontificate . . . We have not ceased to exhort the belligerent peoples and Governments to become once again brothers, even though publicity was not given to all that We have done in order to attain this noble end.

. . . We desire now to put forward some more concrete and practical propositions, and invite the Governments of the belligerents to come to some agreement on the following points, which seem to offer the bases of a just and lasting peace, though leaving to them the duty of adjusting and completing them: First of all, the fundamental point must be that the moral force of right shall be substituted for the material force of arms; thence must follow a just agreement of all for the simultaneous and reciprocal diminution of armaments, in accordance with rules and guarantees to be established hereafter, in a measure sufficient and necessary for the maintenance of public order in each State; next, as a substitute for armies, the institution of arbitration, with its high peace-making function, subject to regulations to be agreed on and sanctions to be determined against the State which should refuse either to submit international questions to arbitration or to accept its decision.

Once the supremacy of right is thus established, let all obstacles to the free intercourse of people be swept aside, in assuring, by means of rules, to be fixed in the same way, the true liberty of and common rights over the sea. . . .

As to the damage to be made good and the cost of the war, We see no other way of solving the question but to lay down, as a general principle, an entire and reciprocal con-donation. . . . If in certain cases there are, on the other hand, particular reasons, let them be weighed justly and equitably.

But these peaceful agreements . . . are not possible without the reciprocal restitution of territories at the moment occupied — consequently, on the part of Germany, a total evacuation of Belgium, with a guarantee of her complete political, military, and economic independence . . . ; similar evacuation of French territory; on the part of the other belligerent Powers, a similar restitution of the German Colonies.

As regards territorial questions . . . there is ground for hope that . . . the disputants would feel disposed to examine them in a conciliatory spirit, giving due weight, within the limits of justice and feasibility . . . to the aspirations of the populations, and, on occasion, bringing their particular interests into harmony with the general welfare of the great community of mankind.

The same spirit of equity and justice must direct the examination of the remaining territorial and political questions, and particularly those which concern . . . the former kingdom of Poland, which . . . has a just claim on the sympathies of all nations.

Such are the principal foundations on which We believe

that the future reorganization of the peoples must be built. They are of a nature to make impossible the return of similar conflicts, and to prepare the solution of the economic question, which is so important for the material well-being of all the belligerent States. . . .

May God inspire you with a decision in harmony with His most holy will. Heaven grant that in meriting the applause of your contemporaries you may assure to yourselves, in the sight of future generations, the noble name of peace-makers. For Us, in close communion in prayer and penitence with all the faithful souls who are sighing for peace, We implore for you from the Divine Spirit enlightenment and counsel.

Benedict's peace proposals were fundamental and practical, offering a reasonable and effective solution to the international chaos which man's stupidity and malice had fashioned. The much lauded Fourteen Points of President Wilson, which historians acclaim as the embodiment of international wisdom, were in substantial respects a plagiarism of them. Winston Churchill's suggestions of twenty years later for vitalizing the World Court reveal an imitative reading of the Pope's proposal concerning that institution. The reparations fiasco contrived by the Treaty of Versailles underscored the soundness of Benedict's advice. Since all this is so, why was the papal peace plan rejected by both the Allies and the Central Powers?

The true answer, unfortunately, is bigotry and short-sightedness. By the secret Treaty of London, signed April 26, 1915, France, Great Britain, and Russia promised the anticlerical government of Italy that they would not admit any mediation by the Holy See. Hence, the reply of the Allies through President Wilson that no faith could be given to the word of the German government was only a partial reason for their rejection of the papal peace plan.

The German government concealed its prejudice in a subterfuge. England, who might have won over the other

Allies, informed Cardinal Gasparri that Germany must categorically agree to restore Belgium before any peace proposals could be considered. Von Bethmann-Hollweg, though he had defended Germany's criminal violation of Belgian neutrality as a necessity of war, was agreeable to this demand. But, before he could reach an agreement with the Allies, he was forced out of office and succeeded as Chancellor by George Michaelis. Michaelis, strongly anti-Catholic, considered a papal peace "a most terrible thing" to be prevented at any cost, lest the Pope, through the prestige which such success would bring him, become an influence in European affairs. Michaelis' first note to the Holy See did not even mention Belgium. Archbishop Pacelli again pleaded with the German Chancellor to meet the Allies' demand. The final German note was equally pointless because, while it discussed the restoration of Belgium, it promised nothing.

The evening when the last German note was received, Archbishop Pacelli and a friend sat in gloomy conversation at the nunciature. "Everything is lost," he sadly remarked, "your poor country too." History would prove the Archbishop a true prophet.

Through the remainder of 1917 and most of 1918 Archbishop Pacelli devoted his efforts to lessening the hardships which the war was causing. The children of blockaded Germany were starving and for them he organized food relief. In German prison camps were confined hundreds of thousands of Allied soldiers. These he visited frequently, preaching to them, distributing food and medical supplies, and transmitting their messages to relatives back home. His remaining hours were given to prayer and pastoral work in Munich and other German cities. In conferences and sermons he urged the people to renew in their lives the spirit of the crucified Christ. A particular act of kindness by the Archbishop was saving the life of Ossip Gabrilo-vitch, an eminent Russian pianist. Arrested on charges of espionage, he was being held for trial and execution. Bruno Walter, then director of the Bavarian Opera House and presently a noted symphony conductor in the United States, appealed to the Nuncio. In a few hours Gabrilo-vitch was cleared of the false charges and freed from prison.

The year 1918 brought personal sorrow to Archbishop Pacelli, for his mother passed away in the early winter and his father followed her in death toward the end of fall. This sad loss he accepted in the spirit of Job: "The Lord hath given, the Lord hath taken away. Blessed be the name of the Lord."

The Ludendorff offensive having failed despite its enor-mous cost in dead and wounded, Germany by the fall of 1918 was compelled to sue for peace. Not only had Allied power become overwhelming, but mutiny had broken out in the German Navy at Kiel and rebellion was sweeping the coastal cities. Michaelis was succeeded as chancellor by Prince Max of Baden, who immediately asked President Wilson for a peace based on the Fourteen Points. The President replied that before peace could be discussed a responsible and reliable government must be established in Germany. The kaiser abdicated and fled to Holland. On November 11 the Armistice was signed and a year later the Treaty of Versailles. Peace — but not the hon-orable and just peace of Benedict XV, not even the Four-teen Points of President Wilson! It was a Carthaginian peace destined to be a cause of another and more hor-rible war. The Treaty of Versailles failed to uproot the causes of war and to plant the perennial of peace because vengeance and greed, not justice and charity, wrote its provisions. While a German hand tossed the match which set off World War II, the hands of the other signatories to the Versailles Peace helped to spread the powder. The spirit, more than the letter, of Versailles made peace impossible.

On the night of November 7–8 revolution broke out in Munich with hungry mobs milling through the streets, roaring for peace. Upon the abdication of King Ludwig and the fall of his ministers, Kurt Eisner, an independent socialist, placed himself at the head of a revolutionary government. Pending the election of a new Bavarian Diet, a provisional Socialist Republic was set up. On February 20, 1919, the day before the opening of the Diet, Eisner was murdered as he climbed the steps of the chancellery. A confused lull preceded the tumult which broke in bloodshed on April 4.

The hammer and sickle of Bolshevist Terror flew over Munich, as Spartacist "gangs" plundered the city. Marauding revolutionists sacked the homes of the wealthy and looted the stores and public buildings. Rival bands, quarreling over loot and struggling for power, battled through the city streets. The death toll mounted. Embassy row was hurriedly deserted by the ambassadors and ministers, but the Nuncio remained to feed the hungry children and to console the terrified populace.

One evening, during the Red Terror, an automobile passing the nunciature sprayed the lower floor with machine-gun bullets. Monsignor Schioppa, an assistant to the Nuncio, narrowly escaped death by throwing himself on the floor. The windows were shattered and the walls were scarred by the bullets. Providentially Archbishop Pacelli was in the workers' section of the city on an errand of charity. Upon his return a few hours later he telephoned at once the Spartacist headquarters and vigorously protested against the outrageous incident. The Communist blackguard in command offered no apologies but made more threats, warning the Nuncio to leave Munich immediately.

Toward twilight of the next day a rude pounding shook the front door of the nunciature. Angry shouts and curses were heard. Archbishop Pacelli, in the oratory on the second floor, paused in his recitation of Vespers and made the sign of the cross. That morning thirteen members of the nobility had been murdered. The clamor continuing, a servant unbolted the door and opened it part way. Seven ruffians, brandishing daggers and rifles, roughly demanded entrance. When the servant hesitated, the looters knocked him down, and forced their way into the reception hall. The leader ordered them to search the house for food and valuables. Their search of the first floor produced nothing, for the scant food supply had already been exhausted in feeding the poor.

The looters were starting up the stairs to the second floor when they abruptly stopped. The Nuncio, dressed in his episcopal robes of purple silk and fingering his pectoral cross, was descending the stairway. A few steps above the intruders he stopped. Then, ignoring the rifles pointed at him, he icily inquired:

"Why are you here?"

There was a moment or more of uneasy silence. The Nuncio repeated his question. Then one of the ruffians muttered:

"We want your food supplies and your valuables. You have money hidden. Give it to us."

"I have no money," replied the Nuncio. "If any food is left, it is scarcely enough for ourselves and the hungry children in our care."

Lowering their rifles the Bolsheviks edged down the stairs. Other victims had cringed in terror and pleaded for mercy. This man merely looked at them with scorn and indignation. The Nuncio descended a few more steps. Then, pointing at their guns, he asked the looters:

"Why have you come armed? There is no one here who will attack and harm you. This is a house of peace, not a den of murderers. Yes, tell me why have you broken into my residence with daggers and rifles?"

There were more moments of uneasy silence. Their bluff called, the bullies lacked both answers and courage. Finally, the leader, cursing and waving his rifle, shouted:

"We can kill you. Give us what we want or we will."

As if asking a question in class, the Nuncio calmly inquired:

"Why would you wish to kill me? I have done you no harm nor will I."

Then in a voice vibrant with angry authority the Nuncio demanded:

"Why have you invaded the papal nunciature? This is not German land but belongs to the Holy See. By international law it is inviolable. Please leave at once."

Quailing before the Nuncio's resolute defiance, the ruffians backed toward the front door. From there the leader growled:

"Where is your car? We want it."

This being a small price for security, the Nuncio replied:

"It is in the garage."

One of the looters ran to the garage, started the automobile, and drove it to the door. All climbed in and still cursing they drove off. The Nuncio watched them from the doorway. Then he shut the door and returned to the oratory to finish Vespers.

Archbishop Pacelli had no intention of allowing the Bolsheviks to keep his automobile, when he needed it for works of mercy. Twice daily he telephoned the Communist chief of police, pointed out that since the automobile was papal property its theft was in violation of international as well as of moral law, and demanded its immediate return. Annoyed by such persistency, the police chief one day said: "Stop calling me or I'll come up and shoot all of you." The intrepid Archbishop replied: "You are welcome." The automobile was returned.

Fearful that the Bolshevik Terror would eventually engulf the entire nation, the Reich government despatched an army from Berlin under General Epp. Fierce fighting swept the streets of Munich as the Communists battled the federal soldiers; but by May 1 the revolution was suppressed, its leaders dead or imprisoned. Peace and order restored, the Socialist government returned to power. The following August a constitution was adopted under which Bavaria became a federated republic of the German Reich. The conduct of foreign affairs, the administration of the army, and the control of the railroads and other public utilities were surrendered to the Reich. After the abortive Ludendorff putsch of November, 1923, a coalition government came into power and remained until the rise of Hitler. Then all semblance of Bavarian autonomy disappeared and the Republic of Bavaria became a part of the Nazi state.

In late summer of 1920 the Apostolic Visitor to Poland, Archbishop Achille Ratti, stopped in Munich on his way from Warsaw to Rome. The two future popes, for the guest became Pius XI in 1922, exchanged experiences with the Communists and discussed the condition of the Church in Central and Eastern Europe. During the Bolshevik invasion of Poland, when most of the foreign representatives fled Warsaw, Archbishop Ratti remained and continued his work of charity among the poor in the devastated areas. After the danger had ended, the Polish Parliament passed a resolution citing the Apostolic Visitor for his bravery, and Marshal Pilsudski conferred upon him Poland's highest decoration, the Order of the White Eagle. The two Archbishops had become friends in Rome, when Monsignor Ratti, Prefect of the Vatican Library, had assisted Monsignor Pacelli in his search for the early laws and regulations of the Church.

In the years that followed the 1918 revolution Archbishop Pacelli was the most popular diplomat in Munich. The papal nunciature, though a gloomy-looking, austere mansion on dignified Brienner Strasse, became the most beloved embassy of the capital. Here lived the saintly Nuncio who was father to the prosperous and needy, to the important and the unknown, to all whom either life or man had burdened with sorrows. His sermons of simple beauty moved the sinner to repentance and the devout to sanctity. To him the bishops and priests of Germany turned for wisdom and inspiration in the complex problems which war had left in its wake. The housewives in the neighborhood of the Brienner Strasse had their own particular reason to be grateful to the Nuncio. So punctual was he that they set their clocks by his morning walk. It was always exactly at eight o'clock.

The Holy See had long desired to maintain diplomatic relations with Germany proper rather than with Bavaria alone. This had been prevented by the opposition of anti-

Catholic and antireligious groups in Prussia. Now that Germany was an international pariah, however, bigotry lost out to her need of friends, and in 1927 Archbishop Pacelli was promoted to Berlin, accredited to Prussia and the Reich government.* By immemorial custom — sanctioned by the Congress of Vienna in 1815 — he became Dean of the Diplomatic Corps, taking precedence over all other ambassadors and envoys. This usage derives from the spiritual dignity of the pope, who as the Vicar of Christ outranks secular rulers and sovereigns. With untiring zeal Archbishop Pacelli continued to labor for the Church and for Germany. Success blessed his every effort.

For the Church he obtained favorable Concordats with Bavaria, ratified June 25, 1925, and with Prussia, ratified July 14, 1929. A concordat is a treaty between the Holy See and a secular government regarding ecclesiastical affairs in the territory of the latter. With the United States there is no need for a concordat because the Church in America is completely free to regulate her affairs, restricted only by the laws applicable to all Americans. This is not true of less fortunate nations. There the government interferes with the Church in matters of education, of appointing pastors and bishops, and of property ownership and administration. A concordat determines the rights and duties of the Church and the particular government in respect to each other. The Concordat with Prussia, for instance, provided that "the Holy See is free to appoint Catholic Bishops, but before publishing its nomination, it will submit the name of its choice to the government, which may

---

* The nunciature in Munich was not abolished when Archbishop Pacelli moved to Berlin. A new nuncio, Archbishop Vasalo di Torregrossa, was appointed to his place. This remained the situation until 1933 when under the Concordat the nunciatures to Bavaria and Prussia were merged into a single nunciature to Germany.

object to his appointment for political reasons." The
Church was given full freedom to educate, subject only to
the general regulations and requirements of the Prussian
ministry of education. The bishops were authorized to
appoint pastors at their own discretion, provided that such
appointees were German nationals. The government
would continue to pay the salaries of the clergy, and would
provide needed funds for building and maintaining
Church property. The provisions of the Concordat with
Bavaria were substantially the same.

The Concordat with Prussia, though nullified by subsequent events, was a remarkable achievement for Archbishop Pacelli. Sixty years before, Bismarck, Germany's
Iron Chancellor, had decreed that the Church must become a servant of the State or she would be destroyed.
Harsh repressive laws were enacted and brutally enforced,
priests were imprisoned, and churches and schools were
closed and confiscated. But Leo XIII and the Catholic
Center party of Germany skillfully outmaneuvered Bismarck, and to save his own power he ended the persecution. Prussia remained bitterly anti-Catholic and the negotiations for the Concordat were fanatically opposed.
Criticism Archbishop Pacelli dispelled with patient explanation; opposition he overcame with tactful persuasion.

The German Protestant Press Service once aptly described Archbishop Pacelli as "a sower amid ruins." He
sowed faith in God and love for one's neighbor in a land
of hate and despair. Burdened with unwise reparations and
impoverished by economic collapse, Germany was a cauldron of unrest. By word and example the Nuncio worked
to maintain peace and to secure harmony. In frequent
sermons at Catholic gatherings he recalled the true glories
of Germany and emphasized her great contributions to

world culture and progress, awakening in the hearts of his audience hope for the future and solace for the present.

Nuncio Pacelli aided greatly in securing justice for Germany in the matter of the Ruhr occupation. When Germany was unable to meet the impossible reparations imposed by the Versailles Treaty, French and Belgian troops occupied the Ruhr, which is the German steel and iron center and contains vast stores of coal. To humiliate the Germans, France included black Senegalese soldiers among her occupation troops. These semisavages lacked even elemental respect for the women of the Ruhr. The situation was disgraceful and unjust, and Pius XI ordered Archbishop Pacelli to prepare a firsthand report. The Nuncio flew to the Ruhr and made a thorough investigation. From his exhaustive report the Pope formulated a letter to the Papal Secretary of State, protesting the French occupation and calling for an immediate and equitable settlement of the entire problem of German reparations. Made public, this letter helped to move international opinion against such unjust treatment of the German people.

The high esteem and affection in which Archbishop Pacelli was held during his stay in Berlin can be found in the opinions of those who knew him. President Von Hindenburg of Germany wrote of "the noble conception Archbishop Pacelli had of his office, his wise objectivity, his inflexible sense of justice, his generous humanity, and his great love for his neighbor." Viscount d' Abernon, the first British ambassador in postwar Berlin, called Archbishop Pacelli the best-informed man in the German capital. Dorothy Thompson, American newspaper and radio commentator, said in one of her columns: "Those of us who were foreign correspondents in Berlin during the days of the Weimar Republic were not unfamiliar with the figure of the dean of the diplomatic corps. Tall, slender, with magnificent eyes, strong features and expressive hands, in his appearance and bearing Archbishop Pacelli looked every inch what he was — a Roman nobleman, of the proudest blood of the western world. In knowledge of German and European affairs and in diplomatic astuteness the Nuncio was without an equal."

Because Archbishop Pacelli preferred the mountains to the sea, his vacations were spent at Stella Maris, a convent at the foot of Mount Rorchasch near Einsiedeln, Switzerland. Every afternoon, the weather permitting, he and Father Tomas Jungt, spiritual director of the convent, would hike through the countryside or climb Mount Rorchasch or another of the many hills in the vicinity. Upon their return one November afternoon of 1929, the Nuncio found a telegram on his desk. Opening it, he read, "Heartiest congratulations," and the name of a friend in Rome. Puzzled, the Archbishop handed the telegram to Father Jungt:

"Do you understand what this means?" he asked.

"The message is very clear to me," replied Father Jungt. "May I also congratulate you on your coming elevation to the cardinalate."

A few days later Archbishop Pacelli was officially notified and instructed to relinquish his post in Berlin and to return to Rome for the ceremonies of elevation. The night of his departure from Berlin he rode in an open carriage through gaily decorated streets to the Anhalter Station. The sidewalks were massed with cheering throngs, and deputations from student clubs, labor unions, and church societies marched before the carriage. On the carpeted and flower-strewn platform of the station, the cabinet and the

diplomatic corps were assembled to bid the Nuncio farewell. Archbishop Pacelli thanked the officials and in a
brief speech told them and the thousands crowding the
station of his love and hopes for a Christian Germany.
Then he boarded the train, and coming to the window of
his compartment again blessed the people of Berlin and
through them the people of all Germany.

CHAPTER IV

PAPAL SECRETARY OF STATE

ON DECEMBER 16, 1929, at a public consistory held in the Sistine Chapel and attended by members of the papal court and the diplomatic corps accredited to the Holy See, Pius XI conferred upon Archbishop Pacelli the Red Hat of the cardinalate. A cardinal's hat is worn on very few occasions; after the owner's death it is fastened to the ceiling of his church, where it remains, gathering dust and cobwebs, until time has had its destructive way. The hat is red, tradition explains, to remind the wearer that he must be willing to suffer and to die, if need be, for the faith and for the papacy. The cardinal's ring of sapphire, engraved on the inner side with the Pope's coat of arms, was bestowed at a later and private consistory. On this occasion Archbishop Pacelli also received his title, Cardinal-Priest of the Church of St. John and St. Paul in Rome.

The new pastor of St. John and St. Paul took formal possession of his church on January 12, 1930. In quiet contrast to the spectacular processions of former times, Cardinal Pacelli went alone, accompanied only by his chauffeur and his chaplain. At the church door he was greeted by the vicar and the clergy, who escorted him to his throne in the sanctuary while the choir chanted the *Ecce Sacerdos Magnus* — "Behold a great priest." After the vicar had read a brief address of congratulation and welcome, Cardinal Pacelli in a simple response sketched the lives of St. John and St. Paul and exhorted his new parishioners to follow their example of holiness and fortitude. SS. John and Paul, who are mentioned in the Canon of the Mass, were Roman knights in the household of Princess Constantia. When commanded by Julian the Apostate to sacrifice to pagan idols, they courageously replied: "Our lives belong to the emperor, but our souls belong only to God." Angered by their refusal to deny Christ, Julian had them beheaded. Their church, which dates from the year 360, is one of Rome's oldest, and one of Christendom's most venerable monuments. It has been a place of pilgrimage through the centuries. The ceremony of taking possession ended with Benediction of the Most Blessed Sacrament. The coat of arms of Cardinal Pacelli was placed over the main entrance, and his portrait was later hung in the nave with that of Pius XI.

The resignation of Cardinal Gasparri as Papal Secretary of State, and Cardinal Pacelli's appointment as his successor, was announced by *L'Osservatore Romano* on February 10, 1930. The seventy-seven year old Cardinal Gasparri had held the office for fifteen years under Benedict XV and Pius XI. Among many great works he had achieved two singular triumphs, the restoration of friendly relations with France and the signing of the Lateran Treaty with Italy. The Pope remembered his services with a gift of a villa on the outskirts of Rome, where the Cardinal lived in quiet study and prayer until his death on November 18, 1934. To evidence its respect for Cardinal Gasparri the Italian government posted a guard of honor before his villa and had King Victor Emmanuel III bestow on him Italy's highest decoration, Collar of the Annunziata Order.

"We have appointed you," wrote the Holy Father to Cardinal Pacelli, "because of your spirit of piety and prayer which cannot fail to draw upon you an abundance of heavenly assistance; and because of the qualities of soul and the talents of intellect with which God has endowed you and which you have always used for His glory and for the service of the Church." In accepting the appointment the new Secretary stated: "Now I am bound more closely and personally to the Holy Father; I am to share more intimately his work and his cares. Now I must pray for him all the more fervently: The Lord keep him safe, give him length of days, and deliver him not into the hands of his enemies."

Sixtus V, one of the greatest popes, wrote of the Papal Secretary of State: "He must know everything, have read everything, understand everything, but he must say nothing." These qualities and many more are indeed necessary, because the Papal Secretary of State is not alone the Pope's Minister of Foreign Affairs but also his Prime Minister. As the former he is responsible for the Church's foreign policy and her relations with the nations of the world. At the present time thirty-three countries are represented at the Vatican by an ambassador or a minister; and the Holy See has thirty-eight nuncios and twenty-five apostolic delegates in foreign nations. The countries having diplomatic relations with the Holy See are: Argentina, Belgium, Bolivia, Brazil, Chile, China, Colombia, Costa Rica, Cuba, Czecho-Slovakia, Dominican Republic, Ecuador, Eire, Finland, France, Great Britain, Guatemala, Haiti, Holland, Honduras, Hungary, Italy, Liberia, Monaco, Nicaragua, Panama, Peru, Poland, Portugal, Rumania, San Marino, San Salvador, Spain, Uruguay, Venezuela, and Yugoslavia.* The Cardinal

* The Order of Malta also maintains diplomatic relations with the

Secretary of State directs* the work of the papal envoys who keep him constantly informed on political and ecclesiastical conditions in the different countries. The foreign envoys to the Vatican discuss with him diplomatic and other matters involving their nations. He counsels the pope on international problems in which the Church is concerned, and frequently acts as his spokesman in time of crisis and difficulty.

The Papal Secretary of State is also the chief advisor and assistant of the Holy Father in the domestic affairs of the Church and Vatican. The pope consults with him on the appointment of bishops to vacant dioceses and of officials to Vatican posts. Administrative problems involving dioceses, religious organizations, church societies, the clergy and the laity are frequently referred to him for disposal. He collaborates with the Holy Father in the writing of important encyclicals, and often speaks for him on moral and doctrinal questions.

Hence, with his appointment as Papal Secretary of State, Cardinal Pacelli became second only to Pius XI in importance and responsibility. For the nine years that followed he would labor zealously and tirelessly to protect and to spread the Kingdom of God throughout the world.

Because his appointment in March, 1930, as Archpriest

Holy See. The representatives of Germany and Japan were withdrawn in 1945 at the command of the Allied governments; Lithuania and Slovakia which *Annuario Pontificio* (1945) lists are today sections of Soviet Russia and Czecho-Slovakia.

* The apostolic delegates are immediately subject not to the Papal Secretariate of State but to either the Congregation of the Consistory, or to the Congregation of Propaganda Fide, or to the Congregation for the Oriental Church, depending on where they are posted. However, the duties and activities of the apostolic delegates are frequently such as to bring them under the supervision and guidance of the Cardinal Secretary of State.

of the Basilica of St. Peter and Prefect of the Congregation of the Fabric of St. Peter's brought Cardinal Pacelli much personal joy, the reader will allow a digression here. Upon the death of Cardinal Merry del Val, who had been Archpriest and Prefect for many years, Pius XI named Cardinal Pacelli as his successor. As Prefect, Cardinal Pacelli was the custodian and administrator of Christendom's largest church, which has an annual budget of $100,000 and employs some five hundred artisans, mechanics, and workmen. In the spring following Cardinal Pacelli's appointment dangerous cracks opened in the great dome designed by Michelangelo. The Holy Father and the Prefect made a thorough inspection, climbing even to the copper cupola which surmounts the dome four hundred and sixty feet above the ground. Methods were devised to seal the cracks and to save the dome from further damage. Other changes made under Cardinal Pacelli's supervision include the restoration of the clock on the façade, the paving of the floor of the apse, and the establishment of the new basilica archives. As Prefect, Cardinal Pacelli also had charge of the Studio del Mosaico, one of the few industries of Vatican City. Here are made the magnificent mosaics which decorate St. Peter's and Catholic churches throughout the world. In 1929 Pius XI presented a mosaic reproduction of Murillo's "Immaculate Conception" to the Shrine of the Immaculate Conception in Washington, D. C.

As Archpriest, Cardinal Pacelli was the pope's immediate assistant at sacred ceremonies, and the first curate of the basilica. It was inspiring to see him participate in ecclesiastical functions, for his every move and act had deep religious significance. He preached often to the throngs that crowded the basilica, especially during

Lent and Holy Week. A listener wrote: "I heard Cardinal Pacelli preach on an Ash Wednesday evening. Sixty thousand of the faithful crowded the basilica. The Holy Father sat on his throne. I was near the pulpit. I saw the Cardinal's beautiful hands weaving arabesques on the walls. In the middle of the sermon the amplifier failed, and I heard his true voice. It was musical, persuasive, very soft in the upper register and poignant in the lower. He was speaking of the parable of the many who are called and the few who are chosen. He made me think of the great St. Bernard with his austere tenderness."

The first major problem confronting the new Papal Secretary of State was the Maltese Question. Malta, which belongs to the British Empire, is a chain of three small islands lying between Sicily and Africa. The population of 260,000 is almost entirely Catholic and traditionally loyal to the Holy See. Somehow Lord Strickland, who considered himself a good Catholic because he was anticlerical, became prime minister in 1927. The ignoble character of the man is shown by his offer in 1921 of a prize for the best arguments why a certain saintly bishop of Malta should be deprived of his diocese. When no contestants came forward, he offered a reward to anyone who would discover and reveal immoral facts in the lives of Malta's bishops and priests. There were no takers.

Because the clergy senators — two of the seventeen members of the Maltese senate were appointed by the archbishop — in July, 1928, voted down his appropriations bill, Lord Strickland hired ruffians to demonstrate publicly against the Church. The protest of Mauro Caruana, O.S.B., Archbishop of Malta, the prime minister termed a declaration of war, and then instituted in his four daily newspapers a vicious campaign of slander against the bishops and priests. It was his declared purpose to destroy the love of the faithful for their shepherds.

Despite sincere efforts of the Vatican to end the quarrel, the lot of the Church in Malta grew more and more unpleasant. The Carta incident brought the situation to a climax and forced a solution. Father Carta, O.F.M., had come from Italy to inspect the Franciscan monasteries. He decided to transfer a certain monk named Guido Micaleef to Italy because of his political activities contrary to the explicit prohibition of the Maltese bishops. Lord Strickland forbade the departure of Father Micaleef and ordered the imprisonment of Father Carta for a harmless violation of the postal regulations. Cardinal Pacelli summoned the British minister to the Vatican and vigorously protested this unwarranted interference with the Church in Malta. Guided solely by the reports of Lord Strickland, the British government made reply in the form of a "Blue Book," so called because of the color of its covers, issued in May, 1930. The book blamed the bishops and priests of Malta for the controversy and accused them of political interference, while clearing Lord Strickland of all fault. The Pope requested Cardinal Pacelli to make a written answer and he published on June 22 a "White Book," entitled *Documented Exposition of the Maltese Question*. This book of one hundred and eighty-seven pages refuted the charges and accusations of the British government against the Church in Malta and presented convincing evidence of Lord Strickland's guilt. So forceful was its impression on the world that Great Britain felt constrained to send a Royal Commission of Investigation to Malta. The Commission's report cleared the Church of all fault and placed the full blame on Lord Strickland.

He was advised to apologize to the Maltese bishops and priests and to the Holy See, which he did, thus closing the matter.

The Maltese Question admitted of a ready and complete solution, because it involved personalities rather than fundamental principles. However, the Catholic Action controversy, which meanwhile was rising in Fascist Italy, had its ultimate cause in the diametric opposition of Catholicism to totalitarianism. Hence there could be no solution, only an uneasy armistice. For an intelligent understanding of the Catholic Action controversy, in which Cardinal Pacelli's role was major and decisive, it will be useful to recall here the history of the Holy See's relations with Italy after 1870 and to review the Lateran Treaty of 1929.

On September 20, 1870, the Italian armies battered down the outer walls and took possession of Rome, the city of the popes and the capital of the Papal States for a thousand and more years. As the attackers were invading his palace on the Quirinal Hill, which had been an official residence of the popes for centuries, Pius IX fled to the Vatican. There he and his successors would keep themselves voluntary prisoners for fifty-nine years. The new Italy, seeking to legalize its aggression and to justify its robbery to a critical world, enacted the Law of Guarantees. This law permitted the pope to use "the Vatican palaces and all gardens and grounds annexed thereto," which were declared the property of the Italian state, placed him on the government pay roll at an annual salary of $1,650,000 (1929 value), and promised him freedom from interference in the exercise of his spiritual powers. Pius IX immediately proclaimed: "We refuse to recognize in the

Italian government any right to grant Us privileges or to make laws for Us." The historic dispute popularly known as the Roman Question had come into being.

To protest publicly the grave injustice done the papacy, Pius IX and his successors issued certain regulations to govern the relations of the Holy See and of Catholics with the new Italy. For many years all subjects of the former Papal States were forbidden to take part in elections, to run for the national legislature, or to accept positions from the new regime. The members of the diplomatic corps of the pope could not speak to or visit with those of the Italian king, nor could their staffs speak or visit. The members of embassies to the king were never permitted to visit the pope nor to enter St. Peter's. The American ambassador to Italy and his staff did not enter St. Peter's until 1931, when Francis J. Spellman, now cardinal archbishop of New York, was consecrated auxiliary bishop of Boston by Cardinal Pacelli. A visitor of the king would not be received by the pope. President Wilson tactfully solved the problem by dividing his visit of 1919 into two distinct parts. First he called on the king. Then he took up residence at the American Embassy. This gave the impression of starting the Rome visit afresh. From the embassy he and Mrs. Wilson went to the Vatican for an audience with Benedict XV.

Not content with having annexed the papal dominions, the Italian government and its anticlerical adherents continued to taunt and to insult the Holy See and the pope. In a previous chapter we told of the shameful incident in connection with the burial of the saintly Pius IX. Soon after the seizure of Rome a monumental statue of Garibaldi, who had looted and plundered the Papal States, was erected on the Janiculum Hill so as to be near and

On board the *Conte de Savoia* as Cardinal Pacelli arrived in the U. S.,
in October, 1936. -- *Acme*.

Cardinal Pacelli in New York. This is said to be a favorite picture with His Holiness. — *Acme.*

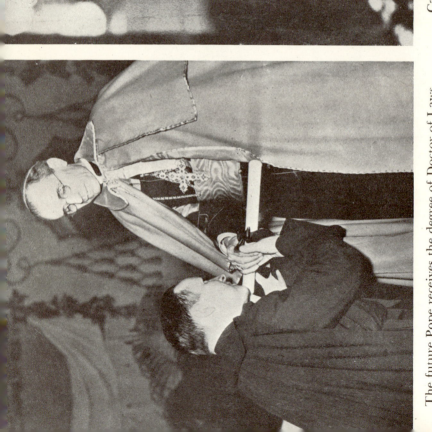

The future Pope receives the degree of Doctor of Laws from the president of Fordham University. — *Acme.*

Cardinals' chairs just after the election of the Pope. The canopy over the chair of Cardinal Pacelli remains in place; the others have been lowered. — *Wide World*.

Cardinal Pacelli, with the committee of Cardinals that governed the Church in the interval between the death of Pius XI and the election of his successor.

overlooking the Vatican. When Benedict XV died in 1922, Premier Ivanoe Bonomi ordered the flags of public buildings lowered to half-mast. That afternoon the anticlericals in Parliament denounced his action in violent speeches of hatred for the Holy See and drove him from office. Each September 20 was jubilantly dedicated to denouncing the Holy See and calling the pope names. On several occasions vulgar caricatures of the reigning Holy Father were paraded through the city. However, throughout the world prayers were being recited after every low Mass that God in His merciful wisdom might restore to the Holy See and His Vicar complete independence and freedom.

There is, of course, another side to the Roman Question, that of Italy and the Italian people, for which truth and fairness demand a hearing. While Europe was a mixture of small kingdoms, duchies, and other principalities, the popes needed the Papal States to secure their safety and to maintain their freedom against foreign domination. The size and the power of the Papal States alone, or in alliance with other European powers, were usually sufficient to dissuade or repel foreign aggression. However, when the modern nations of Europe began to emerge through a series of civil and foreign wars, the Papal States became an anachronism and a liability. Too small and powerless now to protect the popes against foreign aggression, they were burdening them with problems alien to the mission of the Holy See. The popes had enough burdens and cares without those of taxation and banking, agriculture and manufacturing, revolution and lawbreaking. Hence, the annexation of the Papal States and Rome, in one sense, was a blessing, because it placed the popes above European and Italian politics and freed them to work solely for the salvation of the world. By 1870 the popes no more needed the Papal States than a cured cripple needs his crutches.

Moreover, granted that the popes had a legal and an historical right to Rome and the Papal States, the right of the Italian people to become one nation must also be conceded.* The lands and the cities belonged ultimately not to the popes but to the citizens (after God), who had an inalienable right to prefer union with the other Italians. The aggression of Victor Emmanuel, Cavour, and Garibaldi was immoral and cannot be justified, but it can be extenuated by their good objective, a united Italy. Although justice was clearly on the Catholic side of the Roman Question, its proponents too often forgot the right of the Italian people and overlooked the reality of the situation. Pius XI, in his remark, "We do not want subjects," epitomized the fact that the loss of Rome and the Papal States was not an unmixed evil. This fact does not excuse, however, the contemptible and petty attitude of the Italian government, which maliciously worked to hinder and to subordinate the papacy.

However, the contention of the Italian government and of other critics of the Church that the popes had neither a right to nor a need for an independent and sovereign territory was entirely erroneous. They wished to consider the popes Italian citizens and to treat them as such. Because our president is superior to the states, the Founding Fathers established his residence in the District of Columbia, which is an independent and sovereign territory in relation to the states. Likewise, the pope,

---

* However, the Italian people were forbidden by moral law to resort to violence in the exercise of this right, because the popes governed their states justly and democratically. Revolution by force is permissible only against illegal or tyrannical leaders.

because he is the Vicar of Christ, is above any nation or ruler. He cannot be the citizen of any country, as he necessarily would be if he resided within its territory and was subject to its jurisdiction. Moreover, if the Holy Father were a resident and national of any country, the peoples of other nations would suspect his motives and would associate him with the policies of that country. To maintain his dignity as the Vicar of Christ and his position as Father of Christendom the pope must possess an independent and sovereign territory in which he is the sole ruler. For this reason Pius IX and his successors could not consent to the annexation of the Papal States until some part, no matter how small, was returned to them and recognized to be sovereign and independent.

Many efforts were made to solve the Roman Question, but because of anticlerical opposition in the Italian parliament none was successful until 1929. Negotiations were instituted by Leo XIII with the encouragement of the European powers, but the Italian Liberals did all in their power to prevent an agreement. Pius X sought to improve relations between the Holy See and Italy by permitting Catholics to take part in political elections and by encouraging them to influence the civic and social conscience of Italy through example and instruction. A commission of five cardinals was appointed by Benedict XV to find a solution; but beyond exploratory steps and a determination of minimum conditions it made no progress. In the spring of 1919 Monsignor Francis Clement Kelly, now Bishop of Tulsa and Oklahoma City, discussed the Roman Question with Italy's wartime premier, Vittorio Orlando, who was then attending the Versailles Conference at which the Monsignor was an unofficial observer. Monsignor Kelly carried Orlando's proposals, which are said to have included a square mile of territory and an outlet to the sea, to Cardinal Gasparri then Papal Secretary of State. Further conferences were held between Orlando and Vatican officials. After terms of agreement acceptable to both sides had been reached, it was decided to submit the settlement to the Italian parliament for ratification. Orlando, however, had failed to persuade the Versailles Conference to give Italy the small seaport of Fiume, and when he returned to Rome the parliament immediately forced his resignation from office. The proposed solution of the quarrel between Italy and the Holy See was never introduced into parliament.

On February 11, 1929, Cardinal Pietro Gasparri, Papal Secretary of State, and Benito Mussolini, Italian Prime Minister, affixed their signatures to a document which settled the Roman Question. From the fact that it was signed in the Lateran Palace, built by Emperor Constantine for the popes, it is officially known as the Lateran Treaty. In the summer of 1926 Mussolini had instructed Professor Domenico Barone, of the Italian Foreign Office, to inquire of some informed Vatican official what the Holy See would consider as a settlement of the Roman Question. Barone approached Francesco Pacelli, a Vatican lawyer and brother of the then Archbishop Pacelli, who told him that a sovereign territory and the legalization of religious marriages were the basic conditions. Since the Church's requirements were so reasonable, Mussolini gave Barone a formal letter authorizing him to continue negotiations. Apprised of the Italian "peace feeler" by Francesco Pacelli, Cardinal Gasparri instructed him to proceed for the Holy See.

By November 24 Barone and Pacelli had completed a first draft of sixteen articles. Francesco's son Carlo was used for secretarial work in order to assure absolute secrecy. Cardinal Gasparri and Monsignor Borgongini-Duca, Papal Undersecretary of State and later Nuncio to Italy, then joined the negotiators in revising and expanding the preparatory agreement. Each term and phrase was carefully weighed and debated for its legal significance and historical precedence, for the Holy See knew from bitter experience the danger of loose terminology. Before its final acceptance the Lateran Treaty went through twenty-one rewritings. In one hundred and twenty-nine private audiences Francesco Pacelli discussed with the Holy Father all the drafts, modifications, and corrections, receiving from him his reactions and instructions. After the death of Barone on January 4, 1929, Mussolini conducted the parleys directly with Pacelli. The first official announcement was made on February 7 in a statement by Cardinal Gasparri to the diplomatic corps accredited to the Holy See that a treaty was about to be signed. The negotiations had taken two and a half years.

The Lateran Treaty comprises three documents: a political treaty, a financial settlement, and a concordat. The political treaty, which consists of a preamble and twenty-seven articles, established "The City of the Vatican" and defined political relations between Italy and the Holy See. By Article III Italy recognized the full possession, exclusive dominion, and sovereign jurisdiction of the Holy See over the Vatican. This territory, bounded on the north and south by the Leonine walls and on the west and east by the Bernini Colonnade, is only one sixth of a square mile, but, as Pius XI remarked, it is "the largest in the world for it includes the dome of Michelangelo, the treasures of science in the gardens and library, the treasures of art in the museums and galleries, and,

above all, the tomb of the Prince of the Apostles."
Mussolini offered considerably more territory, but Cardinal Gasparri refused with the wry remark: "That much
land would require streetcars, and we do not wish to
worry about strikes." Besides the Vatican Italy returned
to the Holy See fourteen other pieces of territory, including the Lateran Palace, the Basilica of St. John Lateran,
and Castel Gandolfo, which is in the Alban hills twelve
miles southeast of Rome and is now the papal summer
residence. The papal basilicas and certain buildings in
Rome which house the Holy See's congregations and offices.
were declared extraterritorial, that is, they are a part of
Italy but are exempt from Italian authority. In return the
Holy See surrendered its claim to Rome and to the Papal
States and recognized the Kingdom of Italy.

By Article XII Italy recognized the right of the Holy
See to send its own diplomats to foreign countries and to
receive foreign diplomats, even in time of war. Therefore,
though America and Italy were at war, Myron C. Taylor,
the personal representative of the President, was allowed
to confer with the Pope.

By Article XXIV the Holy See "declares that it wishes
to remain aloof from all temporal disputes between nations and from international congresses convoked to settle
such disputes unless the interested parties make a joint
appeal to its mission of peace." Thus the Holy See could
not have "taken sides" in World War II. Moreover, because of this clause, it may not become a member of the
United Nations Organization as membership in that body
involves military obligations against aggressor nations.

As compensation for the economic loss of the Papal
States the Holy See accepted from Italy a billion lire ($50,-
000,000) in Italian state bonds bearing 5 per cent interest,

which it agreed not to sell, and seven hundred and fifty million lire in cash ($37,500,000). This sum is less than what the pope would have received if he had accepted the salary offered him by the Law of Guarantees. Pius XI created a special commission to administer this fund, but with the economic collapse of Italy the bonds are now valueless. Pius was a more prudent financier than his predecessor Benedict XV. Benedict gave so generously to relieve the sorrows of the world that when he died the Holy See was "broke." Cardinal Gasparri had to borrow money to defray the expenses of the Conclave.

The Concordat established Catholicism as the official religion of Italy and guaranteed freedom to the Church in all her activities. Religious instruction was to be given in both elementary and secondary schools, and all textbooks were subject to the approval of the local bishop. Catholic Action was recognized, "if developed independently of any political party and for the diffusion and realization of Catholic principles." Marriages solemnized by priests were made legal and given the same civil effects as those performed by public officials. Cases of nullity and applications for dispensations were reserved to the ecclesiastical courts, whose decisions were made binding on the state courts. "God had been restored to Italy, and Italy had been restored to God."

The Mussolini who signed the Lateran Treaty was also the Duce of Fascism who taught the absolute and all-embracing supremacy of the State. His immoral political principles had to clash sooner or later with the God-given truths of Catholicism. Not long after signing the Lateran Treaty, Mussolini declared in a speech to the Italian Senate that the Church in Italy was not free but was subject to the State. Pius XI made an immediate and forceful reply, describing Mussolini's claim as "heretical and worse than heretical." One Fascist newspaper ominously warned: "No true Fascist can tolerate that the Pope should presume to censure Il Duce who, we will remind him, is not to be discussed." The next year, 1930, passed without incident except that Italy enacted legislation evidently aimed at encouraging the spread of Protestantism. Since Italy was 97.6 per cent Catholic, the Holy Father denounced the efforts of the Italian government to undermine the Church.

But April, 1931, opened with the most violent attacks on the Church by the press and officers of the Fascist party. Monsignor Pizzardo, Papal Undersecretary of State, and Count Della Torre, editor of *L'Osservatore Romano,* were accused of plotting to assassinate Mussolini and to overthrow the government. Members of Catholic Action were charged with sabotaging Fascism by their political activities. Catholic Action in Italy and throughout the world is "a lay organization whose sole purpose is to make its members good Christians and make them live their Christianity." The authentic and fundamental definition is "the participation and collaboration of the laity with the Apostolic Hierarchy." Cardinal Pacelli denied the charges and demanded proof of the government's accusations. The answer was official silence and an outburst of mob violence. Through the late afternoon and night of May 28, squads of Fascist youths rioted in Rome and other cities, shouting "Down with the Pope! Death to the Pope!" They smashed into offices of Catholic Action, burning records and slashing pictures of the Holy Father. Boys belonging to Catholic Action were clubbed wherever found. The Italian police looked on idly, refusing to interfere. On May 30 the Italian government ordered the closing of all offices of Catholic Action, and the next day disbanded the associations of young people and of university students affiliated with it.

Cardinal Pacelli immediately sent a sharp note of protest to the Italian Foreign Office, denouncing the outrages as violations of the Lateran Treaty. The Italian reply rejected all complaints and refused to recall the decree against Catholic Action. Mussolini then came out from behind his henchmen with a radio broadcast in which he said that he had "documents on hand to prove that the Catholic Action groups were hostile to Fascism." One week later the government-controlled press published an unofficial and unsigned document which repeated former accusations and added new and even more malicious charges.

Aware that Mussolini was sensitive to international opinion, Cardinal Pacelli decided to place the Vatican's case before the nations of the world. He would depend on world indignation at the Fascist outrages to force a satisfactory settlement. Pius XI, assisted by Cardinal Pacelli, wrote one of his finest encyclicals entitled *Non Abbiamo Bisogno*. But with the Italian government controlling the telephones and cables, how could the Pope's letter be published abroad? Cardinal Pacelli dramatically leveled the barrier. Monsignor Francis Spellman, at that time attached to the Secretariate of State, was instructed to smuggle the encyclical out of Italy to Paris. He left Rome secretly, outwitted the Italian frontier guards, and arrived in Paris. There he distributed copies of the encyclical to the Associated Press, the United Press, Reuter's, and other news agencies. They "flashed" the encyclical to the world's newspapers which gave it front-page publicity. Mussolini's first knowledge of the encyclical was by way of dispatches from Paris.

The encyclical described the Fascist attack as "a devastating storm which swept suddenly down on the spiritual garden of souls and injured and uprooted the plants and tender flowers growing in God's garden." The unofficial document published by "the hostile press of the party, which is often ordered what it must say" Pius termed a lie. "The history of documents prepared not in the service of truth but in offense of truth and justice is a long and sad story. But we must say, with a certain dismay, that in Our many years of active life rarely have We seen an article so contrary to truth and justice." "Tell Us," Pius demanded, "tell the country, tell the world what documents there are and how many of them there are which treat of politics planned and directed by Catholic Action with all this peril to the State." And, as though answering, said: "Rarely has the fable of the wolf and the lamb been exemplified so strikingly: and history will recall it."

Certain immoral principles of Fascism were unreservedly denounced:

The resolve (already in great measure actually put into effect) to monopolize completely the young, from their tenderest years up to manhood and womanhood, for the exclusive advantage of a party, of a regime based on an ideology which clearly resolves itself into a true, a real pagan worship of the State is . . . no less in contrast with the natural rights of the family than it is in contradiction with the supernatural rights of the Church. . . . What is to be thought about the formula of an oath, which even little boys and girls are obliged to take that they will execute orders without discussion, from an authority which, as we have seen and experienced, can give orders against all truth and justice. . . . Takers of this oath must swear to serve with all their strength, even to the shedding of blood, the cause of a revolution which snatches the young from the Church and from Jesus Christ and which inculcates in its own young people hatred, violence, and irreverence. . . . Such an oath, as it stands, is unlawful.

In closing, the Pope asked: "What new things does the future prepare and threaten?" And he answered: "The future is in the hands of God and God is with us, and 'if God be for us, who is against us.' "

World opinion, informed and aroused by the passionate appeal of Pope Pius XI, became outspokenly indignant against the brutal malice of the Fascists, and so Mussolini decided to make peace with the Vatican. He asked Father Tacchi Ventura, S.J., to discuss a settlement with Cardinal Pacelli. On September 2 it was announced that an agreement had been entered into whereby Catholic Action was permitted to renew its activities. The decree against the Catholic Youth groups was withdrawn, but they were denied the right to sponsor athletic and vocational training programs. Though not winning a complete victory, Cardinal Pacelli succeeded in securing the right of the Church to encourage the growth of the supernatural life through lay organizations of youths and adults. This was the fundamental issue in the controversy and the primary concern of the Holy Father.

Much has been written concerning the Catholic Church and Fascism. Anti-Catholics and anticlericals have tried to label the Vatican as the friend and supporter of Fascism in Italy. The truth is that the Holy See, except for condemning Fascist errors and opposing Fascist crimes, never indicated any interest in Fascism. The accusers cannot cite any papal document or establish any papal action which befriended and supported Fascism. On the other hand, uninformed and biased Catholics, of which there are too many, would now have us believe that the Italian hierarchy and clergy did oppose Fascism. They

err because, while avoiding political activities the majority
of the Italian bishops and priests acquiesced in Fascism,
and some few allowed patriotism to prevail over their
moral principles. The majority of the Italian bishops and
priests, however, did condemn the errors and did oppose
the crimes of Fascism, perhaps not as courageously as the
outside world would wish, but as best they could. Unlike
the drawing-room heroes and microphone crusaders who
criticize them, they had to live with the tiger. The Church
of a country may not actively interfere in its political life
until religion and morality are in danger of extinction,
and Mussolini never forced his evil to that point. Would
the critics have the American Catholic bishops preach
rebellion because our southern Negroes are deprived of
their vote, or because American education is godless, or
because the atomic bombing of cities is considered by
some of our theologians immoral? It is not too hard to
understand the attitude and conduct of Italian churchmen
toward Fascism but there is no explanation for the attempts made by certain American Catholics and certain
American Catholic publications to whitewash Mussolini
and his evil. The suppression of political opponents by
illegal force, the denial of fundamental rights, the in-
vasions of Ethiopia and Albania were crimes which no
good deed, not even the Lateran Treaty, of Mussolini
could justify. The lesson that American Catholics might
well learn from the whole matter is to adhere to the right,
and not allow prejudice or political considerations to
obscure moral judgments.

A most shameful page in the history of North America
is the horrible persecution of the Church in Mexico. Our
newspapers, which today describe in detail the horrors
of Belsen and Buchenwald, passed over in silence

that can hardly have been unplanned the sadistic and obscene cruelties inflicted on the priests and nuns and faithful of Mexico.*

Because the Mexican government had guaranteed formally in 1929 the freedom of the Church, the renewal of persecution in 1931 was all the more cruel and malicious. Laws were enacted drastically limiting the number of priests, e.g., in the State of Vera Cruz only one priest was to exercise the sacred ministry for every 100,000 of the inhabitants. Government agents murdered priests for the crime of celebrating Mass and imprisoned Catholics for the offense of praying in common. That the faithful might be left to stray without shepherds the government "hounded" bishops into exile and hiding. Religious instruction was forbidden in the schools, while irreligion and grossly immoral teachings were made compulsory.

Reports of these bitter conditions flowed into the office of Cardinal Pacelli. On January 1, 1932, he urged the Catholics of Mexico to appeal to the courts, and to refrain from violence. But the courts were "packed," justice could not be obtained and the iniquitous laws were upheld. Cardinal Pacelli then turned to world opinion to ease the lot of the Church in Mexico. On September 29, 1932, Pius XI issued the eloquent and sorrowful encyclical *Acerba Animi,* in which he told the passion of the Mexican bishops and priests and Catholics. He appealed to the world for justice and prophetically warned that the torrent of persecution, if unchecked, would flow to other lands. Unhappily one cannot write that the encyclical gained its end, for the persecution continued. Today the

* *Blood-Drenched Altars* by Bishop Francis Clement Kelley tells the story well and honestly.

Church is tolerated in Mexico, but the persecutors are still in power and the anti-Catholic laws are still on the statute books.

During the Italo-Ethiopian conflict, which extended through 1934 to 1936, Cardinal Pacelli, as Papal Secretary of State, was criticized for the Vatican's alleged failure to condemn Mussolini's aggression. The criticism can be dismissed as self-serving and hypocritical, for the critics uniformly belonged to that group which has always denounced the Church as a "political meddler." The British naval officer who in a letter to the Holy Father demanded that he and Cardinal Pacelli resign unless they stopped Mussolini, would indeed have been wrathful had Cardinal Rampolla and Leo XIII condemned England's rape of the Boer Republic. One can refute the criticism with facts and an explanation. On December 24, 1934, in alluding to "the widely spread rumor of war," the Holy Father exhorted the Lord: "Scatter Thou the nations that delight in war." *L'Osservatore Romano*, August 30, 1935, in commenting on Italy's claim of "a need for expansion," remarked "the need for expansion cannot of itself justify force as a means of acquiring what is necessary." Though urged by the Italian government, the Pope flatly refused to crown Victor Emmanuel as Emperor of Abyssinia. Thus the Vatican by word and by act did condemn Mussolini's aggression. What the critics wanted was a dramatic excommunication of Mussolini and the summoning of all nations to the defense of Abyssinia. The Duce's reply undoubtedly would have been: "Forbid me to enter any church? Refuse me the sacraments? I never go to Mass and never receive the sacraments. Excommunication will not bother me." Finally, it should be remembered that neutrality in conflicts between nations is the traditional policy of the Vatican, for the Church is a spiritual institution and not an international policeman.

The Spanish Civil War brought Cardinal Pacelli a full measure of sorrow. Upon the abdication of Alfonso XIII in 1931, the Republic of Spain was proclaimed with Alcala Zamora at its head. The Vatican immediately recognized the Republic, urging the people of Spain to obey and support it. To his credit President Zamora, a practicing Catholic, earnestly tried to keep the government from plunging into anarchy and persecution. But in January, 1932, the Jesuits were expelled from Spain on the specious grounds that they were unsympathetic to the Republic. Wholesale burning of churches, schools, seminaries, convents, and monasteries followed. Later laws were enacted confiscating all Church property, outlawing all religious orders and societies, and secularizing all education. By protest and entreaty Cardinal Pacelli labored to move Spain to a policy of justice and decency, but with no success. On June 3, 1933, Pius XI gave to the world the encyclical *Dilectissima Nobis* in which he condemned the persecution as Communist in origin and implored the protection of God for the Church in Spain. The same day Cardinal Pacelli issued a statement that all members of the Spanish government were excommunicated and barred from the benefits of the sacraments. Yet, when the Spanish government suggested in 1934 that a concordat be negotiated, Cardinal Pacelli ignored the past and sought to reach an agreement, even visiting Madrid in his efforts. But the government demanded concessions which could not be granted. One may treat with the devil, but one may not treat of truth and justice.

With the so-called republic fast becoming a Bolshevik anarchy, the counterrevolution under General Francisco

Franco broke out on July 19, 1936. We need not relate here the horrors of which both sides were guilty, nor will we discuss the intervention of Russia for the misnamed Loyalists and of Germany and Italy for the Nationalists. A few general observations will be enough. To describe the Spanish Civil War as a struggle between democracy and Fascism is as absurd as to blame the French Revolution on Marie Antoinette's foolish remark: "If the people haven't bread, let them eat cake." The Spanish Civil War had its origin in the social, political, and economic injustices of a century and more. It was basically a struggle to determine how justice was to be restored to Spain and to all her people. But the blood-bath of Communism was no more a solution for Spain's problems than was the guillotine terror of Robespierre for France's. The intervention before and during the Civil War of foreign ideologies and nations prevented a peaceful solution and prolonged the strife.

The Church in Spain was freely condemned by our newspapers as a wealthy leech and a bigoted foe of democracy and freedom. The guilt of the Church was not wealth of possession, for most of her property had been confiscated in the mid-nineteenth century. It was not opposition to freedom and progress, for the Church supported and favored the Republic as long as it was democratic and just.

The guilt of the Church was the complacency of too many of her priests and bishops and lay members in the face of the political and economic injustices oppressing the common people. There were too few voices teaching the papal encyclicals on labor and the social order, too few voices demanding that Catholic leaders and industrialists live their Christianity, and too few hands working to pull the people from the ditch of poverty and misery into which greedy exploitation had shoved them. The martyrdom of 14,000 Spanish priests and bishops, while gloriously atoning for their mistakes, should be a warning to the Church in other lands.

While neither sanctioning nor aiding the counter-revolution in any way, the Vatican hoped for a victory by Franco. Cardinal Pacelli favored Franco, not because he considered him a paragon of virtue, which indeed he is not, but because he judged him a lesser evil and a greater good than the Communists. Apparently Great Britain and the United States came to the same conclusion. British warships prevented the landing of supplies for the Communists and we refused to aid them by lifting the arms embargo. The events following the end of the war in Europe have surely proved the wisdom of Cardinal Pacelli's judgment. The Western Allies are uneasy enough about Russian domination of Europe without having a Stalin-controlled Spain threatening Gibraltar.

History has swept away the concordats which Cardinal Pacelli negotiated with certain European countries, but at the time of their making they were rightly acclaimed triumphs of diplomacy. On October 12, 1932, the Landtag of Baden, then a semi-independent province in south-western Germany, ratified a Concordat with the Vatican. The vote being forty-four ayes and forty-four nays, the presiding officer, a Catholic, exercised his prerogative and voted aye again. A Concordat with Germany was signed on July 20, 1933, by Cardinal Pacelli and Hitler's emissary, Franz Von Papen. On May 2, 1934, Austria and the Vatican signed a Concordat, but it became meaningless after the Anschluss of 1938. The Concordat with Yugo-slavia was signed on July 29, 1935, but it was never ratified by the Yugoslav Parliament because the Serbian Orthodox Church threatened to excommunicate whoever voted to ratify.

The hours that diplomacy did not demand Cardinal Pacelli gave to prayer and priestly duties. With Jesus in the Blessed Sacrament he daily discussed the problems of the Church and the world, drawing from God wisdom and strength. To his customary prayers he added in 1932 those of the Third Order of St. Dominic, which he joined under the name of Brother Albert. The Cardinal had been a member of the Third Order of St. Francis for many years. In 1934 the Holy Father named him protector of the Sisters of St. Mary of the Third Order of St. Francis, whose mother house is in St. Louis, Missouri. He often presided at sacred functions in St. Peter's and other churches of Rome, inspiring the faithful with his intense spirituality and devout attention.

The Church and the nations of the world gratefully acknowledged Cardinal Pacelli's achievements with honors and dignities. Italy bestowed on him the Collar of the Annunziata Order, which gives its wearer the right to call the Italian king "cousin." France honored him with the Grand Cross of the Legion of Honor, Rumania with the Grand Cordon of the Order of King Carol, and the Dominican Republic with the Grand Cross of Duarte. In 1935 Pius XI appointed him Camerlengo of the Holy Roman Church. During the life of the pope the Camerlengo is the administrator of the revenues of the Holy See. Upon the death of the pope he directs the preparations for the Conclave and in general governs the Church and the Vatican. Because of his intellectual interests Cardinal Pacelli was also named Chancellor of the Pontifical Institute of Christian Archeology.

The Thirty-Second International Eucharistic Congress was to open on October 10, 1934, in Buenos Aires, capital of South America's great republic Argentina. Pilgrims were gathering from all corners of the earth to glorify the Blessed Sacrament and to honor their hidden Lord. Fearful of the winds of greed and hate which were troubling the seas of international relations, Pius XI appointed Cardinal Pacelli his personal representative, with the title "Legate," to the Congress. Never before in the history of the Holy See had a Secretary of State been sent to a foreign country on a mission other than diplomatic. The Holy Father, knowing Cardinal Pacelli's thirst for peace, hoped that his presence and eloquence might turn the thoughts of nations and their leaders away from war and conquest. The Legate and his staff, consisting of five prelates, a secretary, a butler, and two members of the Noble Guard, sailed from Genoa on the 26,000-ton Italian liner *Conte Grande*. The voyage through the Mediterranean and across the Atlantic Cardinal Pacelli devoted to "brushing up" on his Spanish and Portuguese. The classroom was his suite on the upper deck, and the tutor was Father Restrepo, S.J., the son of a former president of Colombia.

On the morning of October 9, at dawn, the *Conte Grande* approached the Recalada lightship, which marks the entrance to the Rio de la Plata one hundred and twenty-five miles below Buenos Aires. There it was met by an escort squadron of six Argentine warships. When the flotilla entered the four-mile channel leading to the harbor, the flagship of the escort hoisted the papal flag of white and gold to the masthead and thundered forth a twenty-one gun salute, which by international usage is reserved for ruling sovereigns. Shore batteries echoed the royal salute and the bells of Buenos Aires' one hundred and three churches pealed a joyous welcome. At the pier President Justo, together with federal and municipal officers, boarded the *Conte Grande* to greet the Legate and his party.

Wearing robes of scarlet silk and a cross and chain of heavy gold, Cardinal Pacelli set out for the cathedral in a state carriage drawn by shining black horses. Brilliantly uniformed grenadier guards rode ahead and behind the carriage, as thousands crowding the way shouted, "Long live Cardinal Pacelli." The flags of the thirty-four nations represented at the Congress fluttered in the warm breeze of a perfect spring day (our autumn is spring for the Argentineans). One side of the boulevards was lined with soldiers and sailors stiffly at attention; on the other side boys and girls in white suits and dresses waved flags and sang hymns. From balconies and windows flowers of gorgeous hues floated down, so that soon the streets were a carpet of petals. As Cardinal Pacelli stepped into the century-old cathedral a choir of five hundred and sixty voices proclaimed: "Thou art Peter. And upon this rock I shall build my Church and the gates of hell shall not prevail against it." Prayers of thanksgiving for the safe journey and of petition for the success of the Congress were said. Cardinal Pacelli then proceeded to the mansion of Senora Adela de Olivas, which would be his residence while in Buenos Aires. That evening at six he made a formal call on President Justo at the executive mansion.

The morning of October 10 the Eucharistic Congress opened in Palermo Park, where a huge white cross, one hundred and thirty-five feet high, had been erected at the juncture of four broad avenues. A half million men and women devoutly assisted at the inaugural Mass. In flawless Spanish Cardinal Pacelli pleaded with the pilgrims to pray for universal peace and especially for peace among the nations of South America. Bolivia and Paraguay were still fighting their war of many months in the dust and heat of the Chaco. "Before the immaculate host may each heart raise the ardent cry: 'Jesus Christ, King of Peace, bring true peace to the world.' " After receiving the diplomatic corps in the early evening, Cardinal Pacelli presided at the midnight Holy Hour for the clergy.

Thursday, October 11, was children's day. Clothed in white and wearing the colors of the Congress, gold and white, and the colors of Argentina, white and blue, diagonally over the left shoulder, one hundred thousand boys and girls prayed in unison, while Cardinals Hlond of Poland, Gonçalves of Portugal, Leme of Brazil, and Verdier of France, celebrated Mass at the beautiful altars erected on each side of the cross. Moving reverently amid the youthful adorers, three hundred priests distributed Holy Communion. The children were then served a breakfast of cocoa and rolls by groups of nuns. Cardinal Pacelli arrived unexpectedly as the children were eating. He immediately asked that cocoa and rolls be served him at his throne. Very pleased the boys and girls applauded their breakfast companion. When he and they were finished, Cardinal Pacelli spoke to the children, urging them to keep always their present innocence.

On Columbus Day, one of Argentina's great holidays, Cardinal Pacelli consecrated in Buenos Aires the Church of Santa Rosa de Lima. St. Rose, who glorified Lima, Peru, with her sanctity and miracles, is the patroness of South America and as yet the only canonized saint born in the Western Hemisphere. Saturday was dedicated to the Blessed Mother under the title of Our Lady of Lujan, a town located some forty miles from Buenos Aires and

revered as the Lourdes of Argentina. As the Image of
Lujan, which had been brought to the capital by ox cart
the evening before, was placed on the main altar, airplanes
overhead released a great shower of roses while batteries
of artillery roared a twenty-one gun salute. At the close of
the Mass Cardinal Pacelli gave a short sermon on Mary,
Queen of Peace.

The Congress closed Sunday, October 14, before a million people in Palermo Park. By radio from the Vatican
Pius XI extended his apostolic blessing. The pontifical
Mass was celebrated by Cardinal Pacelli, who also delivered the final address.

Our International Eucharistic Congress wishes to be nothing
more than a powerful cry, whose echoes will ring to the ends
of the earth, proclaiming in sweeping victory the Kingship
of Jesus Christ. Here love is concentrated, and from the depths
of all hearts rise voices of reparation and of triumph, which
seem to say: "No, Jesus will not now die amid the humilia-
tions and sorrows of Calvary." Faith will conquer apostasy.
We shall share the good fortune of the multitudes which of
old accompanied Him on the day of His triumph. With His
help we shall raise a throne for Him in every heart. We
shall make Him loved by every soul, and by all the peoples
of the world. . . . Once touched by love, one must be possessed
entirely by it. The soul feels impatient until Christ sets up
His Kingdom in her and longs to be able to say: "The Lord
possesses me." Such is the watchword of the kingdom. She
burns with apostolic zeal for the extension of the Church's
borders. Being subject to sweet agony she repeats: "I desire
to be dissolved and to be with Christ," and at the same time
she feels able to carry out all her generous resolves, trusting
in love. "I can do all things in Him who strengtheneth me."

Tuesday morning Cardinal Pacelli took farewell of
Buenos Aires, whose affection and admiration he had so
securely won. As the *Conte Grande* moved slowly down
the River Plate, hundreds of white doves were released to

soar over the liner. Standing on the top deck, the Cardinal continued to bless the cheering crowds until they faded from sight. That night powerful searchlights designed a luminous cross above Buenos Aires in memory of the blessing which the Pope's legate had brought the capital and the nation.

After a brief visit in Montevideo, Uruguay, Cardinal Pacelli arrived in Rio de Janeiro, Brazil, the morning of Saturday, October 20. President Getulio Vargas and hundreds of thousands of Brazilians welcomed him. After visiting the gigantic statue of Christ the Redeemer which overlooks Rio's harbor, the Cardinal addressed the Brazilian Deputies assembled in Parliament. Speaking in faultless Portuguese, which he is said to have learned in fifteen days, he exhorted the legislators to work for peace by upholding and promoting justice. That evening he was the guest of honor at a state dinner given by President Vargas and attended by the political and industrial leaders of Brazil. He was presented the Brazilian Order of the Southern Cross, and in turn decorated President Vargas with the Great Cross of the Order of Pius IX. The next morning he preached to the vast crowds which had gathered in beautiful Parque Republica to attend the open-air Mass and to demonstrate their love and homage for the Pope's Secretary of State. At four P.M. the *Conte Grande* weighed anchor and headed past Sugar Loaf Hill to the open sea and Rome.

As Cardinal Pacelli entered the papal library, the Holy Father rose from his desk to greet him. For two hours they talked of what the Legate had seen and learned in South America. The Pope congratulated him on his successful mission and praised him for the good he had accomplished. The evident sanctity and the brilliant talents of the Papal

Secretary of State had greatly increased the prestige and influence of the Holy See on the South American continent. Honors and attentions hitherto withheld even from foreign princes and rulers had been joyously accorded him. More of the world would meet the man whom Pius XI affectionately termed "Our closest collaborator."

One of his priests suggested to the late Cardinal Bourne, Archbishop of Westminster, England, that the bishops and priests of the world should gather together in one place to pray for peace among nations. In a private audience, a short time thereafter, Cardinal Bourne mentioned the suggestion to Pius XI. His Holiness immediately approved the plan and selected the Shrine of Lourdes, high in the Pyrenees Mountains of southern France. There in 1858 the Mother of God revealed herself to Bernadette Soubirous and to the world under the title of "The Immaculate Conception." Our Lady still obtains from her Son miracles of grace and health for those who pray at that hallowed place. Before the war a million pilgrims visited Lourdes each year. It was further decided that the gathering of the priests and bishops to pray for peace should take the form of a Triduum (three days of prayer), and that it should mark the closing of the Holy Year of Redemption, which the Pope had proclaimed in April, 1934, to commemorate the nineteenth centenary of Christ's death.

At first the Holy Father himself planned to go to Lourdes, but reluctantly yielded to his physicians who feared the trip might prove too tiring for a man in his late seventies. His Holiness then appointed Cardinal Pacelli to represent him as Legate. "We have entrusted this most honored mission to you, Our beloved son, because you so intimately serve the welfare of the Church in Our daily activity that you may be called Our closest collaborator, because you are a prince of the Church, and because of the sublime achievements you have accomplished for the salvation of souls."

Entering France at Nice, Cardinal Pacelli and his entourage of prelates, servants, and Noble Guards, were received by Louis Morin, the Minister of State, and other officials. Alpine chasseurs in dark blue uniforms and silver plumed helmets presented arms, as bands played the French and the papal anthems. With unprecedented pomp the visitors were escorted across France, which thirty years before had expelled the religious orders and had sought to establish an independent national church. So reverent and joyful was the reception wherever his train stopped that the Cardinal asked a member of his party: "Is this the France that has been renowned as nonreligious and anticlerical? No. It has always been the France of St. Louis and Jeanne d' Arc." During the journey he gave the first press interview of his life. It was to Charles Pichon of *L'Echo de Paris*. One remark in the interview is worth repeating today, when patriotism is valued by too many as higher than service to God. "There are two forms of patriotism. The false in which one makes of his country a heathen idol thirsting for war and bloodshed and superior to the principles of justice and charity. The other is true in which one loves his country as a mother who is loved not with fear but with respect and honor according to the laws of God."

At four o'clock in the morning of Friday, April 26, 1935, the Triduum opened with the offering of holy Mass for world peace. By special permission of the Holy Father, Mass would be celebrated every half hour of the day and night for the next three days. In all, one hundred and forty Masses were offered that "the dawn of better times might smile upon mankind." Bishop James Kearney of Salt Lake City, Utah, was the celebrant of one. Arriving toward noon, Cardinal Pacelli was welcomed to Lourdes by the three cardinals of France, sixty bishops of the world over, and throngs of cheering pilgrims. The hours not given to prayer and preaching Cardinal Pacelli devoted to the sick who had come hoping to be cured at the miraculous spring. His kind friendliness and pious simplicity deeply impressed the people, who eagerly sought his blessing. The people of France quickly recognized in Cardinal Pacelli the nobility of character which comes only from sanctity.

For the closing Mass Sunday afternoon, April 28, at which Cardinal Pacelli pontificated, 200,000 men, women, and children gathered before the Grotto of Massabielle, where the Immaculate Virgin appeared to Bernadette. Their prayers rose to heaven with those of the millions all over France and the world, who had dedicated the day to the Queen of Peace. In his sermon Cardinal Pacelli outspokenly attacked the program of dictatorship, Nazi, Fascist, and Communist, which was driving humanity into the fires of war. "Whether they are possessed by superstition of race and blood or by a false conception of the social and economic world, their philosophy rests upon principles essentially opposed to those of the Christian faith. And on such principles the Church may not and will not form a compact, no matter how bitter the price of refusal." Toward the end he warned the enemies of Christ that: "The Church of the Catacombs, the Church of the Popes and the Bishops, the intrepid and heroic Church, is not just history. It is a living reality. In all ages, past, present, and future, by the grace of God she has been and always will be active, strong, and inflexible. Flattery cannot make her deviate nor menace make her tremble." Speaking from the Vatican by radio, the Pope closed the Triduum with his apostolic blessing.

They prayed for peace; war was their sorrow four years later. Was the Triduum, then, a hollow mockery, or a proof that prayer is silly gibberish, foolish prattle? Fools, of course, and there are plenty of them, will argue that it was. But the fact is that countless thousands of those who prayed for peace obtained it in their own hearts, even when shells rumbled overhead. And who can say that the Triduum of Lourdes did not soften God's anger against sinful mankind? Five years of war was a light punishment for the decades of sin in which the world wallowed since 1918.

CHAPTER V

THE TRANSATLANTIC CARDINAL

URING the last three weeks of September, 1936, there were persistent rumors in Rome that Cardinal Pacelli would forego his customary vacation at Stella Maris convent in the Swiss Alps to visit the United States of America. In 1931 he had expressed a desire to see the United States, because "America is a young and progressive nation, and the Americans have a vigorousness which I would like to experience." Vatican circles continued to deny these rumors until the evening of September 29, when it was officially announced that Cardinal Pacelli would sail from Naples October 1 on the *Conte di Savoia* for New York City. The next morning the Holy Father returned to the Vatican from Castel Gandolfo, the papal summer residence, to wish his Secretary of State Godspeed.

At once the secular press of all nations began to guess the motives behind the Cardinal's visit to the United States. *Der Berliner Tageblatt,* a Nazi propaganda organ, authoritatively stated that the Cardinal would "deliver" the Catholic vote to President Roosevelt, 1936 being an election year, in exchange for diplomatic recognition of the Holy See by the United States. *The New York Times,* which once ran an editorial suggesting that Pius XI write an encyclical "on vacation and holidays and their high uses," learned from "unimpeachable sources" that Cardinal Pacelli would discuss with President Roosevelt an international conference of the heads of state. Many American newspapers were quite certain that he was coming to investigate and prohibit the political activities of Father Charles E. Coughlin, who was then sponsoring the Union Party with Congressman William Lemke as candidate for the presidency. *The New Republic,* a pseudo-liberal magazine published in New York City, having the intellectual vision of a snipe hunter, disclosed that Cardinal Pacelli wished to obtain the assistance of the United States for the Vatican's campaign against Communism, and then loftily advised him: "The Communist menace is about as real as the Japanese menace." To the newspapers, avid for the unusual, the Cardinal's need of a vacation and his interest in the United States were too colorless to be true.

Early Thursday morning, October 8, a cutter brought down to Quarantine His Excellency Archbishop Cicognani, the Apostolic Delegate to the United States, Francis J. Spellman, then Auxiliary Bishop of Boston, and the prelates representing the four American cardinals. Boarding the *Conte di Savoia,* they met Cardinal Pacelli and Count Enrico Galeazzi, his personal aide, in one of the ship's spacious salons. As greetings were being exchanged, fifty or more reporters and cameramen from the New York dailies and the principal press services hustled into the salon. Forewarned that American newsmen are inclined to misquote and to garble, Cardinal Pacelli smilingly refused to comment on the presidential election, on Hitler, on conditions in Europe, on Father Coughlin, and down the list. Instead he distributed among the reporters a written statement, which read in part:

On this my first visit to the United States there is no need of a lengthy statement to have you understand my desire, cherished for a long time, to see with my own eyes this country and to feel the pulsation of its life and labors. What could be more natural for me than the desire to know at first-hand this great and powerful nation, which by the force of its labor and organization, by its ideals, by its inexhaustible sources of wealth, has done such great things in the past and promises so much for the future, not only for this country but for all humanity. I am indeed happy to find myself within the territory of a great people who know how to unite so beautifully and successfully a sense of discipline with the exercise of a just, legitimate, and well-ordered liberty. May all the sons and daughters of the North American continent enjoy a noble and decent existence, which is the prerequisite of a true and lasting peace.

His "journalistic tax of entry" paid, Cardinal Pacelli went down to the foredeck to be photographed. Flash bulbs "popped" and newsreel cameras whirred as the visitor was "shot" from every possible angle. One cameraman, who was perched on a lifeboat for greater advantage, shouted excitedly: "Hey, Mr. Pope, look this way," thus showing himself a prophet even if not an authority on ecclesiastical etiquette. Wearing a black cassock piped in scarlet, a heavy gold cross and chain, and a scarlet skullcap, the first Papal Secretary of State to visit the United States was an impressive figure. It should be noted, however, that he does not photograph well, for the camera hides the gentle kindness of his face and accentuates his austere features.

The cameramen were still "shooting," when the *Conte di Savoia* docked. A crowd of clergy and laity, many of whom wore on their coat lapels button pictures of Cardinal Pacelli framed in the American and papal colors, were shouting a welcome. Followed by his aide and visitors, the Cardinal walked down the gangplank toward a waiting limousine. Before entering he turned and blessed the crowd, which knelt in reverence on the cold pier wet from the morning fog.

Arriving at the Archbishop's House on Madison Avenue, the papal visitor was joyfully greeted by His Eminence Patrick Hayes, New York's Cardinal of Charity, whom he had called friend for many years. The two princes of the Church then went to St. Patrick's Cathedral where prayers of thanksgiving for the safe journey across the Atlantic were offered. With Cardinal Hayes acting as guide, they inspected the cathedral's treasures, among which are the magnificent windows, the Little Flower altar, and Our Lady of Victory Chapel. Afterward Cardinal Pacelli was driven to Inisfada at Manhasset, Long Island.

Inisfada, which is today a Jesuit seminary, was the elegant estate of Mrs. Nicholas Brady, the widow of New York's traction tycoon. Of Tudor-Elizabethan architecture, the main house had eighty-seven rooms, including a beautiful chapel which Cardinal Bonzano, later Papal Legate to the International Eucharistic Congress at Chicago, consecrated in 1920. For her open-handed contributions to the Church and to charity, Mrs. Brady was made a Papal Duchess by Pope Pius XI, through whom she and her husband became admiring friends of Cardinal Pacelli. On her annual pilgrimage to Rome in the spring of 1936 Mrs. Brady invited the Papal Secretary of State to be her guest at Inisfada.

On Saturday Cardinal Pacelli lunched at Cardinal Hayes' residence with Nicholas Murray Butler, President of Columbia University. They had known each other for a number of years, as Mr. Butler had been a member of the committee for the reorganization of the Vatican Library. The return route to Inisfada led over the seventeen miles long Triborough Bridge, and Cardinal Pacelli had the chauffeur stop three times so that he could get out and study the spectacular structure. Sunday morning the papal visitor presided at the pontifical Mass commemorating the twenty-sixth anniversary of the consecration of St. Patrick's Cathedral. That afternoon Cardinal Pacelli received in private audience the former queen of Spain, Victoria.

On Monday Angelo Spugnardi, tailor extraordinary to the Eastern bishops, measured the Cardinal for a black suit — size 38 coat, 34 inches in the waist, and the trousers 32 inches long. Of his distinguished customer Angelo said: "He never fidgeted, but asked me so many questions about things in the United States."

The next day, October 13, Cardinal Pacelli with Bishop Spellman and Count Galeazzi motored to Boston, stopping at Hartford, Connecticut, to be luncheon guests of Bishop McAuliffe. After a lengthy chat with Cardinal William O'Connell, Boston's renowned archbishop, Cardinal Pacelli went to the Sacred Heart rectory, Newton Center, Massachusetts, to be the guest of its pastor, Bishop Spellman.

The next morning the children of the Sacred Heart school presented a special program in honor of their visitor. Introducing Cardinal Pacelli, the pastor said: "No parish priest would have had the courage to ask Your Eminence to stay at a small parish, unless he knew you, as I know you, and knew your love for the poor and the lowly. I have seen Your Eminence among the lowly in the mountains of Italy and among the children of the shepherd folk. Therefore I knew that I was not courageous in asking you to come." His Eminence then spoke in English to the children, concluding with "I congratulate you on your splendid program, and I wish to tell you that I thoroughly enjoyed it. I realize that you must have worked very hard. And therefore I grant you two holidays, today and tomorrow." Remembering his own school days, the Cardinal accepted the thunderous applause as gratitude for the free days rather than tribute to himself.

Thursday Cardinal Pacelli returned to Inisfada where he remained, receiving distinguished members of the laity and clergy, until the following Monday. Then he drove to the Jesuit house of St. Isaac Jogues at Wernersville, Pennsylvania. Proceeding to Philadelphia the papal visitor was received by Denis Cardinal Dougherty, who accompanied him to Independence Hall. Cardinal Pacelli signed the register and, after viewing the Liberty Bell, sat in the chair once occupied by George Washington. Visits also were made to St. Charles Borromeo Seminary, to Rosemount College, and to other Catholic institutions.

Wednesday afternoon, October 21, Cardinal Pacelli left Philadelphia by train for Washington, D. C., where he would be the guest of the Apostolic Delegate, Archbishop Cicognani. When the new delegation was erected on Massachusetts Avenue, the furniture of the bedroom occupied by Cardinal Pacelli together with pictures of his visit was placed in a special room marked with a plaque as "Cardinal Pacelli's Room." After Mass and breakfast the next morning, His Eminence visited the Catholic University of America to address the faculty and the student body. "May yours be the grace," he told the professors, "of an intimate realization of the greatness, the nobility, and the responsibility of those who, in the designs of God, are destined to be the servants and custodians of learning. After the priesthood of the altar there is none greater than the priesthood of truth."

At eleven o'clock Cardinal Pacelli toured the Library of Congress, studying with great interest the original documents of the Declaration of Independence and the Constitution and an original score of Abbé Franz Liszt, the

Hungarian pianist and composer. He signed the guest register "E. Card. Pacelli." After a brief call at the headquarters of the National Catholic Welfare Conference, whose admirable work for the Church in America he praised and blessed, he proceeded to the National Press Club where he was the luncheon guest of some four hundred correspondents. Addressing his hosts on world peace, he told them: "The Holy Father appeals to you, who have great responsibility in reporting facts and in inspiring public opinion, to work for peace."

From the National Press Club Cardinal Pacelli motored across the Potomac River to Mount Vernon, the ancestral estate of George Washington. He placed memorial wreaths at the tombs of George and Martha Washington, and pausing before the room where America's first president died, said a prayer for the repose of his soul. Two honeymoon couples who were visiting Mount Vernon at the same time asked and received Cardinal Pacelli's blessing. Late that afternoon His Eminence visited Georgetown University, where before a distinguished assembly of the laity and clergy the honorary degree of doctor of canon and civil law was conferred upon him.

On Saturday evening, October 24, a brilliant reception was held for Cardinal Pacelli at Inisfada. Seven hundred candles lighted the quarter-mile drive leading from the main gateway to the door. Among the guests were renowned prelates, Cardinals Hayes and Villeneuve, and distinguished members of New York society. At another social function honoring Cardinal Pacelli, Dunninger of stage and radio fame attempted to read his mind. To the mentalist's confusion the Cardinal was thinking in Latin, a language which Dunninger did not understand.

Ten o'clock Sunday morning, Cardinal Pacelli, Basil

Harris, Bishop Spellman, and Count Galeazzi boarded a chartered plane of the United Airlines at Roosevelt Field, Long Island, for an air tour of the United States. Captain Jack O'Brien was the pilot, and the stewardess was Miss Madeline Quirici, who speaks both English and Italian. Over the congested cities of New Jersey and eastern Pennsylvania, the Allegheny and Appalachian mountains, the flat lands of Ohio, the plane made its way to South Bend, Indiana. Here at the famed Notre Dame University Cardinal Pacelli received an honorary LL.D. The chilling rain could not dampen the enthusiasm of the students, encouraged by the gift of a holiday.

Because of a thick fog enveloping the airport Cardinal Pacelli's plane was an hour late into Chicago. The Archbishop of Chicago, Cardinal Mundelein, the bishops of the other dioceses in Illinois, and a delegation of civic and government officials were at the airport to greet and welcome the Papal Secretary of State to America's second largest city. The evening was spent at the Archbishop's house in conversation with Cardinal Mundelein and priests of the Chicago diocese, who found their guest more desirous of hearing their views than of expressing his own. Cardinal Pacelli had come to learn of America and of Americans in the Midwest, and so most of his conversation was in the form of questions. Monday His Eminence visited the St. Mary of the Lake Seminary, whose prestige and beauty bespeak the greatness of its founder, the late Cardinal Mundelein, and then the papal visitor flew northward to St. Paul, arriving in the late afternoon. The next morning he celebrated Mass in St. Paul's Cathedral and spoke briefly to a congregation of clergy, seminarians, and laity. The prairies robbed by the harvest, the Rocky Mountains piercing the clouds, the deserts lying in leaden slumber, and then San Francisco, where Cardinal Pacelli was given a civic reception by Archbishop Mitty and Mayor Rossi, and, afterward, blessed the gigantic Golden Gate Bridge spanning the bay.

After a pause at Los Angeles, Cardinal Pacelli's plane turned eastward, flying low over Grand Canyon and circling Boulder Dam for a better view. A delay in refueling at Kansas City, Missouri, gave the Cardinal and Bishop Thomas Lillis time for a prolonged conversation as they paced the runway in the cold midnight air. In Cincinnati His Eminence blessed the cornerstone of a new school for Monsignor Edward J. Quinn, with whom he had taken a vacation trip from Naples to Gibraltar in 1933. A detour over Niagara Falls and Cardinal Pacelli was back in New York City, October 31, at 3:28 p.m. In seven days he had traveled eight thousand miles, visited twelve of the then sixteen archdioceses, and met seventy-nine bishops. He had viewed industrial centers, farming areas, and the sources of America's natural wealth, and had inspected schools, churches, hospitals, and homes for the aged and the orphaned.

On Sunday afternoon, November 1, Fordham University of New York City accorded Cardinal Pacelli a most enthusiastic welcome, in which the presidents of ten universities and the consular representatives of many foreign countries joined. The Papal Secretary of State told the audience of five thousand people: "It is my fervent prayer that all the citizens of the United States may profess in deeds as well as in words their absolute adherence to the following fundamental truth of all good government: 'Unless the Lord build the house, they labor in vain who build it. Unless the Lord keep the city, he watcheth in vain that keepeth it.'" Standing today at the summit of world power and gazing down upon conquered foes and dependent allies, we would do well daily to pray the prayer of Cardinal Pacelli in word and in deed.

The presidential election over, Cardinal Pacelli lunched with President and Mrs. Roosevelt on November 5 at Hyde Park. When pressed for a comment by the ever persistent reporters, he escaped smilingly: "I enjoyed lunching with a typical American family. I am very happy to have had the opportunity of seeing and congratulating the President." On the return trip to New York City Cardinal Pacelli stopped at Bronxville to have tea with Mr. Joseph Kennedy, formerly American ambassador to Great Britain, and his family. The youngest member of the family, Teddy, then five years old, was unable to open the medal case which the Cardinal had given him. To the embarrassment of his parents but to the delight of their guest, Teddy climbed up on Cardinal Pacelli's lap and had him open the case.

Saturday morning, November 6, Cardinal Pacelli knelt with Cardinal Hayes in St. Patrick's Cathedral and recited the *Itinerarium,* which is the prayer said before departing on a journey. Afterward the two Cardinals, Archbishop Cicognani, Bishop Spellman, and representatives of the clergy and laity crossed Manhattan to Pier 59 on the North River where a reception was held aboard the *Conte di Savoia.* To the ever present press Cardinal Pacelli gave a written statement which is quoted here only in part: "I have enjoyed all I have seen and done in America. I am leaving America with gratitude in my heart to all with whom I have come in contact, and with a prayer that almighty God may continue to bless this great nation, that its citizens may be happy and prosperous, and that the influence of the United States may always be exerted for

the promotion of peace among peoples." As the color
guard on the pier dipped the flags of the United States and
the Holy See, the liner moved out into the river. Standing
at the deck rail, Cardinal Pacelli continued to bless America and all Americans until New York City was lost to
view.

The *Conte di Savoia* reached Naples November 14, and,
after lunching with Cardinal Ascalesi, the Neapolitan
Archbishop, Cardinal Pacelli entrained for Rome. A large
gathering of papal officials and foreign diplomats greeted
him at the station, from which he motored to Vatican City.
As Cardinal Pacelli entered the papal study, the Pope rose
from his desk to greet him. They talked for two hours,
with the Holy Father asking numerous questions about the
United States and its people, and the Secretary of State
making a detailed report on his journey. At the end of the
audience Pius XI gave Cardinal Pacelli his picture autographed "To Our Beloved Transatlantic Cardinal." When
he reached his own office, Cardinal Pacelli immediately
wrote President Roosevelt, saying among other things:
"My travels in the United States left on me the deepest
impression of my whole life."

During Cardinal Pacelli's visit to the United States,
reports continued to reach his desk of violations of the
Concordat which he had signed with Nazi Germany in
1933. By that agreement Hitler guaranteed the Church of
Germany freedom to educate her children, to maintain her
institutions, and to fulfill her divine mission of saving
souls. The striking triumph which Cardinal Pacelli seemed
to have gained quickly proved a tragic failure, as Hitler,
after solidifying his position, turned like a venomous snake
against the Church of Germany. Catholic boys and girls
were driven by physical violence into Nazi youth organiza-

tions whose loathsome paganism made them slaves to sin and vice. In a Bavarian forest lie the unmarked graves of some one hundred Catholic boys whom Gestapo agents beat to death. These innocents were slain because they refused to deny their God and Saviour in the name of a degenerate leader. Thousands of Catholic schools were closed, and those not closed were harassed and undermined by subtle persecution. In an effort to discredit their shepherds with the faithful, the government basely accused monks and priests of sexual perversion and political treason. After trials like that of Christ before Caiphas these servants of God were flung into infamous concentration camps where clubbings and tortures ended the lives of many. The club-footed Satan, Goebbels, by monstrous lies and vicious falsehoods strove to uproot the Church of Germany which he smeared as treacherous and depraved and whose doctrines he ridiculed as degenerate and obsolete. The foul-mouthed Julius Streicher told the German people: "It is only in one or two exceptional points that Christ and Hitler stand comparison, for Hitler is far too big to be compared with one so petty." The Nazis had declared total war against the Church and the Catholics of Germany, and indeed against Christianity.

Though cheated by Hitler, Cardinal Pacelli had not been hoodwinked nor was he now defeated. His years as Nuncio to Germany had given him an intimate awareness of Nazi dishonesty and evil, but solicitude for the eternal salvation of the German people necessarily prevailed over political skepticism. The Papal Secretary of State is first a priest, and only secondarily a statesman. Hitler had been given an opportunity to prove himself and had failed. Cardinal Pacelli now was free and obligated to fight. Each new violation of the Concordat was firmly denounced in sharply worded notes to the German ambassador at the Vatican or to the German foreign minister at Berlin. Time and time again the Holy Father condemned with mounting emphasis the Nazi paganism in all its vile forms. "Anti-Semitism is a movement which we Christians cannot share. We are Semites spiritually. Propaganda against the Jews assumes proportions unworthy of twenty centuries of Christian civilization."

Cardinal Pacelli encouraged the German clergy and faithful to resist the Nazi warfare against Christ and His Church, and they did so in a manner worthy of the early Christian martyrs. Determined that the German Catholics and the entire Christian world should know Hitler as another Nero and learn the fundamental opposition of Catholicism to Nazism, Pius XI, with the help of Cardinal Pacelli, wrote the now famous encyclical *Mit Brennender Sorge*. The mails and the telegraphs being closely censored by the brutal Gestapo, the resourceful Secretary of State had copies of the encyclical smuggled into Germany by priests and laymen returning from a pilgrimage to Rome. Each bishop received a copy, and secretly had additional ones printed and distributed to the parish priests. Palm Sunday morning, March 21, 1937, and again that evening the Holy Father's letter was read from the pulpit of every Catholic church in Germany.

Unmasking the hypocrisy of the Nazis, the Pope declared:

In the furrows where We tried to sow the seed of a sincere peace, other men, like the "enemy" of Holy Scripture, over-sowed the cockle of distrust, unrest, hatred, calumny, and a determined enmity, secret or open . . . against Christ and His Church.

The encyclical proceeded to condemn basic doctrines of

Nazism, which even today with Hitler dead and Berlin occupied, hold sway in the Balkans and in Eastern Europe as so-called democracy:

Whoever exalts the race, or the people, or the State, or a particular form of State, or the depositories of power, or any other fundamental value of the human community . . . above their standard value and divinizes them to an idolatrous level, and deifies, distorts and perverts an order of the world planned and created by God. . . . He who sacrilegiously disregards the yawning abyss between God and man, and dares to place any mortal, were he the greatest of all times, beside Christ, or worse, above Him and against Him, is a false prophet in whom the words of Scripture find terrible application: "He that dwelleth in heaven, shall laugh at them."

Scorning the Swastika, the Holy Father proclaimed:

The Cross of Christ, though the mere name may have become to many a folly and a scandal, is still for the Christian the hallowed sign of redemption, the standard of moral greatness and strength. In its shadow we live. In its kiss we die. On our graves it shall stand to proclaim our faith, to witness our hope turned towards the eternal light.

Advice which the postwar world should heed, even though Nazism is destroyed, was forcefully given:

The principle "What helps the people is right." should be inverted to read: "Never is anything useful, if it is not at the same time morally good." . . . He who sings the songs of loyalty to his earthly country must not become a deserter and a traitor to God, to his Church, and to his eternal country. . . . They who expel Christianity from instruction and education, from the formation of social and public life, are treading the ways of spiritual impoverishment and decline.

The Holy Father in eloquent terms praised the courage and devotion of the German clergy and people whose faith was "being tried like pure gold in the fire of tribulation and concealed and open persecution." Then in prophetic tone he told them: "The enemies of the Church who fancy that her hour has come will soon recognize that they rejoiced too soon and were too quick to dig her grave."

Outwitted by the Vatican the Nazis struck back in fury, confiscating the presses which had printed the encyclical and increasing their oppressive measures against the Church and loyal Catholics. The encyclical did not lighten the burden of the German Catholics, but it did demonstrate to the world and to history the uncompromising opposition of the Holy See to Hitler's Nazism. With the Anschluss the Nazi persecutors began to scourge the Church of Austria, but were steadfastly resisted by the Austrian clergy and faithful under the guidance of Cardinal Pacelli. When certain members of the Austrian hierarchy tended to compromise slightly with the Nazis, the Papal Secretary of State summoned their leader to the Vatican and "laid down the law" to him in a stinging rebuke.

His warfare against Nazism did not obscure for Cardinal Pacelli the dangers and evils of another enemy of Christianity and civilization, atheistic communism. This plague struck Russia at the end of World War I, when defeat, famine, and chaos walked through the land in murderous kinship. Wading through slaughter to despotic power, the Communists under the leadership of Lenin, and later of Stalin, became the masters of the Russian people. Manacled by the cruel OGPU, after which Hitler modeled his Gestapo, the Russian people saw their churches defiled, their clergy martyred, and their children befouled by atheistic and immoral propaganda in soviet schools, newspapers, and organizations. The people themselves became the groveling slaves of the State, which treated them as subhuman beings without rights and without value. When the peasants resisted Stalin's robbery of their few acres, he confiscated their food supplies and they starved to death, not a few hundred thousands but several millions. Others he placed in boxcars during the winter and had his soldiers dump their corpses on the frozen wastes of Siberia.

Because Communism is basically an international, rather than a national, movement, it did not, and will not, confine itself within the borders of Soviet Russia. Bela Kun made Hungary a shambles in his unsuccessful efforts to communize that country in 1919; the Communists changed Spain's orderly revolution into a bloody civil war; in Mexico they fomented the inhuman persecution of the Church and loyal Catholics; and in France, the United States, and other countries they have continued to incite social and industrial strife. Today Communism terrorizes in absolute, if concealed, power Bulgaria, Yugoslavia, Hungary, Rumania, Poland, and the Baltic Republics, Lithuania, Esthonia, and Latvia, and it is reaching with hideous hands toward Italy, France, Germany, and the Lowland countries, Belgium and Holland.

Because Communism, like its political twin Nazism, is destructive of Christianity and civilization, the Church has fought it without cease or compromise. As early as 1846, Pius IX solemnly condemned "that infamous doctrine of Communism which, if once adopted, would utterly destroy the rights, property, and possessions of all men, and even society itself." His successor, Leo XIII, likewise denounced Communism as atheistic (denial of God) and totalitarian (denial of human and political rights — liberty, self-government, free speech and worship). Having experienced at first hand the horrors of Communism, while Apostolic Visitor to Poland, Pius XI marshaled the full influence and strength of the Church against this barbarism. Frequently and insistently in encyclicals and addresses he called public attention to the communist danger. Cardinal Pacelli guided a world-wide attack, obtaining and supplying information on conditions in Russia, advising the bishops how to oppose the communist campaign in their countries, and encouraging them to awaken their people to its evils. In 1937 he collaborated with the Holy Father on the encyclical *Divini Redemptoris* (Divine Redeemer), which is a "must" on the reading list of any intelligent Catholic or non-Catholic.

The basic teachings of Communism are stated and analyzed:

According to this doctrine there is in the world only one reality, matter, the blind forces of which evolve into plant, animal, and man. Even human society is nothing but a form of matter, evolving in the same way. By a law of inexorable necessity and through a perpetual conflict of forces, matter moves toward a classless society. In such a doctrine, as is evident, there is no room for the idea of God; there is no difference between matter and spirit, between soul and body; there is neither survival of the soul after death nor any hope in a future life . . . the Communists claim that the conflict which carries the world towards its final synthesis [a classless society] can be accelerated by man. Hence they endeavor to sharpen the antagonisms which arise between the various classes of society. Thus the class struggle with its consequent violent hate and destruction takes on the aspect of a crusade for the progress of humanity. On the other hand, all other forces whatever, as long as they resist such systematic violence, must be annihilated as hostile to the human race.

Communism, moreover, strips man of his liberty, robs human personality of all its dignity, and removes all the moral restraints that check the eruptions of blind impulse. There is no recognition of any right of the individual in his relations to the collectivity; no natural right is accorded to the human being, who is a mere cogwheel in the Communist system. . . . Nor is the individual granted any property rights over material goods or the means of production . . . all forms of private property must be eradicated, for they are at the origin of all economic enslavement.

Refusing to human life any sacred or spiritual character, such a doctrine logically makes of marriage and the family a purely artificial and civil institution . . . the notion of an indissoluble marriage tie is scouted. Communism is particularly characterized by the rejection of any link that binds woman to the family and the home, and her emancipation is proclaimed as a basic principle. She is withdrawn from the family and the care of her children, to be thrust, instead, into public life and collective production under the same conditions as man. The care of home and children devolves then upon the collectivity.

Finally, the right of education is denied to parents, for it is conceived as the exclusive prerogative of the community, in whose name and by whose mandate alone parents may exercise this right.

. . . Communism is by its nature antireligious. It considers religion as "the opiate of the people," because the principles of religion which speak of a life beyond the grave dissuade the proletariat from the dream of a Soviet paradise which is of this world.

Because mere opposition will not prevent the spread of Communism, the Holy Father set forth a constructive program for removing the social and economic abuses upon which it feeds:

. . . The fundamental remedy today lies in a sincere renewal of private and public life according to the principles of the Gospel by all those who belong to the fold of Christ. . . .

. . . Even in Catholic countries there are still too many who are Catholics hardly more than in name. . . . The Catholic who does not live really and sincerely according to the faith he professes will not long be master of himself in these days when the winds of strife and persecution blow so fiercely, but will be swept away defenseless in this new deluge which threatens the world. . . .

. . . Let [the rich] be mindful of the account they must render [of their earthly goods] to their Lord and master, and value them as precious means that God has put into their hands for doing good.

. . . But the poor too, in their turn, while engaged . . . in acquiring the necessities of life and in bettering their condition, should always remain "poor in spirit," and hold spiritual goods in higher esteem than earthly property and pleasures. Let them remember that the world will never be able to rid itself of misery, sorrow, and tribulation, which are the portion even of those who seem most prosperous. Patience, therefore, is the need of all. . . .

Still more important as a remedy for the evil we are considering, or certainly more directly calculated to cure it, is the precept of charity. We have in mind that Christian charity, "patient and kind," which avoids all semblance of demeaning paternalism, and all ostentation. . . . Its faithful observance will pour into the heart an inner peace which the world knows not, and will finally cure the ills which oppress humanity.

But charity will never be true charity unless it takes justice into constant account . . . a "charity" which deprives the workingman of the salary to which he has a strict title in justice, is not charity at all, but only its empty name and hollow semblance. The wage-earner is not to receive as alms which is his due in justice. And let no one attempt with trifling charitable donations to exempt himself from the great duties imposed by justice. . . .

Social justice cannot be said to have been satisfied as long as workingmen are denied a salary that will enable them to secure proper sustenance for themselves and for their families; as long as they are denied the opportunity of acquiring a modest fortune and forestalling the plague of universal pauperism; as long as they cannot make suitable provision through public or private insurance for old age, for periods of illness and unemployment . . . it is of the utmost importance to foster in all classes of society an intensive program of social education adapted to the varying degrees of intellectual culture. It is necessary with all care and diligence to procure the widest possible diffusion of the teachings of the Church, especially among the working-classes. . . .

. . . as a final and most efficacious remedy We recommend the spirit of prayer joined with Christian penance . . . the evil which today torments humanity can be conquered only by a world-wide holy crusade of prayer and penance.

The courageous stand of the Russian people against Nazi aggression has gained for them the admiration and gratitude of the other United Nations. It is essential for world peace that the United States and Soviet Russia maintain friendly and co-operative relations. But "Communism is intrinsically wrong, and no one who would save Christian civilization may collaborate with it in any undertaking whatsoever. Those who permit themselves to be deceived into lending their aid toward the triumph of Communism in their own country, will be the first to fall victims of their error." It is, indeed, the moral and patriotic duty of every American, of whatever creed and whatever political party, to oppose the spread of Communism in our Republic.

Expose the diabolic propaganda of the Communists in newspapers, magazines, books, movies, plays, and radio programs. "Little by little Communistic propaganda penetrates into all classes of the people and even reaches the better-minded groups of the community, with the result that few are aware of the poison which increasingly pervades their minds and hearts." Remove from positions of influence and power the Communists in schools, labor organizations, business establishments, and government bureaus. An American citizen cannot obey both the Constitution and the Communist Manifesto, for in supporting one he must destroy the other. Above all, eradicate the social, economic, and political abuses which foster the growth of Communism in the United States. The Negro, who incidentally is both a human being and an American citizen, surely has an excuse for turning in despair to Communism. Jim Crowism, mob lynchings, pigsty housing, and persecution in countless ways make hollow and hypocritical any argument for the Declaration of Independence and the Constitution. And unless the American workingman is freed, soon and permanently, from the economic slavery of depression, unjust wages, and job insecurity,

Communism will glide to power. Jobless men with hungry and ragged families are easily led astray because a full stomach is a stronger argument than a free ballot. Finally, "when religion is banished from the school, from education, and from public life, are we not really fostering the materialism which is the fertile soil of Communism? Neither force, however well organized it be, nor earthly ideals however lofty and noble, can halt a movement whose roots lie in excessive esteem for the goods of this world."

In his struggle against Nazism and Communism Pius XI often sought the intercession of the Little Flower, St. Thérèse of Lisieux, whom he had canonized and whom he affectionately called "Star of Our Pontificate." Therefore he chose his chief collaborator in that struggle, Cardinal Pacelli, to consecrate the newly erected Basilica of St. Thérèse at Lisieux. It would be a symbol of universal peace and brotherhood, because the peoples of all nations had contributed to its erection.

The Papal Legate and his party arrived in Paris on June 10, at nine in the morning. President Albert Lebrun and his ministers, Cardinal Verdier and other ecclesiastics welcomed him to France. The station echoed with the cheers of excited thousands, as the band played the "Marseillaise" and "Long Live the Pope." After inspecting the special guard of soldiers drawn up on the railway platform, Cardinal Pacelli celebrated Mass in the famous Sacred Heart Basilica on Montmarte. In the early afternoon he visited the Missionary Exposition, where the work of the Catholic missions throughout the French Empire was on display.

Cardinal Pacelli reached Lisieux at five-thirty the same afternoon. After the pontifical letter of appointment had been officially read in the chapel of the Carmelite convent, the Papal Legate went to the Bishop's House for dinner and a night's rest. The consecration of the basilica began Sunday morning with pontifical Mass, of which Cardinal Pacelli was the celebrant and the great multitude crowding the shrine and overflowing into the square and adjacent streets was the choir. The Cardinal's sermon in French was two hours long, but the beauty of thought and language saved it from being tiresome.

Why do we call this Basilica the House of God? Has God need of a dwelling place as a refuge from thunder and lightning, storms, and the tempests of this world — a God who separated the light from the darkness and who created the stars, the moon, and the sun, and hung them in the heaven?

The procession of the Blessed Sacrament started at four in the afternoon, and extending for two miles under triumphal arches lasted until seven. The Papal Legate, holding the Blessed Sacrament in an ostensorium of beautifully wrought gold, moved through the streets on a chariot decorated with lilies and wake robins. From the grateful hearts of the kneeling thousands rose the glorious strains of the *Pange Lingua,* the *Lauda Sion,* and other eucharistic hymns. The Little Flower, who had never given God anything but love, must have rejoiced in heaven at the homage being paid the Eucharistic King in her own Lisieux.

After solemn benediction of the Blessed Sacrament closed the day, Cardinal Pacelli was received within the walls of the Carmelite Convent, holy with memories of St. Thérèse. Her sister Pauline, the Prioress, and Celine, the youngest sister, met the visitor in the convent parlor. He conversed with them for a half hour, telling of the Holy Father's special love for their sister and asking the prayers of the community for world peace. Then he visited the cell of Marie, the eldest sister, bedridden for many

years, and bestowed on her his blessing. The next morning
Cardinal Pacelli returned to the Convent and offered Mass
in the infirmary, now a chapel, where the Little Flower
had died.

Tuesday morning the Papal Legate pontificated in historic Notre Dame, the Cathedral of Paris and all France.
In his sermon he glorified the France of history and
warned the France of today against internal strife and
religious indifference. After the luncheon given in his
honor by President Lebrun, Cardinal Pacelli placed a
wreath on the tomb of France's unknown soldier of World
War I. A formal reception at the Hôtel de Ville, and then
Cardinal Pacelli boarded the train for Rome. The account
of his journey which Cardinal Pacelli wrote for *L'Osservatore Romano* closed with lines of special significance:
"As soon as nations realize that there is a definite correla-
tion between the mission of the Church of Christ and their
own progress and greatness, so soon shall occur the harmony which God desires. This must be the goal of all
peoples of good will."

The Thirty-Fourth International Eucharistic Congress
was to be held May 23–29, 1938, in Budapest, Hungary's
romantic capital on the River Danube. Pius XI named
Cardinal Pacelli Legate to the Congress, because he wished
his Secretary of State to study the condition of the Church
in Hungary and Eastern Europe. The Papal Legate and
the Pontifical Mission arrived at Budapest on Monday, the
opening day of the Congress, and were met by the Regent,
Admiral Horthy, and the Primate, Cardinal Seredi. A
state drive through streets bright with flower arches and
multicolored flags took the Legate to the Royal Palace,
which was to be his residence during the Congress. On
Tuesday and Wednesday Cardinal Pacelli presided at the

morning Masses and attended the afternoon conferences, where prelates from various countries discussed with the pilgrims religious, moral, and modern problems.

Children's Day was Thursday, the Feast of the Ascension. In City Park 50,000 children assisted at outdoor Mass and received Holy Communion. That evening while thousands of pilgrims, each holding a flaming torch, lined the banks, a flotilla of lighted and decorated barges moved down the Danube between Buda and Pest. The center barge carried an immense altar on which rested a golden monstrance, so huge that it was easily visible to the worshipers on the banks. Before it knelt Cardinal Pacelli, whose lips moved in fervent prayer as the devout pilgrims chanted the *"O Salutaris Hostia."*

The closing day, Sunday, was set aside as general Communion day for the million pilgrims attending the Congress from fifty-seven nations. In one of his greatest speeches Cardinal Pacelli challenged and denounced the militant godlessness of our day:

The philosophers of godlessness, in breaking the bonds which bind man to his Creator, have at the same time, without knowing and, perhaps, even without wishing it, destroyed those spiritual forces which gave to the human community its dignity, its cohesion, and its very existence, and which drew their strength and their effectiveness from faith in the heavenly Father. The deniers of the Christian revelation have defiled man in his private and social life; and have robbed man's relations with man of their high nobility and sacred character.

A slow but continuous work of disintegration has separated intellectual and moral life from the unshakable rock, faith in God and in Christ, on which it was originally founded. Blind presumption has little by little weakened and finally broken the link between the duty of man and the principles of the eternal law without having been able to substitute anything else except earthly morals, which have neither foundation nor sanction. Drunk with the pride of a purely material progress, the philosophers of godlessness have detached education from the foundation which God gave it. And today we contemplate, with horror, the fruit of their work: instead of the proud humanity, conscious and free, which had been promised us, we see a world in chaos without joy or peace, a sorry product of godless errors and mistakes.

Has the world ever known such bitter hatred, divisions, and deep discords as those within which it is today hopelessly involved? Has the value of the given word ever been lower than it is today, when utilitarian materialism has been openly and officially substituted for the eternal moral principles? In a world in which the idea of the fear of God is lost and the teachings of Christ are not applied in real life, ought we to be surprised to see hatred rule between class and class, between man and man, between nation and nation, hatred which has arrived at such a degree that its brutal force threatens any moment to cause a catastrophe?

Until those who are on both sides of the line have their hearts penetrated by the spirit of Bethlehem, by the example of Nazareth, by the doctrines of the Sermon on the Mount, all the official laws, all human efforts will remain impotent at the great risk of arriving one day at the full bankruptcy of their promises.

These words, spoken in 1937, are surely of even greater application today, when the world claims to be building a new era. The militant godlessness of the Nazis and the Fascists has ended in total defeat, only to appear in somewhat different garb, in the social, political, moral, and educational philosophy of its conquerors. Is there today, or will there be tomorrow, less hatred, division, and discord than in 1937?

Cardinal Pacelli's visits to the United States, France, and Hungary were shadowed by the lingering illness of Pius XI. From 1936 on, the Holy Father had resisted approaching death with fierce, at times sarcastic, determination. When a certain cardinal remarked to him that he was not looking well, the Pope sharply replied: "Eminence, the

Lord has blessed you with many talents, but a clinical eye is not among them." On his seventy-ninth birthday he said to Count Ratti who had suggested that he take care of himself, "Thanks very much, my dear nephew, for your kind advice. Rest assured that I shall take it to heart, when I am old." But death was not to be cheated forever, and on Friday morning, February 10, 1939, at 5:31, His Holiness Pope Pius XI returned to his Maker and his Judge. Hardening arteries, a weak heart, bad circulation, and eighty-one years of struggle — this was the trouble.

Glorious and courageous was the pontificate of Pius XI. He reconciled Italy with the Church and founded Vatican City. His zeal in spreading the Kingdom of Christ to pagan lands gained for him the title, "Pope of the Missions." He was a fighter against war and oppression, for justice and morality. His encyclicals "On the Condition of the Workingman," "On Education," "On Christian Marriage," "Against Fascism," "Against Nazism," "Against Communism," place him with history's great champions of humanity and Christianity. The annals of the popes, which extend through twenty centuries, tell of two hundred and sixty-two popes, but of very few greater than Pius XI.

As Camerlengo of the holy Roman Church Cardinal Pacelli notified the Sacred College of Cardinals, the diplomatic corps accredited to the Holy See, and the papal nuncios and apostolic delegates abroad that their Sovereign Pontiff was dead. Then he returned to the Pope's bedroom and, kneeling with the papal household, recited the *De Profundis:*

Out of the depths I have cried to thee, O Lord:
Lord, hear my voice.
Let thy ears be attentive to the voice of my supplication,
If thou, O Lord, wilt mark iniquities:

Lord, who shall stand it?
For with thee there is merciful forgiveness: and by reason of
the law
I have waited for thee, O Lord.
My soul hath relied on his word: my soul hath hoped in the
Lord.
From the morning watch even until night,
Let Israel hope in the Lord.
Because with the Lord there is mercy; and with him plenti-
ful redemption
And he shall redeem Israel from all his iniquities.

The Confessors of St. Peter then dressed the body in a
white cassock and sash, a lace alb, a gold miter, slippers
embroidered with crosses, and a red chasuble. Red is the
color of mourning for a pope, because the early pontiffs
were martyrs. The first day the body lay on a blue and gold
catafalque in the Sistine Chapel, to which were admitted
only ecclesiastical dignitaries and foreign diplomats. The
next day the body was taken in procession to the Blessed
Sacrament Chapel of St. Peter's, and placed on an open
bier, which was surrounded by twenty-four tall candles in
golden candlesticks and guarded at each corner by a Noble
Guard in dark uniform and silver helmet. A half-million
and more persons filed past the bier and kissed the crosses
on the Holy Father's feet, which extended through the
wrought-iron gates of the chapel.

On orders of Cardinal Pacelli the papal apartments in
the Vatican and Castel Gandolfo were locked, and all personal documents and papers of the late Pope were placed
under seal. The will of Pius XI was later read to the Sacred
College of Cardinals, but its contents have not been divulged, though it is known that he left his chalice to Cardinal Pacelli. The matrix, from which lead impressions
bearing the name of Pope Pius XI had been made and the
Fisherman's Ring, the symbol of papal authority, were

placed in a red silk bag and were broken. The commissions charged with the administration of the Church and the Holy See until the election of a new pope began to function under the authority of Cardinal Pacelli. Expressions of condolence and tributes from the rulers and nations of the world began to arrive at the Vatican. Secretary of State Cordell Hull sent the following message to Cardinal Pacelli: "The President desires me to express to Your Eminence profound condolences on the death of His Holiness Pope Pius XI. His great spiritual qualities and his zeal for peace and tolerance won for him a place in the hearts of all races and creeds. Word of his passing has been received with deep sorrow throughout the United States."

The burial of Pope Pius XI took place in the afternoon of February 14, the fourth of the Novendials or the nine consecutive days on which funeral services are held for a deceased pontiff. St. Peter's was completely bare and unornamented, only twelve candles being lighted — six on the papal altar beneath the dome and six on the altar of the cathedra. The body lay on a trestle, not far from the place where the enormous triple coffin was waiting to receive it. Archbishop Roberto Vicentini recited the prayers for the dead to which the choir sang the responses. The body was then placed in the coffin, and the face and hands were covered with a white cloth and the whole body with a crimson cloth. A copy of Monsignor Bacci's eulogy enclosed in a brass tube and three red velvet bags, one containing seventeen gold coins, a second, seventeen silver, and a third, seventeen copper — one coin of each metal for each year of his pontificate, were placed at the Pope's feet. A wooden lid bearing a large black cross was fastened to the inner coffin of cypress. Cardinal Pacelli tied two ribbons of violet silk across the inner coffin and sealed the knots with wax. A bronze lid was soldered to the middle coffin, made of lead. This cover had a cross at the top, a skull and crossbones in the middle, and the Pope's coat of arms at the bottom. The middle coffin was also tied with two violet ribbons and their knots were sealed with lead. A walnut lid was fastened to the outer coffin of the same wood with gold-plated screws, which Cardinal Pacelli inserted and started.

The coffin was covered with a pall of violet wool and borne to the Confession, which is directly above the tomb of St. Peter and leads to the crypt of the Basilica. As the choir chanted the *Miserere*, the cardinals filed past the coffin and imparted their blessing. Then it was lowered to the crypt and placed in the tomb which Pius XI had prepared for himself near the tombs of Pius X and Benedict XV.

The death of Pius XI was a lonely sorrow to Cardinal Pacelli for they had become as father and son. Under God Pius XII owes most to his great predecessor who taught him in daily collaboration over a period of nine years how to be a saintly and wise pope.

CHAPTER VI

"THOU ART PETER"

O N SUNDAY morning, March 12, 1939, silver trumpets sounded from the huge dome of the Basilica of St. Peter. The massive bronze gates of the main entrance opened to admit the coronation procession of Eugenio Pacelli, whom twelve days earlier the Sacred College of Cardinals had elected the Vicar of Jesus Christ on earth and the Sovereign of Vatican City. Papal gendarmes in buff tunics, white breeches, and black busbies followed the Auditor of the Rota who, walking between seven acolytes of noble birth, held aloft a golden spear-headed cross. There were friars in brown robes, monks in white habits, and priests in black cassocks and lace surplices. The Sistine Choristers in violet dress began to chant "Thou art Peter," as the music of the papal march echoed away.

Then came a platoon of the Palatine Guards in blue tunics and trousers with red and gold trim and black shakoes with a slender red plume in front. The purple robes of the monsignori, bishops, and patriarchs contrasted with the white chasubles of the Confessors of St. Peter's. Bearded missionaries and sandaled monks walked with black-skinned priests from Africa and slant-eyed priests from the Orient. A papal chaplain escorted by two Noble Guards carried the gleaming tiara on a velvet cushion, and chamberlains in purple robes and ermine capes carried the papal jewels of priceless worth and exquisite craftsmanship. There were heralds in red and gold uniforms, mace bearers in black doublets and violet capes, and princes in medieval dress with lace ruffs, chains of gold, and glittering decorations. Their white cloaks emblazoned with crimson crosses, the Knights of Malta marched with the Knights of St. Gregory and the Knights of the Holy Sepulcher. Each carrying his scarlet train over the left arm, the cardinals wore golden robes and silvery miters, whose jeweled beading caught and reflected the myriad lights of the Basilica.

Above the magnificent procession, His Holiness Pope Pius XII was carried on the *sedia gestatoria* (a portable throne), which rested on the shoulders of twelve *sediarii* (chair bearers) in crimson knee breeches and red damask liveries. He was robed in a flowing cope of cloth of gold, which was caught at the neck by a large golden clasp set with precious stones. On his head was a silver miter adorned with blazing jewels. White gloves of embroidered silk covered his hands, and on the third finger of the right hand was the symbol of his authority, the Fisherman's Ring. Over the Pope's head floated a cream canopy ornamented in gold and resting on eight poles carried by chamberlains, in lace rochets and purple capes. Prelates on either side of the sedia waved ostrich fans (*flabella*), which in ancient days were emblems of royal authority. The three cardinals who would assist the Pope in celebrating Mass walked in front, each wearing a cope of silver lamé. Officers of the Noble Guard in white breeches, scarlet tunics with golden epaulets, and silver helmets flanked the sedia. A platoon of Swiss Guards in shining medieval armor, each shouldering a halberd, closed the procession.

The seventy thousand people crowding the basilica

greeted the Holy Father with thunderous handclaps and shouts of "Long live the Pope!" "Long live Pius the Twelfth!" Pale and grave, His Holiness showed no awareness of the applause and pomp, but ceaselessly made the sign of the cross in blessing. The mammoth basilica began to fill at sunrise and by seven-thirty the gates had to be shut. The fortunate ones represented every class of society, every race of mankind, and every Christian nation of the world. In the front row of the unreserved section was a little peasant woman — a shabby figure with hands roughened by toil and face furrowed by time, wearing a black cotton dress and shawl. To her right stood an aristocratic gentleman in formal clothes and displaying papal decorations, and to her left a fashionable woman in black moire and lace mantilla. Beneath the gallery of St. Veronica were seminarians from the Ethiopian College, and near them stood students from the Oriental College, Chinese, Hindus, and Malays. In a special tribunal erected on the Gospel side of the central nave were to be seen the members of thirty-five special missions and the entire diplomatic corps accredited to the Holy See. Joseph P. Kennedy, then our ambassador to England, represented the United States. The representative of King George VI and Great Britain was the Duke of Norfolk, a Catholic and a prominent member of the English peerage. Paul Claudel, former ambassador from France to the United States and the Catholic author of "Satin Slipper" and other beautiful poems, represented his country. Eamon de Valera, Prime Minister of Eire, attended the coronation in person. The Scandinavian kingdoms and the South American republics, the Iberian Peninsula and the Balkans, the Lowland countries and the Baltic nations, had sent envoys to represent them.

Moving slowly down the center aisle, the procession paused at the Chapel of the Most Holy Trinity. The Pope left the sedia for a moment of adoration before the most Blessed Sacrament and of petition for world peace. Resuming the royal sedia, he was reminded of the mortality of all men. A master of ceremonies with a lighted taper in the right hand and a tuft of flax soaked in oil and attached to a silver wand in the left knelt before the Sovereign Pontiff. Touching the taper to the flax, which was quickly consumed, he sang out: "Holy Father, thus passes the glory of the world." The warning was repeated when His Holiness passed the bronze statue* of the first pope, St. Peter, and again when he entered the sanctuary. The Pope was then carried to the apse where a throne awaited him and where the ceremony of homage began. Each cardinal and bishop, escorted by two prelates, approached the throne, genuflected, and kissed the cross on the slippered foot, the knee, and the ring of the Holy Father.

Vested in the pontifical robes, over which was placed the fanon, a gauzelike material, striped in blue, gold, and red, and symbolizing the high priest, His Holiness Pope Pius XII began the celebration of solemn pontifical Mass at the central altar reserved for him alone. After the *Confiteor* he returned to his throne and seated himself. Then the Dean of the Cardinal-Deacons placed the pallium on the Pope's shoulders, saying: ."Receive the pallium with the fullness of papal authority, to the honor of almighty God, of the glorious Virgin and Mother Mary, of the blessed Apostles Peter and Paul, and of the holy Roman Church." The pallium, a narrow collar of white

---

* At papal coronations this ancient statue (at least fifteen hundred years old) is always attired in a pontifical cope and crowned with a tiara.

wool on which are worked five black crosses, symbolizes the government of the pope over the bishops. The wool for the pallium, which is obtained from two lambs blessed and sheared at the Church of St. Agnes in Rome, is kept until needed in a golden casket near the tomb of St. Peter. Archbishops also wear the pallium as a sign that they share in the pope's authority.*

After the *Gloria* of the Mass, a cardinal-bishop descended to the tomb of St. Peter, which is in front of and below the main altar, and intoned the *Laudes*. This beautiful litany, chanted only at coronations, dates back to the sixth century. The *Laudes* are intoned at the time of the Epistle by the Dean of the Cardinal Deacons, who is answered by the Apostolic Subdeacons of the Rota, the Consistorial Advocates, and the other officials of the Pontifical Court.

They begin with the invocation: "Hear us, O Christ!"

Then the others answer: "To our lord Pius, by God appointed Sovereign Pontiff and universal Pope, life!"

The Cardinal Protodeacon then sings three times: "Saviour of the world!" And the others answer: "Do Thou help him."

The Cardinal sings twice: "Holy Mary!" And the others reply: "Do thou help him."

Then the following invocations are repeated, each once, and after each of them is answered: "Do thou help him!" The invocations are:

St. Michael	St. Paul	St. Benedict
St. Gabriel	St. Andrew	St. Basil

* Tradition says that the pallium has its origin in the mantle of Elias, which fell upon the shoulders of Eliseus as his master was taken to heaven in a fiery chariot. It was a sign that Eliseus was to take the place of Elias as prophet and lawgiver of the Jewish people.

St. Raphael	St. Stephen	St. Agnes
St. John Baptist	St. Leo	St. Cecilia
St. Peter	St. Gregory	St. Lucy

At the conclusion of the *Laudes,* the solemn Papal Mass continued with its usual ceremonies. From his throne the Pope presided over the double chanting of the Epistle and Gospel, once in Greek and once in Latin. The use of the two languages recalls the early centuries when Greek was the official, and Latin the ordinary, language of the Church and when many of the popes and saints were of Greek origin.

As the Holy Father bowed to consecrate the Host a word of command sounded through the sanctuary. The Swiss Guards, who formed a circle before the altar, dropped to their right knees, at the same time bringing their left hands to their helmets in salute. The Noble Guards near the papal throne and the Palatine Guards lining the center aisle did the same. As the Pope lifted the Host on high, the cardinals, the other prelates, and the faithful knelt in adoration. At that moment the famous Vatican silver trumpets, whose players were hidden in the highest recesses of the Basilica's dome, filled the air with music. Communion over and the blessing given, Cardinal Gerlier presented the Holy Father with twenty-five gold coins in a white silk purse, saying: "Your Holiness, the Chapter and the Canons of this holy Basilica offer you the customary gift for a Mass well sung."

Again the majestic procession was formed, and the Pope was borne in the *sedia gestatoria* along the main aisle to the Stairway of Constantine and up to the outer balcony of St. Peter's. The square below and the neighboring streets were packed with over five hundred thousand people who had waited there from dawn, and it was now well past one. Thunderous cheers rolled up, as the Holy Father, robed in a cope of cream-colored silk, occupied the throne of red velvet. After the silvery miter had been removed from the Pope's head, Cardinal Caccia Dominioni lifted the gem-studded tiara from a red-velvet cushion. Standing to the left of His Holiness, the Cardinal said: "Receive the triple-crowned tiara, and know that you are the Father of Princes and Kings, the Pastor of the Universe, and the Vicar on earth of our Lord Jesus Christ, to whom belongs honor and glory, now and forever, world without end." As Cardinal Caccia Dominioni placed the tiara on the head of His Holiness Pope Pius XII, the hidden Sistine choir and the vast crowd answered "Amen." Then, assisted by one of the cardinals, the Holy Father arose from the throne and gave his blessing "to the city and to the world."

The coronation ceremonies, beginning at eight-thirty, had continued for five hours, and for the first time in history had been broadcast by radio to the world. The tiara used was given by Queen Isabella of Spain to Pius IX, the last pope prior to Pius XII to be crowned in public. Subsequent unfriendly relations between the Holy See and Italy had made it necessary that the other popes be crowned either in the Basilica or in the Sistine Chapel. The tiara of Pius IX is studded with one hundred and forty-six jewels — eleven diamonds and thirty rubies. It is surmounted by a diamond cross on a gold globe enameled in blue. There are many explanations of the triple crown — some say that it signifies the Church Militant, the Church Suffering, and the Church Triumphant; others claim that it refers to the threefold role of the pope as lawgiver, judge, and teacher. It should be noted that the coronation of a pope, unlike that of kings and emperors, is not a necessary ceremony, since the election itself confers upon him the fullness of papal authority and power.

As the quarters of the Secretary of State were now unoccupied, Pius XII remained there while the papal apartments were completely renovated under the direction of Count Enrico Galeazzi. These apartments comprise eighteen rooms on the top floor of the east wing of the Vatican Palace, bedroom, study, dining room, library, throne room, chapel, and rooms for guests and servants. The principal rooms have floors of polychrome marble and the inner rooms floors of fumed oak. The drawing-room floor has in its center the coat of arms of the present Holy Father, a dove holding an olive branch in his beak with the motto *Opus Justitiae Pax* (The Work of Justice is Peace). This is repeated in the frieze which runs around the ceiling. The bedroom is small and austere, its only furnishings a plain brass bed, a simple desk, and an ordinary dresser. When Pius X entered the papal bedroom for the first night, an attendant solicitously said: "It's a comfortable bed." "No doubt," replied the Pope somewhat sadly, "but I shall have to die in it."

The Holy Father rises every morning at six o'clock, and after shaving with an electric razor of American make, puts on a white cassock with an elbow length cape and a wide sash, a gold chain and pectoral cross, a white skull-cap, red slippers embroidered with gold crosses, and a ring on the right hand. He offers Mass at seven o'clock in the papal chapel. During the Pope's thanksgiving another Mass is celebrated there by his secretary. Before going to the library, Pius eats a frugal breakfast of rolls and coffee heavily diluted with hot milk. The library, a beautiful corner room overlooking St. Peter's Square, is furnished with a large walnut desk — on which rest a white statue of Christ and a crucifix — three tall bookcases, and occasional chairs of ornate design. Of the three wide windows two are curtained, and the center one, immediately behind the Pope's chair, has stained glass panes depicting the Madonna and Child. In this room take place all private audiences, in which the dignitaries and leaders of the Church and the world pay homage to the Sovereign Pontiff.

The business day begins with the examination of written reports from nuncios and apostolic delegates abroad, and with private correspondence. The Holy Father is an efficient typist, but he generally dictates to his several secretaries or uses an ediphone. At nine o'clock the Substitute Secretary of State,* Monsignor Montini, enters, his briefcase bulging with confidential dispatches, memoranda on the previous day's conferences with foreign diplomats, and bulletins received during the night. He discusses with the Holy Father whatever problems are confronting the Church on the diplomatic front, and the policy to be pursued. The Substitute Secretary of State is followed by the cardinal-prefects of the various congregations and the lay and clerical chiefs of Vatican offices and departments, who must make at least weekly reports on their work and problems. Then come audiences with foreign bishops who are making their *ad limina* visits to Rome. Canon Law requires a bishop personally to visit the tomb of St. Peter once every five years (bishops who reside outside of Europe may make their visits once every ten years) and to report to the Holy Father on the state of his diocese. Through these meetings the Pope keeps

* Since the death of Cardinal Luigi Maglione in 1944, the post of Secretary of State has been vacant.

intimately informed on the progress and problems of the Church in all parts of the world. Afterward foreign diplomats and rulers and prominent laymen, Catholic and non-Catholic, are received in audience during which international matters are discussed and views exchanged.

At one-thirty Giovanni Stefanori, the Pope's personal servant for many years, serves him lunch in the dining room of the papal apartments. The simple meal — a light meat and a vegetable dish — is prepared by the German nuns who have cooked the Holy Father's meals since he was Nuncio to Germany. He has no preference in foods, does not smoke, but delights in an occasional glass of wine of ancient vintage. In accordance with papal etiquette the Pope eats alone, his only companions being two canaries which are released from their cages as soon as he enters. They fly around during the meal, perching on the Holy Father's shoulders or pecking at the food which he serves them on two saucers. On very rare occasions the Pope has official guests for lunch, but they eat at a separate and lower table, and, of course, are served last.

An hour of rest follows lunch, and then the Pope returns to the library where he works until four o'clock. At that hour he is driven in an automobile to the Vatican Gardens. Here he walks for an hour with a quick, elastic step, followed at a distance by his chamberlain and a Swiss guard. The Pope, disliking the hot sun, has ordered that the trees along his promenade be trimmed long so he can walk in the deep shade. The Vatican Gardens boast the beauty of eternal spring, because Pius XI had an irrigation system installed which keeps the flower beds always blooming and the lawns always emerald green.

As the bells of Rome's many churches ring six o'clock, the Holy Father gathers his servants and secretaries around him for the Angelus and the Rosary. Dinner is as simple as lunch, and much of the time allotted for the meal is spent reading newspapers from many lands. Then the Pope allows himself an hour or more of relaxation, conversing with friends or enjoying the music of Wagner, Verdi, and other composers. He has all the works of Wagner that have been recorded. Afterward he returns to the library, where he prepares speeches, outlines future encyclicals, and keeps up on his reading of current and religious publications. Before retiring at midnight, often one o'clock, the Pope is said to work on a theological treatise which he began many years ago. During his apprenticeship in the Secretariate of State Pius XII published several works on Canon Law, copies of which are to be found in the Library of Congress, Washington, D. C.

Each Wednesday morning at ten o'clock public audiences are held in the Hall of the Consistory. This is an immense room magnificent with murals and paintings and leading to eight smaller halls. Admittance is by ticket only, which one can readily obtain from the Majordomo's office. Preceded by Swiss Guards, the Holy Father arrives promptly at ten and addresses the visitors in their own tongue, if he knows it, or through an interpreter. At the end of the audience the Pope walks through the crowd, blessing the people and giving each his ring to kiss. For very large gatherings the public audiences are held in the Courtyard of St. Damasus, which can accommodate ten thousand people. During the tourist season the public audiences are repeated several times a week.

The gentle kindness of Pius XII has shown itself on many occasions during public audiences. One day as he approached a group of nuns and children, a young girl among them burst into tears. Bending down, the Pope questioned her and then ordered the others to move away. He led her by the hand to the center of the hall and, after hearing her confession, gave her absolution and his blessing. On another occasion a group of children from the Trastevere slums of Rome pounded on the outer gates of the Vatican Palace, demanding to see the Pope. His Holiness, informed of their presence by the startled guard, ordered that they be brought at once to his drawing room.

"Who brought you to my home?" he asked.

"I did," replied a tattered girl of ten. "The parish priest said we should visit the Pope. Here we are. We are all good boys and girls."

Much pleased, Pius spoke to the children of God and the Blessed Mother, and then dismissed them, each clutching a rosary and a medal of their Holy Father. Another young visitor to the Pope was not so good. When the Holy Father asked him where his parents were, he contritely admitted that he had run away from home. His Holiness lectured him on the sin of disobedience, and sent him home with a blessing for his family.

Why do people come from the far corners of the world to visit Pius XII? It cannot be to seek favors, because he has neither silver nor gold nor political favors to give them. Although a man of profound sanctity, he works no miracles and utters no prophecies. It cannot be out of fear, because he rules the hearts, not the bodies, of men, and these through love not coercive force. Although a man of international fame, he has no personal press agent nor propaganda machine. Then why? Take up the New Testament, which God Himself wrote through the Apostles and the Evangelists, and read in the Gospel:

"And when Jesus had come into the district of Caesarea Philippi, he questioned his disciples, saying, 'Whom do

men say that the Son of Man is?' And they said, 'Some,
John the Baptist; and others, Elias; and others, Jeremiah,
or one of the prophets.' He saith to them, 'But whom say
ye that I am?' And Simon Peter answered and said, 'Thou
art the Christ, the Son of the living God.' Jesus answered
and said to him: 'Blessed art thou, Simon Bar-Jonah, because flesh and blood hath not revealed this to thee, but
my Father in the heavens. And I do say to thee, thou art
Peter, and upon this rock I will build my church, and the
gates of hell shall not prevail against it. I will give thee
the keys of the kingdom of the heavens; and whatsoever
thou shalt bind upon earth shall be bound in the heavens,
and whatsoever thou shalt loose upon earth shall be loosed
in the heavens" (Matt. 16:13–19).

"When therefore they had breakfasted, Jesus saith to
Simon Peter, 'Simon, son of John, lovest thou me more
than do these?' He saith to him, 'Yea, Lord, thou knowest
that I love thee.' He saith to him, 'Feed my lambs.' He
saith to him again a second time, 'Simon, son of John,
lovest thou me?' He saith to him, 'Yea, Lord, thou knowest
that I love thee.' He saith to him, 'Shepherd my sheep.'
He saith to him a third time, 'Simon, son of John, lovest
thou me?' Peter was grieved because he said to him the
third time, 'Lovest thou me?' And he said to him, 'Lord,
thou knowest all things; thou knowest that I love thee.'
Jesus saith to him, 'Feed my sheep' " (John 21:15–19).

With these promises and commands Christ, who is God,
appointed St. Peter to take His place as the master of
the Apostles, as the earthly head of the Church, and as
the spiritual shepherd of the entire world and of all men.
Because he was His Vicar on earth, Peter alone would possess all the authority and power which was Christ's when
He walked among men. Peter would confer upon men the

right and the power to spread the kingdom of God and to preach the Gospel of Christ. Peter would decide what was the word of God. Peter would judge the actions and the lives of individuals, of rulers, and of nations, and would open or close to them the gates of heaven. All men would be subject to Peter, but he would be subject to no one except Christ.

Peter became the first Bishop of Rome, where he was martyred on the Vatican hill in A.D. 67. His successor as Bishop of Rome, Linus, necessarily inherited from Peter all the authority and the power conferred on him by Christ. Because the Church is to last until the end of time, our Lord made His promises and gave His commands not to Peter alone but to his successors. Hence, whoever succeeds Peter as Bishop of Rome, becomes like him the Vicar of Jesus Christ on earth.

Pius XII is the two hundred and sixty-second successor of St. Peter. Hence, he is the master of the successors of the other Apostles, the bishops, is the sole and supreme head of the Catholic Church, which is the only true Church of Christ, and is the spiritual ruler of the clergy, the faithful, and all men regardless of belief, race, or nationality. In the governor-general the people of Canada see and honor their sovereign, King George VI. Similarly when people come from the far reaches of the earth to visit Pius XII, they behold and do homage to their God and Saviour, Jesus Christ.

As it was Christ's, so it is the duty of Pius XII to save mankind, not by another sacrifice of Calvary, but through the Church which is the continuation of the cross. There being about 350,000,000 Catholics and 1,750,000,000 non-Catholics and pagans who though outside the fold are yet part of his charge, the Pope employs an extensive and complex organization to assist him in fulfilling his duty. This organization, or central authority of the Church, is commonly called the Vatican, in the same sense as one speaks of our Federal Government as "Washington."

The Vatican consists of the Roman Congregations, the Roman Tribunals, the Offices of the Curia (Court), and the Pontifical Court. The twelve Roman Congregations may be likened to the executive departments of our Federal Government, the cardinal-prefects corresponding to the cabinet members. They are the usual organs for the administration and governing of the Church, each congregation being charged with certain specific duties. The Congregation of the Holy Office deals with all matters concerning faith or morals, judges heresy and schism, and applies and enforces the penalties incurred. The Pope himself is the prefect of this Congregation. The creation of new dioceses and the nomination of bishops is the duty of the Congregation of the Consistory, which maintains a round-the-clock contact with the bishops in every country where the Church is no longer in the missionary state. It keeps detailed records of the lands, the churches, the schools, the colleges, and the hospitals under Catholic ownership. This Congregation also has the Holy Father as its prefect. The missionary activities of the Church are entrusted to the Congregation of the Propagation of the Faith, whose cardinal-prefect is popularly called "the Red Pope" because of his great powers and widespread jurisdiction.

The other Congregations are: Congregation on the Discipline of the Sacraments, Congregation of the Council, Congregation of Religious, Congregation of Sacred Rites, Congregation of the Eastern Church, Ceremonial Congregation, Congregation of Extraordinary Ecclesiastical Affairs, Congregation of Seminaries, Universities, and Studies, and Congregation of the Fabric of St. Peter's.

The judicial power of the Church is exercised by three tribunals: the Sacred Poenitentiaria, the Sacred Roman Rota, and the Apostolic Signatura. Questions of conscience submitted by bishops throughout the world are decided by the Sacred Poenitentiaria. Certain sins, for example, the murder of a priest or the defilement of the Blessed Sacrament, cannot be forgiven by a priest or bishop, save in time of death, and absolution must be sought from the pope through this tribunal. Most of the cases with which the Sacred Roman Rota deals are matrimonial cases, for although the Church cannot dissolve a validly contracted and consummated marriage, it declares null and void marriages which are invalid in origin. A divorce admits that a valid marriage did exist, whereas an annulment denies that any marriage ever existed because of some defect, called a nullifying impediment, which made it impossible for a contract of marriage to be executed. In each diocese there is a matrimonial court where cases of validity are argued and decided. If the decision is unsatisfactory, an appeal may be taken to a court of higher instance, in most cases the matrimonial court of the archdiocese of the province. From the latter a further appeal may be taken to the Rota, which is also empowered to hear cases at the beginning.

Protestants and too many Catholics often claim: "If you can afford it, the Church will give you a divorce." This charge can be answered by the record. In 1944 the Rota heard and decided sixty-seven cases dealing with marriages alleged to be null and void. In thirty-four cases the Court declared the nullity of the marriage, and in thirty-three cases it maintained the validity of the marriage. Twenty-nine cases were handled free, not even the filing fee being paid, and in eleven of these annulments (not divorces) were granted.

From the Rota an appeal may be taken to the Apostolic Signatura, which is composed of cardinals, and is similar to our Supreme Court. They do not decide on the merits of the case, but may consider only whether there has been an error of procedure sufficiently important to remand the case to the Rota where it will be tried again by a new set of judges.

The Secretariate of State, which we have already discussed, is the most important of the five Offices of the Curia. The Apostolic Chancery, another office, sends out bulls, which are papal letters used for such solemn matters as canonizing a saint or establishing a new diocese. The letter is called a bull because of the lead seal, *bulla* in Latin, which is sometimes attached to it. The Apostolic Datary distributes benefices, that is, positions with a regular income supplied by an endowment. Many of the European churches possess funds provided by generous Catholics with the understanding that the priest who receives the income will pray for the souls of the benefactor and his family. The Apostolic Camera administers the property of the Holy See when the papal throne is vacant, and is presided over by the Camerlengo. The Secretariate of Briefs prepares the letters which the Holy Father sends to the rulers of nations.

The Pontifical Court is divided into two main categories: the papal court and the papal household. The cardinals and the prelates who take part in the religious ceremonies which the pope attends make up the first. The second consists of those cardinals, such as the Secretary of State, and those prelates, such as the papal sacristan, who perform duties closely connected with the pope's daily life. The Pontifical Court also includes the representatives of those religious orders to which certain ecclesiastical posts have been entrusted for centuries. The Advent and Lenten sermons are always preached before the pope and his court by a Capuchin. A Dominican is the Master of the Sacred Palaces, or the Theologian of the Pontifical Court. The official confessor of the Holy Father is always a Servite. The members of the Pontifical Court may be likened to the various persons attached to the White House staff.

With the assistance of the Vatican Pius XII has done much during the troubled years of war to promote the kingdom of Christ on earth. The pages that follow present only the more interesting high lights; the ceaseless labors and the excellent achievements of our Holy Father are too many to be recounted here. In April, 1942, His Holiness ordered that the *Missale Romanum* (the large book used by the priest at Mass) be brought up to date, something that had not been done for many years. In addition to certain revisions and rearrangements a special Mass honoring the thirty-one canonized popes was inserted. By a *Motu Proprio*, an unofficial decree whose name means in English "by Our own accord," Pius erected in the Sacred Congregation of Seminaries and Universities a Pontifical Society for priestly vocations. It is the duty of this Society to intensify among the faithful the desire of promoting and assisting ecclesiastical vocations and to disseminate among all peoples right information on the dignity and necessity of the Catholic priesthood. In a papal brief, which is a letter less formal than a bull, the Pope recommended that diocesan synods be held more frequently as a means of consolidating parish and diocesan activities and of making Christian life more flourishing and fruitful. A synod is the meeting of the priests of a diocese under the authority of their bishop, to legislate for the diocese in religious and practical matters. The conferences are usually held in the cathedral and in accordance with a procedure which is a thousand and more years old.

The war interrupted the work of many and increased the hardships of all the seventy-nine thousand missionaries under the guidance of Pius XII. Since the Maryknollers were American citizens, he approved their removal from Japan and Japanese controlled areas, and assigned them to the Pando district in northern Bolivia. As Vicar Apostolic of the Pando he named Monsignor Alonso Escalarte, M.M., the first North American to be appointed bishop in South America. On October 29, 1940, the Pope consecrated twelve missionary priests bishops in the Basilica of St. Peter, two Americans, two native Africans, an Indian, a Chinese, and citizens of a half-dozen European countries. As required by ancient custom, each bishop offered the Pope a gilded and a silvered loaf of bread, two candles, a cask of wine, and a cask of water. After Mass the twelve new apostles descended to the tomb of St. Peter, and after praying returned to his successor for the apostolic blessing. The establishment of a native episcopacy in Africa and Asia is an anxious desire of Pius XII, because, reading the history of ancient civilizations swept away by war and sin, he knows the future. Some day, many generations hence perhaps, the centers of civilization and Christianity will move from the rubble of Europe and the Americas to what are now missionary lands. Some day from the Church which Pius XII is strengthening in Africa and Asia may come a successor to St. Peter, who whatever his color or race will be the Vicar of Christ on earth.

Each year His Holiness designates a Sunday of October as Mission Sunday, and exhorts Catholics to give of their prayers and money to the missions. In recent decades only American Catholics have been able to give much support to the missions, because the European Catholics, whose forefathers financed the missionaries to the United States, have been impoverished. From a purely selfish, or from a humanitarian point of view — disregarding the religious viewpoint entirely — experiences of our servicemen and women, in the Pacific areas particularly, have shown the value of our missionary endeavors. Countless stories have come out of this war of the courage, and charity, and helpfulness of the missionary priests and sisters.

On November 13, 1939, the Catholic University of America, Washington, D. C., celebrated the golden anniversary of its founding. Addressing the faculty and students by radio from Vatican City, the Holy Father congratulated the University on its growth and warned: "The Christian education of youth was never of more decisive or vital importance than it is today. Our chief hope after God rests in the schools of Christian culture." Because youth is educated more beyond than within the walls of school, the Pope in receiving a group of Hollywood producers, July 14, 1945, said: "O, the immense amount of good that the motion picture can effect. That is why the evil spirit, always so active in this world, wishes to pervert this instrument for some impious purpose. It is for public opinion to support wholeheartedly and effectively every legitimate effort to purify the films and keep them clean, to improve them and increase their usefulness."

During the first year of Pius' pontificate the Knights of Columbus built an oratory near St. Peter's complete with theater, chapel, gymnasium, and schoolrooms. The Holy Father gave the chapel several religious paintings and a beautiful tabernacle. The Knights have built and support five playgrounds in Rome, as a means of counteracting the proselytizing efforts of the Protestants. Another gift to His Holiness was a statue of our Lady of Guadeloupe which the Catholics of Mexico had placed in the Vatican Gardens. The popes receive many and varied gifts from the great and the little of the world. A tactless prelate once announced that Pope Leo XIII needed a pair of slippers for his aching feet. In a very short time the Vatican Palace was "swamped" with slippers and remedies for sore feet, and as the Pope remarked: "I can wear only one pair at a time." When Haile Selassie, the Emperor of Ethiopia, visited Pius XI, he presented the Pope a purse of gold and a full-grown lion. The author does not know what the Holy Father did with the lion.

Obeying the divine command "Feed my lambs. Feed my sheep," Pius XII has written two letters of spiritual guidance for Christ's flock. These are his encyclicals "On the Promotion of Biblical Studies" (*Divino Afflante Spiritu*) and "On the Mystical Body of Christ" (*Mystici Corporis*). Because he who hears the Pope hears Christ, every Christian and non-Christian should read and study these inspiring encyclicals.

The *Divino Afflante Spiritu* was issued on September 30, 1943, the Feast of St. Jerome, the greatest doctor of the Church in the exposition of the Sacred Scriptures. The Introduction and Part One recall the work of Pope

Leo XIII and his successors in safeguarding the Bible and encouraging its study. Certain teachings of the Church are reaffirmed:

> The books of the Bible are sacred and canonical not because, having been composed by human industry, they were afterwards approved by the authority of the Church, nor merely because they contain revelation without error, but because having been written under the inspiration of the Holy Spirit, they have God for their author, and as such were handed down to the Church herself. It is absolutely wrong and forbidden either to narrow inspiration to certain passages of Holy Scripture, or to admit that the sacred writer has erred, since divine inspiration not only is essentially incompatible with error but excludes and rejects it absolutely and necessarily, as it is impossible that God Himself, the supreme Truth, can utter that which is not true. This heaven-sent treasure [the Bible] holy Church considers the most precious source of doctrine on faith and morals.

Part Two discusses biblical studies at the present day and instructs the clergy and the faithful on the use and value of the divine word. Though the Catholic Bible "is free from any error whatsoever in matters of faith and morals," the Pope urges that it "be purified from the corruptions due to the carelessness of the copyists, and be freed, as far as possible, from glosses and omissions, from the interchange and repetition of words and from all other kinds of mistakes, which are wont to make their way gradually into writings handed down through many centuries." This is to be accomplished by the comparison of ancient texts and the study of scientific findings through excavations in Palestine and other biblical lands. Answering those persons who charge the Bible with error because certain of its expressions, e.g., Josue stopped the sun, today seem incorrect, the encyclical points out:

> What is the literal sense of a passage is not always as obvious in the speeches and writings of the ancient authors of the East,

as it is in the works of the writers of our own time. For the ancient peoples of the East, in order to express their ideas, did not always employ those forms or kinds of speech which we use today, but rather those used by the men of their time and countries.

Refuting again that puerile lie: "Catholics may not read the Bible," the Holy Father orders:

Let the bishops favor and lend help to those pious associations whose aim it is to spread copies of the Sacred Letters, especially of the Gospels, among the faithful, and to procure by every means that in Christian families the same be read daily with piety and devotion. Let they themselves give public conferences or dissertations on biblical subjects, or see that they are given by other public orators well-versed in the matter. . . . Men will more fully know, more ardently love and more faithfully imitate Christ, the author of salvation, in proportion as they are more assiduously urged to know and meditate the Sacred Letters, especially the New Testament, for, as St. Jerome says, "To ignore the Scripture is to ignore Christ."

Though always a jewel in the treasury of dogma, the doctrine of the Mystical Body of Christ faded from the awareness of the faithful with the decline of early Christian fervor. The revived interest in sacred liturgy, the more widely spread custom of frequent Communion, and the more fervent devotion to the Sacred Heart, which are characteristic of today, have uncovered for many the inexhaustible riches of this doctrine. But it is not a doctrine easy to understand, and inaccurate and thoroughly false ideas have been disseminated. To correct these errors and to set forth the true teaching of the Church, Pius XII on June 29, 1943, issued the encyclical *Mystici Corporis*. Space permits only a brief digest here, but every reader ought to read and to study this encyclical.

Part One of the encyclical defines and explains the doctrine of the Mystical Body of Christ.

As He hung upon the cross, Christ Jesus won for us, His brethren, an ineffable flow of graces. It was possible for Him of Himself to impart these graces to mankind directly; but He willed to do so only through a visible Church made up of men, so that through her all might co-operate with Him in dispensing the graces of Redemption. If we would define and describe this true Church of Jesus Christ — which is the one, holy, catholic, apostolic Roman Church — we should find nothing more noble, more sublime, or more divine than the expression "the Mystical Body of Christ."

One must not think that this Body contains only hierarchical elements [bishops and priests], or only those who enjoy miraculous powers. That those who exercise sacred power in this Body are its first and chief members must be maintained uncompromisingly. *But** when the Fathers of the Church sing the praises of this Mystical Body of Christ, they are thinking not only of those who have received Holy Orders, but also of all those who follow the evangelical counsels, passing their lives actively among men or hidden in the silence of the cloister, of those who, though living in the world, consecrate themselves wholeheartedly to spiritual and corporal works of mercy, and of those who live in the state of Holy Matrimony.

However, only those are to be included as members of the Church who have been baptized and profess the true faith, and who have not separated themselves from the unity of the Body or have been excluded by legitimate authority for grave fault committed. *But one must not* imagine that the Body of the Church, just because it bears the name of Christ, is made up during the days of its earthly pilgrimage only of members conspicuous for their holiness. Not every sin, however grave it may be, is such as of its own nature to sever a man from the Body of Christ — *only* schism or apostasy does that. Let everyone abhor sin, which defiles the mystical members of our Redeemer; but if anyone unhappily falls and his obstinacy has not made him unworthy of communion with the faithful, let him be received with great joy and let eager charity see in him a weak member of Jesus Christ.

Our Lord is the Founder, the Head, the Support and the Saviour of this Mystical Body. *He* began the building of the mystical temple of the Church when by His preaching He made known His precepts; He completed it when He hung

* Words in italics have been inserted by the author for the sake of clarity.

glorified on the cross; and He manifested and proclaimed it when He sent the Holy Spirit in visible form on His disciples. The Son of God and of the Blessed Virgin is to be called the Head of the Body, *the Church,* by reason of His singular pre-eminence. Who is in a higher place than Christ God, who, as the word of the eternal Father, must be acknowledged to be the first born of every creature? Because Christ is so exalted, He alone by every right rules and governs the Church. It is He who reigns within the minds and hearts of men, and bends and subjects their wills to His good pleasure, even when rebellious. But we must not think that He rules only in a hidden and extraordinary manner. On the contrary, our divine Redeemer also governs His Mystical Body in a visible and normal way through His Vicar on earth, *the Pope.* What we have said of the Universal Church must be understood also of the individual Christian communities, *dioceses,* which go to make up the one Catholic Church. For they, too, are ruled by Jesus Christ through the voice of their respective bishops.

As our Saviour does not rule the Church directly in a visible manner, He wills to be helpèd by the members of His Body in carrying out the work of redemption. This is not because He is indigent and weak, but rather because He has so willed it for the greater glory of His spotless Spouse, *the Church.* This is a deep mystery that the salvation of many depends on the prayers and voluntary penances which the members of the Mystical Body of Jesus Christ offer and on the co-operation of pastors of souls and of the faithful, especially of fathers and mothers of families. As the human body is given the proper means to provide for its own life, health, and growth, and for that of all its members, similarly, the Saviour of mankind out of His infinite goodness has provided in a wonderful way for His Mystical Body, endowing it with the Sacraments, so that *through an unbroken* series of graces its members should be sustained from birth to death.

Christ by His own divine power permeates His whole Body and nourishes and sustains each of the members according to the place which they occupy in the Body, in the same way as the vine nourishes and makes fruitful the branches which are joined to it. This presence and activity of Jesus Christ is described by Leo XIII in these words: "Let it suffice to say that, as Christ is the Head of the Church, so is the Holy Spirit her soul."

In the second and third parts of his encyclical the Pope instructs us how to be worthy members of the Church, the Mystical Body of Christ.

As her children it is our duty not only to *love the Church* for her maternal goodness, but also to respect the authority which she has received from Christ. Thus we are commanded to obey her laws and moral precepts, even if at times they are difficult to our fallen nature. True love of the Church requires not only that we should be mutually solicitous for one another as members of the same Body, rejoicing in the glory of the other members and sharing in their suffering; but likewise that we should recognize in other men, although they are not yet joined to us in the Body of the Church, our brothers in Christ according to the flesh, called, together with us, to the same eternal salvation. All who claim the Church as their mother should seriously consider that not only the clergy and those who have consecrated themselves to God in the religious life, but the other members of the Mystical Body of Jesus Christ as well have each in his degree the obligation of working hard and constantly for the building up and increase of this Body. We wish this to be borne in mind especially by members of Catholic Action who assist the bishops and the priests in their apostolic labors, and also by those members of pious associations which work for the same end.

The Holy Father concludes with a prayer to the Blessed Virgin Mary:

May the most holy mother of all the members of Christ, to whose Immaculate Heart we have trustfully dedicated all mankind, and who now reigns in heaven with her Son, never cease to beg from Him that copious streams of grace may flow from its exalted head into all the members of the Mystical Body. May she throw about the Church today, as in times gone by, the mantle of her protection and obtain from God that now at last the Church and all mankind may enjoy more peaceful days.

On May 2, 1940, His Holiness canonized Gemma Galgani and Mary St. Euphrasia Pelletier, who was the foundress of the Good Shepherd Sisters. Eleven days later Rose Philippine Duchesne, foundress of the Sisters of the

Sacred Heart in the United States, was beatified. During the first half of the nineteenth century Blessed Rose worked among the pioneers of the Midwest and later among the Indians of the Far West. On February 6, 1942, the Pope issued a decree formally acknowledging the heroic virtues of Kateri Tekakwitha, the Mohawk maiden, and granting her the title of Venerable.

The steps which lead to the honors of the altar, as beatification and canonization, are sometimes called, are lengthy but interesting. They begin with an informal inquiry into the reputation for holiness of the person proposed and into the soundness of his or her writings, if any. The inquiries are conducted under the authority of the bishop of the diocese or dioceses where the person resided, and the findings are sent in documentary form to the Sacred Congregation of Rites. If the cardinals of the Congregation agree that the documents indicate that the person practiced the cardinal and theological virtues to an heroic degree, the Holy Father appoints a commission to make a formal inquiry and grants the person the title of Venerable.

The commission interviews at great length and with meticulous care people who personally knew or heard of the person. Their testimony of life is minutely winnowed to separate truth from edifying legend. Proof of the three miracles which the Church requires to have been performed by God through the intercession of the person is then investigated, witnesses being called and doctors being questioned as to the validity of the cures. The findings of the commission are sent in documentary form to the Sacred Congregation of Rites, which has copies printed and distributed among its members. If it is determined after extended debate that the person is worthy of beatification, the Holy Father issues a brief permitting public veneration of the Blessed in specified places only. As soon as it has been proved that two miracles have been worked at the intercession of the Blessed subsequent to his or her beatification, the Pope issues a bull of canonization commanding the public veneration of the Saint by the universal Church. When Rose of Lima was beatified, only the Church of Peru was allowed to offer prayers in her honor; but after she was canonized the Church of every country was required to venerate her by a special Mass and Office (the prayers which a priest must say daily). This account of the steps to the altar is very sketchy, and so the reader ought to consult the article "Beatification and Canonization" in Volume II of the *Catholic Encyclopedia*.

The solemnity of beatification and canonization usually takes place in the Basilica of St. Peter, which is decorated for the occasion with portraits of the person or persons to be beatified or canonized. His Holiness is requested three times to register the name of the person in the catalog of the saints or of the blessed, the first request being followed by the recitation of the litany of the saints and the second by the chanting of the *Veni Creator*. After the third request the Vicar of Christ decrees that the name of the person be so inscribed and that his or her memory be duly honored. In the evening the façade and dome of the Basilica are outlined in dancing lights, today by reflected lighting and formerly by tallow candles in vellum lamps.

On Ascension Thursday, May 18, 1939, Pius XII took possession of his cathedral, the Basilica of St. John Lateran. The mother and queen of all churches, the Cathedral of Rome was first built in 324, and in 1370 was rebuilt for the third time, having been destroyed once by earthquake and twice by fire. Solicitous of their spiritual welfare the Bishop of Rome dedicated the Romans to the Immaculate Heart of Mary by a prayer of his own composition. Often during the war years he gathered them into the Cathedral for a holy hour of adoration and petition, during which he instructed them in the truths of their religion and in the ways of spiritual perfection. They joyfully celebrated with their Bishop the Silver Jubilee of his episcopal consecration, May 13, 1942, which was honored in this country by religious services and a national broadcast from the Catholic University.

For the Church of America the Holy Father has established to date three archdioceses (Denver, Indianapolis, and Omaha) and seven dioceses (Evansville, Ind., Gallup, N. M., Lafayette, Ind., Madison, Wis., Pueblo, Colo., Steubenville, Ohio, and Youngstown, Ohio). He has appointed eight archbishops, thirty residential bishops (heads of dioceses), eleven coadjutor-bishops (assistant to a residential bishop with right to succeed him), and twelve auxiliary bishops (assistant to a residential bishop but without right to succeed him). By what procedure does a priest become a bishop? In the United States, every two years the archbishop and suffragan bishops of the province submit to the Congregation of the Consistory a list of priests, who, because of ability and achievement, are worthy and capable of being bishops. When a diocese becomes vacant, or a residential bishop needs an assistant, the Congregation, after considering the recommendations of the Apostolic Delegate and of bishops acquainted with the needs of the diocese and the qualifications of Father X on its list, nominates him to the Holy Father. He consults with the Sacred College of Cardinals and through the Secretariate of State sends the name to the apostolic

delegate. Father X receives a letter from the latter notify-
ing him that the pope wishes to appoint him bishop of
the Diocese of Y and asking him whether he accepts the
appointment. Father X may seek the advice of his own
bishop, who has also received a letter of notification from
the apostolic delegate, and one other person. He then
communicates to the apostolic delegate his decision, and,
if he has accepted, awaits an official announcement by the
Apostolic Delegation. Only then may he begin to order
his episcopal robes.* Bishop-Elect X later receives the
official document of appointment, which also authorizes
him to be consecrated by a bishop other than the pope,
who alone has the absolute right to confer apostolic
succession.

On the Feast of All Saints, 1939, the Church of the
United States celebrated the one hundred and fiftieth
anniversary of the establishment of the American hierarchy. On November 6, 1789, Pope Pius VI gave us our
first bishop in the person of John Carroll, and set him
over the Diocese of Baltimore. In honor of the anniversary
Pius XII wrote to the American cardinals, archbishops,
and bishops the encyclical letter *Sertum Laetitiae*. Below
are quoted certain passages which should warn and guide
us today when we are beginning to build a new and
better United States.

We confess that we feel a special paternal affection, which is
certainly inspired of heaven, for the Negro people dwelling
among you; for, in the field of religion and education we know
that they need special care and comfort and are very deserving
of it. . . . We raise our voice in strong, albeit paternal, com-
plaint that in so many schools of your land Christ is often
despised or ignored, the explanation of the universe and mankind is forced within the narrow limits of materialism or of

* At times a vacant diocese is filled by transferring a residential bishop
from another diocese or by elevating an auxiliary bishop.

rationalism, and new educational systems are sought after which cannot but produce a sorrowful harvest in the intellectual and moral life of the nation. . . . Oh! If only your country had come to know from the experience of others rather than from examples at home of the accumulation of ills which derive from the plague of divorce. Let reverence for religion, let fidelity toward the great American people counsel energetic action that this disease, alas so widespread, may be cured by extirpation. . . . With regard to those marriages in which one or the other party does not accept the Catholic teaching or has not been baptized — such are rarely happy and occasion grave loss to the Catholic Church.

The fundamental point of the social question is this, that the goods created by God for all men should in the same way reach all, justice guiding and charity helping. The history of every age teaches that there were always rich and poor; that it will always be so we may gather from the unchanging tenor of human destinies. But God does not wish that some have exaggerated riches while others are in such straits that they lack the bare necessities of life. . . . The salaries of the workers, as is just, are to be such that they are sufficient to maintain them and their families. May it also be brought about that each and every able-bodied man may receive an equal opportunity for work in order to earn the daily bread for himself and his own. We deeply lament the lot of those — and their number in the United States is large indeed — who though robust, capable, and willing cannot have the work for which they are anxiously waiting.

Because sociability is one of man's natural requirements and since it is legitimate to promote by common effort decent livelihood, it is not possible without injustice to deny or to limit either to the producers or to the laboring and farming classes the free faculty of uniting in associations by means of which they may defend their proper rights and secure the betterment of the goods of soul and of body, as well as the honest comforts of life. But let the unions draw their vital force from principles of wholesome liberty; let them take their form from the lofty rules of justice and of honesty; let them act in such a manner that in their care for the interests of their class they violate no one's rights; let them continue to strive for harmony and respect the common weal of civil society. . . . What a proud boast it will be for the American people, by nature inclined to great undertakings and to liberality, if they untie the knotty and difficult social question by following the sure paths illuminated by the light of the Gospel and thus lay the basis of a happier age.

One might expect that Pius XII, burdened by innumerable duties and problems, would not find the time for scholarly pursuits. That this is not true, however, he has shown time after time. In a discourse to the Pontifical Academy of Science, in February of 1943, for example, the Holy Father forecast the development of atomic energy. After discussing the disintegration which uranium undergoes when bombarded by neutrons, His Holiness expressed the hope that its force would be harnessed for the service of man and not released for his destruction. Again, *The New York Times* carried a brief item under the dateline of September 19, 1945: "Pope Pius this morning received Sir Alexander Fleming and discussed with him new uses of penicillin. The discoverer of penicillin presented the Pontiff a plate for cultivating mold to be used in research. Sir Alexander, after a twenty-minute audience, declared he was astonished at the Pope's knowledge of his discovery."

CHAPTER VII

PIUS XII AND WORLD WAR II

HIS family name contains the Italian word for peace, *Pace*lli, his every speech as nuncio and cardinal argued for peace, his coat of arms pleads for peace, yet Pius XII was a wartime pope. Before recounting the story of the Holy Father's greatest sorrow, it may be well to outline the traditional policy of the Church in time of war, and then to discuss the international position of the Vatican on the eve of World War II.

Political neutrality but moral belligerency is the traditional policy of the Church in time of war. Since the Church is not a political institution but a spiritual one whose mission is to obtain the eternal salvation of all men, of every race and country, and since her children are among the peoples of all nations, the Church cannot ally herself with or against any nation or nations. Nor may she seek by diplomacy, propaganda, or other means the victory of one side and the defeat of the other. History and wisdom as well dictate a policy of absolute neutrality. In centuries past the Church, largely because of circumstances, did "take sides" in disputes among nations, and at the price of internal corruption and lost prestige learned that politics is a hellish captivity. And the wise Church knows that she would be a mere tool for the aims of her allies, who would scream "Keep religion out of politics," if she dared to question their motives. Finally, intervention by the Church would be futile, because the Catholics of the enemy nation would copy the reply of the Irish, "Religion from Rome, but politics from Dublin," and would begin novenas that the pope be liberated from his wicked allies.

Moral belligerency, however, is the right and the duty of the Church in time of war. The Spouse of Christ cannot remain silent while the commandments of His Father are being broken by the nations, while His teachings are being supplanted by the so-called necessities of war, and while the rights of His brethren are being crushed by force. She must tell the nations of the world what Christian morality permits and forbids in the prosecution of war; she must condemn crimes against justice and charity done in the name of national defense; and she must ease the sufferings of the war's victims. Moreover, the spiritual mother of mankind may not remain idle while the evils of war are devastating civilization and changing the sons of God into pawns of Satan. She must work to open the road to peace and to uproot the weeds of hatred and injustice which would choke the wheat of tomorrow's hopes. Thus, the Church, although neutral as to the political aspects of war, is forcefully belligerent as to its moral aspects, and in that restricted sense may be said to favor or to oppose a particular side.

However, the Church of a nation at war, because of its patriotic obligations, cannot remain politically neutral but, necessarily and rightfully, supports the war effort. The previous statement is correct and acceptable, if the particular nation is fighting a just war. But what ought to be the position and attitude of the Church of an aggressor nation? To this there is no precise answer, only a halting explanation. The Church of an aggressor nation has the right (but not the absolute duty) to forbid Catholics to aid the war effort in any way. Such a prohibition, however, would be both foolish and useless, because those who obeyed would be shot for treason while the majority would disobey in the face of threats and propaganda. The individual citizen can take part in an unjust war without incurring personal guilt, for, since he cannot know all the facts and the motives of both sides, he may substitute for his own the judgment of his government that the war is just. Therefore, the Church of that nation wisely refrains from increasing the moral difficulties of her people by a decision as to the justice of the particular war, a decision which in fact she herself, because of lack of knowledge, may not be able to make with complete correctness. In the prosecution of a war, just or unjust, the Church of any belligerent nation has the right to condemn immoral actions and to demand adherence to Christian principles. Human prudence and the limits of the possible require that this right be exercised with sane regard to the difficulties of the nation and of the Church herself. The American bishops could have publicly condemned saturation bombing of German cities, for it was wrong, but they prudently protested only by private memorandum to the government. It may be, of course, that such prudence is neither heroic nor zealous, but, as Menander once said, "We live not as we wish but as we can."

On the eve of World War II the international position of the Vatican was dangerous and difficult. The anti-Semitic decrees enacted by Mussolini in 1938 were causing bitter conflicts between Italy and the Holy See. Pius XI had condemned the decrees as heretical, and had encouraged the Catholic Action societies to resist them. The

Fascist press replied with a smear campaign, and Fascist thugs with beatings and burnings. Hitler's vile persecution of the Church in Germany, Austria, and Czechoslovakia was prefacing the atrocities of Belsen and Buchenwald. German Catholics were among the first to suffer and to die, in Dachau and Muelhausen, for their opposition to Nazism. Because the Vatican was organizing and stiffening the Catholic resistance, the Nazis had labeled it "an enemy to be destroyed." Between the Rome-Berlin Axis and Vatican City stood a stone wall built in the ninth century and five hundred guards armed with swords and rifles.

The Vatican's opposition to the paganism and aggression of Fascism and Nazism established a link of understanding with Great Britain, France, and the United States. Though the democratic nations were partly responsible for conditions leading to the war, they were sincerely desirous of a peaceful solution and eager to co-operate with the Holy See to that end. Prime Minister Chamberlain visited Pius XI in January of 1939 and discussed with him means to prevent the imminent disaster. The American and French newspapers prominently displayed and editorially approved the efforts and appeals of Pius XI and Pius XII for peace. And one reading the conscience of the Axis powers and then the conscience of the democratic nations found the weight of justice and morality on our side. Therefore, it can be said with confidence that the Vatican hoped and prayed that the democratic nations might prevail.

Pius XII ascended the throne of the popes as War was unlocking his arsenals and unpacking his tools. Hitler had seized Austria and the Sudeten land, and now was "casing" Czechoslovakia and Poland. Mussolini had stolen Ethiopia, and now wanted parts of France and all of Albania. England and France were hurriedly rearming, having discovered to their surprise that aggression like appetite grows with feeding — a lesson that they seem to be learning again with Russia as the teacher. Although persuaded that war was more likely than not, the new Holy Father began at once to fight for peace.

The morning following his election the Pope appealed by radio to the peoples of the world to lay aside their quarrels and to enjoy "peace, the fairest of all God's gifts." In an address to the Sacred College of Cardinals, the day after his coronation, he stressed: "We assume the government of the Bark of Peter to direct it amid so many woes and tempests toward the port of peace, the boon that humanity desires above all others." Preaching in the Basilica of St. Peter, Easter Sunday, April 9, the Holy Father sadly said: "Today, more perhaps than at any other time, it is the words of Jeremias that best describe the situation, who portrays for us men crying, 'Peace, Peace: and there is no peace.' We, therefore, exhort all, as this fearful storm approaches, to make their way back to the King of Peace." In a letter to Cardinal Luigi Maglione, the Papal Secretary of State, he invited the faithful to join a crusade of prayer for peace during the month of May.

More direct action soon became necessary, as Hitler, having invaded Czechoslovakia, began "a war of nerves" against Poland, and Mussolini, having seized Albania, began to demand Nice and Tunisia from France. Among the countless errors of the Versailles Treaty were the cutting of a Polish corridor through German territory and the establishment of Danzig as a Free City. It was evident to the Pope and to all reasonable men that these errors could be corrected and justice could be done to both

Poland and Germany without war. The papal representatives to Germany, Italy, France, Poland, and England were instructed to confer with the rulers and the officials of these nations to learn whether mediation by the Pope would be considered. They would suggest, as an alternative, a general conference of all the European powers or bilateral conversations of the parties to the Danzig question and to the Nice-Tunisia question. Nuncio Cesare Orsenigo saw Hitler at Berchtesgaden on May 5, and a few days later Foreign Minister Beck received Nuncio Filippo Cortesi at Warsaw. The advice and suggestions of Pius were received by Hitler and Beck, as well as by Mussolini, Daladier, and Chamberlain, with respect and deference — and evasiveness. Hitler had decided on war, and the others were remembering Munich.

Fortified by prayer and mortification, the Holy Father would not despair of peace, even though as a diplomat he saw war approaching. During June and July he continued his efforts to mobilize world opinion against war and to foster among the quarreling nations "a spirit of serene judgment of events." Through the papal representatives accredited to them the small nations of Europe were urged to form a pressure bloc against the will to war of the major powers. In almost daily conferences with their envoys Pius counseled and exhorted Poland, France, England, Germany, and Italy to find a peaceful solution. However, he did not seek peace at any price. In receiving the new ambassador of Poland, Casimir Papée, the Pope spoke of "a true and substantial peace, based on justice, honor, and the liberty of the nations."

On July 24, Pius XII moved to Castel Gandolfo, the papal summer residence some thirty miles north of Rome in the Alban hills. Troops marching to frontiers, warships taking up positions, civilians receiving gas masks, Europe was all but at war. Stalin allied himself with Hitler on August 23, and Germany was free to "deal" with Poland. To hope for peace was futile, but the Shepherd of Christianity would make another despairing plea. On the morning of August 24 he received in private audience the representatives of England, France, Poland, and Italy, and handing each the text of a speech asked them to convey it to their respective governments. That evening at seven o'clock he read the speech to the world. The few sentences quoted below surely prove the Pope's deep love for mankind and his unselfish work for peace.

The danger is imminent, but there is still time. Nothing is lost with peace; all may be lost with war. Let men return to mutual understanding! Let them begin negotiations anew, conferring with good will and with respect for reciprocal rights. Then will they find that to sincere and conscientious negotiations an honorable solution is never precluded. They will feel a sense of greatness in the true sense of the word, if, by silencing the voices of passion — be it collective or private — and by leaving to reason its rightful rule, they will have spared the blood of their fellow men and saved their countries from ruin. . . .

We beseech them by the Blood of Christ, whose conquering force in the world was His mildness in life and in death. . . . We have with Us all those who are upright of heart, all those who hunger and thirst after justice, all those who suffer every sorrow through the evils of life. We have with Us the hearts of mothers which beat as one with Ours; of fathers who would be obliged to abandon their families; of the lowly who labor and do not understand; of the innocent, upon whom weighs heavily the awful threat; of the young men, generous knights of purest and noblest ideals. . . . With Us all humanity seeks justice, bread, and freedom, not steel which kills and destroys. With Us is that Christ, who has made His solemn commandment, love of one's brother, the very substance of His religion and the promise of salvation for individuals and for nations.

The last week of August, England and France were

feverishly seeking a compromise, but Germany's evil genius chose the avalanche of steel and blood. On August 31 Cardinal Maglione summoned the representatives of France, Germany, Italy, Poland, and England, and handed them the eleventh-hour appeal of Pius XII. "The Holy Father cannot abandon hope that conversations now being held may bring about a just and peaceful solution such as the whole world has not ceased to implore. Therefore, His Holiness beseeches, in the Name of God, the governments of Germany and Poland to do everything possible to avoid any incident whatsoever, and to abstain from taking any measure capable of aggravating the present tension. He asks the governments of England, France, and Italy to support this, his request." The rest of the message suggested that Germany and Poland agree to a fifteen-day truce, during which an international conference of the five nations directly concerned together with Belgium, Holland, Switzerland, and the United States might be held. Its purpose would be to revise the Versailles Treaty, settle peacefully the Danzig and other problems, and give Europe a permanent peace.

At six o'clock the next morning Nuncio Orsenigo in Berlin telephoned Hitler's answer to Cardinal Maglione: "Nazi troops have crossed the Polish frontier at five points." The Papal Secretary of State, in turn, notified the Pope at Castel Gandolfo. His Holiness replaced the receiver, walked to the chapel, and knelt in prayer before the image of the Prince of peace.

With all hope of peace gone, Pius XII took up the sad burden of comforting the sorrowful and of assisting the persecuted. Poland soon collapsed under the Nazi panzers and the Communist dagger, which treacherous Stalin thrust in her back. In an editorial condemning the Russian

An excellent study of Pope Pius XII as he bestows the
Apostolic blessing. — *Wide World.*

Pius XII blessing the crowds in St. Peter's. — *International News Photo.*

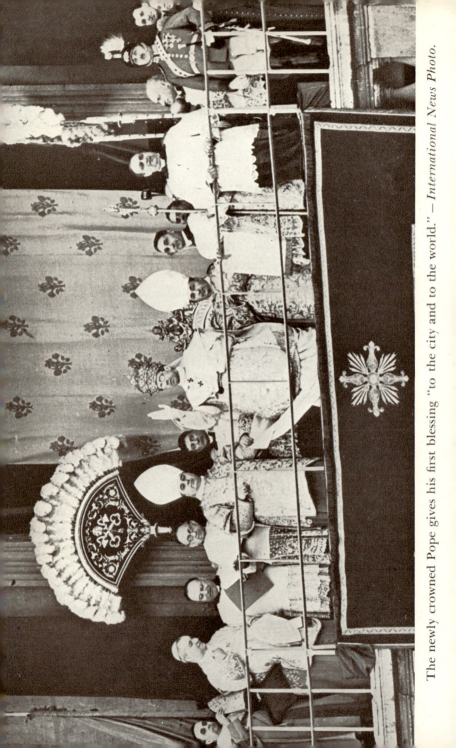

The newly crowned Pope gives his first blessing "to the city and to the world." — *International News Photo.*

Pope Pius receives Myron C. Taylor, representative of the President of the United States to the Vatican. — *International News Photo*.

His Holiness with a group of servicemen from Poland, Canada, and the United States. — *Acme.*

invasion of Poland, *The New York Times,* September 18, 1939, declared: "At last the issue stands clear. Hitlerism is brown communism, Stalinism is red fascism. The world will now understand that the only real ideological issue is one between democracy, liberty, and peace on the one hand, and despotism, terror, and war on the other." Crushed between two forces, Poland began a martyrdom which history has not recorded before but which the world has already forgotten. On October 11, 1939, *Bezbozknik* (Godless), a Moscow newspaper, praised a Red army soldier who tossed several hand grenades into a group of priests and religious. Who can read *The Black Book of Poland* or Cardinal Hlond's report to the Vatican without becoming nauseated at the Nazi bestiality? The sadistic brutality of the Nazi devils toward the Poles has added to history its blackest account of man's inhumanity to man.

The Polish people, loyal to God and Poland, were not forsaken by their Holy Father. The morning of September 30 he received in audience at Castel Gandolfo Cardinal Hlond, Archbishop of Gniezno and Poznan, Dr. Casimir Papée, Polish Ambassador to the Holy See, and two hundred Polish refugees and residents of Rome. His dark tired eyes flooded with tears, the Pope spoke words of consolation and of hope to his despairing children. "Like the flowers of your country, which under a thick blanket of winter snow wait for the warm breezes of spring, so you will know that you too may expect the hour of heavenly consolation. May Christ who wept over Lazarus and over the ruins of his fatherland some day repay you for the tears which you spill over your dead and over the Poland, *which does not intend to die.*"

A papal relief mission was established at Bucharest, Rumania, by Nuncio Cortesi who had escaped from Warsaw before the nunciature was gutted by fire bombs. The Pope sent him large sums of money with which to secure food, clothes, and shelter for the refugees from Poland. Later, a similar mission was sent to Poland to feed and clothe the wretched victims of Nazi aggression, and through Nuncio Orsenigo at Berlin the Polish prisoners of war were given boxes of food and other necessities. The Secretariate of State established a bureau to obtain and furnish to families information of relatives still in Poland.

Pius XII's condemnation of Hitler's crime against Poland was made even more explicit in his first encyclical, *Summi Pontificatus*, issued October 27, 1939. "The blood of countless human beings," he declared, "even noncombatants, raises a piteous dirge over a nation such as Our dear Poland which, for its fidelity to the Church, for its services in the defense of Christian civilization, written in indelible characters in the annals of history, has a right to the generous and brotherly sympathy of the whole world, while it awaits, relying on the powerful intercession of Mary, Help of Christians, the hour of a resurrection in harmony with the principles of justice and true peace." Spurning Nazi objections, the Vatican extended diplomatic recognition to the Polish government in exile first at Paris and later at London. When in January, 1940, the Vatican radio broadcasted a detailed account of Nazi savagery against the Polish people, Diego Von Bergen, Hitler's ambassador to the Holy See, protested to Cardinal Maglione. The answer was a curt suggestion that conditions be remedied.

In the previous March Stalin had promised to defend "the victims of aggression who fight for the independence of their country," but in December his armies invaded Finland and his bombers smashed her cities and villages.

L'Osservatore Romano bitterly denounced the wanton aggression as cowardly and cruel and ridiculed the myth of Russian democracy. In his Christmas message to the cardinals, December 24, 1939, the Holy Father condemned "premeditated aggression against a small, industrious, and peaceful people on the pretext of a threat that neither exists nor is desired nor is possible." To the victims of Stalin's aggression the Pope sent money for food and clothing.

In receiving Adrian Nieuwenhuys, Ambassador of Belgium to the Holy See, September 14, 1939, Pius XII declared that he would now work "to open new roads to peace before the present fire is transformed into a universal conflagration." This being also the objective of the United States, President Roosevelt wrote the Pope on December 23 that he had named Myron C. Taylor, an Episcopalian and former chairman of the United States Steel Corporation, his personal envoy to the Holy See with rank of ambassador. The President was sending Ambassador Taylor to the Vatican "in order that our parallel endeavors for peace and the alleviation of suffering may be assisted. Only by friendly association between the seekers of light and the seekers of peace everywhere can the forces of evil be overcome."

The Protestant churches did not greet the announcement with the same joy as Pius XII, but spent columns of newspaper space and hours of Sunday sermons in denouncing the appointment. Although their opposition was understandable and sincerely motivated, they were overlooking the important fact that Ambassador Taylor would represent not the United States but President Roosevelt alone, and were forgetting the history of diplomatic relations between the United States and the Holy See.

As long ago as 1757, when two British privateers brought into the port of New York a ship flying the papal flag, our country, then a British colony, recognized the sovereignty of the Holy See. The admiralty court to which the owner appealed ordered the privateers to return the ship and to pay damages of $5,000, the judge pointing out that the Holy See was a sovereign nation whose flag and neutrality ought to be respected. The first American accredited to the Vatican was Jacob Martin, from North Carolina, who went to Rome with the rank of chargé d'affaires in 1848. He was succeeded in 1849 by Lewis Cass, of Michigan, who rose to the rank of Minister in 1854. Cass was followed by John Stockton, of New Jersey, Alexander Randall, of Wisconsin, Richard Blatchford, of New York, and Rufus King, of Wisconsin. Congress of 1867 was so hostile to President Johnson that it grasped at any pretext to thwart him. Hence when he asked for the annual appropriation to maintain a minister at the Holy See, some bigoted congressman objected on antipopery grounds, and Congress seized the pretext to abolish the post. Minister King left Rome on January 1, 1868.

During the years 1848–1868, however, the Holy See did not have a diplomatic representative at Washington because such an appointment was inadvisable and unnecessary. The Church in America was then in the missionary stage and was meeting considerable opposition and prejudice. The first apostolic delegate (a papal representative to the Church but not to the government of a country) was Archbishop Francesco Satolli, a Franciscan, whose appointment in 1893 was shrilly denounced by bigots. He was succeeded in 1896 by Archbishop Sebastian Martinelli, who later became cardinal-prefect of the Sacred Congregation of Rites. The third apostolic delegate was Archbishop Diomede

Falconio (1902–1911), and the fourth was Archbishop Giovanni Bonzano (1911–1922). Archbishop, by that time Cardinal, Bonzano returned in 1926 as Papal Legate to the International Eucharistic Congress at Chicago.

The predecessor of His Excellency Archbishop Amleto Giovanni Cicognani, the present apostolic delegate, was Archbishop Pietro Fumasoni-Biondi, who resigned in 1933 to become the cardinal-prefect of the Congregation of the Propagation of the Faith. Although Archbishop Cicognani has no official diplomatic standing, his character and ability have gained him the respect and esteem of our government. The notable growth of the American Catholic Church in the past decade must be credited in great part to the Delegate's wise counsel and able guidance.

Should the United States extend diplomatic recognition to the Holy See? Protestant churches vociferously answer no, arguing that such recognition would violate the American principle of the separation of Church and State and would impair their freedom of worship. Catholics, knowing that Protestant England, whose king is its religious head, and pagan China maintain diplomatic relations with the Holy See, answer, "Why not?" If the United States extends diplomatic recognition to the Holy See, it would not thereby recognize Pius XII as the Head of the Roman Catholic Church but solely as the Sovereign of the Vatican State, which is an international entity and autonomous power in the same sense as France or Cuba. When, in the past, our country maintained diplomatic relations with Japan, we did not thereby recognize Hirohito as the son of god. The fears of some Protestants that diplomatic recognition would herald the invasion and enslavement of the United States by the "papacy" are quite groundless. After twenty-eight years of diplomatic relations with the Holy

See, English Protestants still celebrate Guy Fawkes Day, during which the papacy is roundly cursed and the pope is burned in effigy. (See *Life,* December 11, 1945.)

As a matter of fact, it would be to our practical advantage to extend diplomatic recognition to the Holy See, because Vatican City is the information center of the world. Our State Department on innumerable occasions turned to the Apostolic Delegate for information on missing soldiers, prisoners of war, and civilian internees. The first report that the War Department received on the number and condition of the American fliers shot down in the Ploesti raids was furnished by the Apostolic Delegation. But more important than the question itself of diplomatic relations between the Holy See and the United States is the need of discussing the matter fairly, charitably, and with some regard for facts. He is a poor American who meets every Protestant objection with the shout of "Bigotry" and every Catholic argument with the cry of "Popery."

The year 1939 closed for the Holy Father with an historical visit and a disastrous fire. On December 28 His Holiness paid a ceremonial call on King Victor Emmanuel III and Queen Elena at the Quirinal Palace, from which his predecessor, Pius IX, fled one September morning in 1870. A cold rain was falling but the Pope rode in an open car to the Palace so that the happy Romans, who lined the boulevards in cheering thousands, could see him. The visit was to return that made by the King and Queen a week earlier, and also to signalize the Vatican's support of Italy's then neutrality. On New Year's Eve fire destroyed the Apostolic Chancery, one of Rome's most notable examples of Renaissance architecture. Completed in 1520 it had a façade of travertine stones from the Colosseum and a court of forty-four granite columns from the Theater of

Pompeii. The halls were gloriously frescoed by Giorgio Vasari and Andrea del Sarto, and were hung with paintings by the great artists of the Italian Renaissance.

The winter and early spring of 1940 were lighted by the efforts of the Holy See and the United States to restore peace or, at least, to prevent the further spread of war. In a letter delivered by Archbishop Cicognani on January 20, Pius praised President Roosevelt's work for peace and acknowledged the personal appointment of Ambassador Taylor. The latter arrived in Naples February 24 and, in the company of Monsignor Hurley, then an official of the Papal Secretariate of State, and now bishop of St. Augustine, Florida, proceeded to Rome. The morning of February 27 two chamberlains of the Sword and Cape called for the Ambassador and his secretary, Harold J. Tittman, Jr., at the Hotel Excelsior. As their car, flying the papal and American flags, entered the Courtyard of St. Damasus, a platoon of Palatine Guards presented arms. From the courtyard Ambassador Taylor ascended to the Clementine Hall, and passing a platoon of Swiss Guards at rigid attention, entered the Hall of the Little Throne. After bowing thrice, as is required by papal etiquette, the Ambassador presented his credentials to the Holy Father, who welcomed him cordially and bade him to be seated. In the hour that followed they discussed the European situation and explored possible avenues to peace. At the end of the audience Ambassador Taylor withdrew to call upon the Secretary of State. Cardinal Maglione returned the call that afternoon at the Ambassador's hotel.

For the papal audience the Hall of the Little Throne was used, instead of the Hall of Thrones in which representatives of countries having diplomatic relations with the Holy See are invariably received, in order to indicate that

Ambassador Taylor represented President Roosevelt and not the United States. Setting aside tradition and custom, His Holiness granted permission to record the conversations between himself and Ambassador Taylor and to photograph the entire audience. As a fashion note, it might be added that Ambassador Taylor wore full evening dress and black spats.

Eleven days later Joachim Von Ribbentrop, the Nazi Foreign Minister, was received in audience by the Pope — at the Nazi's own request as the Vatican pointedly announced. The reception was not cordial. Bluntly and sharply His Holiness protested to the Foreign Minister against Hitler's persecution of the German Catholics and the Polish Catholics. The Concordat had been flouted on countless occasions, the protests of the Holy See had been answered with contempt or evasion, the subhuman treatment of the Polish people called to heaven for vengeance, and heaven would answer. Von Ribbentrop replied arrogantly that the Church was at fault and that Der Fuehrer was right and virtuous in his every action. During the audience the Nazi submitted a peace offer, whose eleven points would have made Hitler master of Europe and would have given him additional time for further aggression. It was coldly received and completely ignored.

On March 18 Pius XII discussed the European situation with Sumner Welles, our Undersecretary of State, who was completing a mission to the belligerent nations for President Roosevelt. It was the President's hope that Germany and the Allies might find common grounds for ending the war. However, the Pope and Mr. Welles reluctantly agreed that the viewpoints and objectives of England and France could not be reconciled with the mad ambitions of Hitler. The Brenner Pass meeting the same day between Hitler and Mussolini would soon prove the correctness of this conclusion.

On April 9 the Nazi armies crushed Denmark, and through stealth and deceit invaded Norway. *L'Osservatore Romano* scathingly condemned Hitler's crime, accusing Germany of being the first belligerent to trample the rights of neutral nations. In praise of Norwegian resistance the editorial declared that "shedding of blood for the defense of the rights and liberties of one's Fatherland is not a useless, futile gesture." On May 10 the forces of evil crossed the borders of Holland, Belgium, and Luxembourg, nations which Hitler had promised to respect. Pius XII then took the most courageous step of his pontificate. In messages to the sovereigns of these three countries he pledged them his moral support and condemned the crime of their common enemy. His note to Queen Wilhelmina of Holland read: "We learn with great sorrow that Your Majesty's efforts for peace have not been able to preserve your noble people from becoming, against their will and their rights, the theater of war. We pray to God, the Supreme Arbiter of the destinies of nations, to hasten with His almighty help the re-establishment of justice and liberty. Pius PP. XII." The messages to King Leopold of Belgium and to Grand Duchess Charlotte of Luxembourg, though different in form, were identical in purpose.

The publication of these messages in *L'Osservatore Romano,* which added its own stinging denunciation, provoked the wrath of Italy's Fascist government. The Italian people were against war, but their gambling Duce wanted a casualty list to show Hitler at the victory feast, of which they were then so certain. To dissuade Mussolini from this folly and to keep Italy out of the conflagration, Pius XII left no stone unturned. That he failed is due solely to the one whom the heavens seeking to destroy first made mad. Archbishop Borgongini-Duca, Papal Nuncio to Italy, was instructed as early as April of 1939 to use every opportunity to influence the Italian government against war. In frequent conversations with Foreign Minister Ciano, he pleaded the wisdom of peace, and to his honor Count Ciano worked hard for neutrality. The Pope in audiences with Dino Alfieri, the Italian Ambassador to the Vatican, in visits with the sovereigns of Italy, and in sermons to the Italian people again and again voiced his anxiety that their country be spared the horrors of war. But Mussolini needed arguments, even though they be corpses and amputees, for the expected division of spoils.

In a conversation with Cardinal Maglione, April 10, 1940, Ambassador Alfieri protested that "in many parts of Italy there are manifestations and sermons about peace, perhaps as the result of instructions from the Vatican." The Cardinal denied the supposed instructions as unnecessary since the Italian people desired peace so profoundly. Then the Ambassador objected that L'Osservatore Romano had an attitude different from that of the Italian press, the war news not "being played up" and too much space being given to the glories of peace. Cardinal Maglione curtly reminded him that L'Osservatore Romano is the daily of the Holy See, and implied that its attitude ought to be imitated by the Italian press, "excited, kindled to white heat."*

Two weeks later the Holy Father wrote Mussolini a personal letter in which he pleaded with him to save "our and your country from so great a calamity." The reply was

* In his entry for May 12, 1940, Ciano notes that on orders from Mussolini he had sent an ultimatum on L'Osservatore Romano, threatening to prohibit its circulation in Italy unless it ceased its "subtle propaganda against the axis" (cf. op. cit., p. 248).

respectfully evasive. Sunday, May 5, His Holiness went to the Basilica of Santa Maria Sopra Minnerva for solemn ceremonies in honor of St. Catherine of Siena and St. Francis of Assisi, whom about a year before he had named special patrons of Italy. Before the anxious multitude that crowded the ancient church he preached a heart-moving sermon on peace for the world and peace for Italy. As a result Mussolini informed the Pope, through Ambassador Alfieri, that he was exceedingly irritated with him and his sermons and that it would be advisable for him to remain silent about peace. The Vicar of Christ coolly replied that he had followed the dictates of his conscience, and warned that he could not be frightened from doing his duty by the displeasure of others or the threats of enemies. "We are not afraid, even of being sent to a concentration camp," the Bishop of Rome added with courage worthy of the first Bishop, whom Nero martyred on the Vatican hill.

On June 10 Italy declared war on France and England. Vatican City was now surrounded by a nation at war, and it took necessary steps to protect its residents and to preserve its neutrality. Gas masks were distributed and air-raid shelters were constructed. A special three-room shelter, electrically heated and connected by an elevator with the papal apartments, was built for Pius XII, but he refused to use it. Whenever the siren sounded, the Holy Father turned to the cross on his desk and began the prayers for the dying. At the Pope's request Great Britain and France agreed not to bomb Rome, but the alleged necessities of war eventually set aside that promise. A total blackout, beginning at six-thirty and continuing until dawn, was rigorously enforced.

The representatives to the Holy See of France, Great Britain, Poland, and Belgium found refuge in the Hospice of St. Marta, which is to the left of the Bernini colonnade. Their embassies, churches, and other buildings were placed under the protection of the Holy See, and the Nuncio to Italy was appointed custodian of them. All citizens and residents of Vatican City, as well as visitors, were forbidden to discuss publicly political matters or to communicate secretly with foreign powers. A defenseless householder does not needlessly kick the unfriendly tiger prowling before his door.

Because *L'Osservatore Romano* alone in Italy presented a complete and unbiased picture of international events, its circulation jumped from about 25,000 in prewar days to over 150,000 copies in early 1940. The people of Rome and other cities in which it was sold eagerly snatched every copy to find the truth, which the Fascist press sought to kill with lies and propaganda. This was not to the liking of Mussolini; he needed a misinformed people if his insane scheme was to succeed. Therefore, buyers and sellers of *L'Osservatore Romano* were beaten, and their copies burned by Fascist thugs. The Holy Father, thereupon, banned distribution of the paper outside Vatican City, and after the entry of Italy into the war he restricted its columns to ecclesiastical news. Later, *L'Osservatore Romano* resumed publishing of and commenting upon international events, and again is one of Europe's most authoritative dailies.

With her armies in retreat and her cities defenseless before the Luftwaffe, France surrendered to the Nazis on June 25, 1940. At Compiègne, where the Germans surrendered to Foch on November 11, 1918, an armistice was signed, leaving the southern section of France unoccupied and nominally subject to the Vichy government of Petain and Laval. Today the Petain government has been convicted of treason and collaboration (a judgment which impartial history may not sustain), but at the time it appeared to be France's only salvation. Furthermore, it was the legal government of France, a fact which the United States admitted by sending Admiral Leahy to Vichy as our diplomatic representative. For these reasons the Vatican extended recognition to the Vichy government and, without reference to political aspects, exerted its influence to revive France. In a letter to the French bishops, which Robert Farinacci, former secretary of the Fascist party, angrily attacked as anti-Axis, the Pope deplored "the unprecedented disaster which crossed your fatherland," and prayed that the independence and prestige of France would soon be restored. On several occasions in 1940 the Holy Father urged that the peace, then being discussed between France and the Axis, be one not only of justice but especially of charity. Steps toward a concordat were taken, but the swirl of international events prevented their completion, although many of the oppressive laws enacted against the Church in the early part of this century were repealed.

The spread of the war was cause for Pius XII to increase greatly his charity to the persecuted and the desolate. Until the Nazis expelled his representatives and relief missions, he fed and clothed the Catholics and non-Catholics of Belgium and Holland, Denmark and Norway. The French of both the occupied and the unoccupied zones received generously of the papal charity. Money for food and clothing was sent to the refugee Rumanians fleeing the Russian annexation of Bessarabia and Bukovina. Nor were the Jews, the most pitiable of Hitler's victims, forgotten by the all-embracing heart of Christ's Vicar. The *New York Times,* October 10, 1945, reported that "The Hadassah

Society of America has cabled ten thousand dollars to Pope Pius XII in grateful recognition of his charity to the Jews of Europe during the war."

It has been said, in ignorance or malice, that the Holy See, terrified by the Nazi victories, favored the Axis during the early years of the war. Voluminous evidence to the contrary might be introduced, and the accusers still not be convinced, for prejudice like death is not open to argument. These sentences, however, broadcast by the Vatican radio *in the fall of 1940, when Hitler and Mussolini were at the zenith of their power and conquest,* should be of some weight. "Those who allege that they will be able to create a new order [then the Nazi boast] in the world are prefacing the destruction of the people whom they allegedly wish to make happy. It is a world order as dry as the desert and is being achieved by the exploitation of human life. What these false benefactors call life is death." It should also be pointed out that the Holy See through *L'Osservatore Romano* bluntly denied every claim of the Axis radio and press that the Pope favored its designs and principles. The Holy Father, through his bountiful charity to the oppressed and the enslaved, clearly demonstrated that his sympathies were not with the victors but their victims.

The 1940 Christmas tree of Pius XII was laden with gifts for the children of his nephews and of his guards and officials. But the gift which he had asked of the belligerent nations was not there. In a letter authorizing the celebration of the midnight Mass in the late afternoon, he had asked for a Christmas truce. The answer was no.

Mussolini's invasion of Greece, pompously launched from Albania in late fall of 1940, had bogged down to a disgraceful debacle, his armies in Libya and Ethiopia were in retreat, and his Nazi ally was sending agents, troops, and administrators into Italy. To spur on the Italian people, weary of war and equally fearful of defeat by the Allies or enslavement by the Germans, Il Duce proclaimed on February 23, 1941, a campaign of "cold and implacable hatred against the enemy in every heart and every home." Because Christ taught "love thine enemy" His Vicar again became a moral belligerent. *L'Osservatore Romano* in a series of sharp editorials rebuked the Fascist press for its appeals to hate, declaring that even in time of war charity is still the greatest of all virtues. In audiences with Italian pilgrims the Holy Father, appealing for a humane and just treatment of conquered people, extolled the virtue of fraternal love and denounced the vice of fratricidal hate.

The Fascists retaliated by confiscating the Catholic newspapers which echoed the Pope's words and by ringing Vatican City with spies and informers. The official newspaper of Catholic Action was seized because it quoted with approval these words of a chaplain in the Italian army. "Hatred is one of the most base feelings and dishonors any uniform. Respect your enemy and do not utter words of hatred — they bring dishonor to your country." The telephone wires to Vatican City were tapped by OVRA, the Italian secret police, visitors were followed, and efforts were made to bribe papal employees. Pius XII, who had scorned the threats of Communist assassins, would not be intimidated by such pressure tactics, and continued to preach love of neighbor and to demand a peace of justice and charity. "Nothing can impede or restrain Us from using the weapons of truth and prayer and love to secure and safeguard just rights, true human brotherhood, and genuine peace, wherever the sacred duty of Our Office prompts Us."

Fascist hostility against the Holy Father mounted after the invasion of Yugoslavia and Greece by the Nazis and the entry of Russia into the war. The Yugoslav Minister to the Holy See was offered refuge in the Hospice of St. Marta, but Italy, in flagrant violation of the Lateran Treaty, deported him to Switzerland. This the Secretariate of State protested vigorously but not successfully. The Vatican's protests against Nazi cruelties to the people of Yugoslavia and Greece met with even less success, the Wilhelmstrasse refusing to answer the papal notes. The martyrdom of the Catholic Slovenes and Croats, citizens of Yugoslavia, has been little publicized, but its brutality equalled that of tragic Poland. The clergy and religious were massacred or imprisoned — in one diocese of 80,000 Catholics only three priests were left by the Gestapo, two of them enfeebled with age. Education was Nazified, *Mein Kampf* replacing the New Testament, and Christianity became treason, punishable by torture and death.

To the persecuted people of Yugoslavia and Greece the Holy See gave its moral support and material aid. When the Axis forced upon Croatia a foreign king and a Quisling premier, the Pope refused recognition, continuing to maintain diplomatic relations with the Yugoslav government in exile. Papal relief missions were sent to both countries. The Vatican Bureau of War Prisoners and Missing Persons, which during the war averaged a thousand requests a day, consoled with accurate and prompt information anxious friends and relatives. This charitable work was performed by a corps of clergy and laity under the direct supervision of the Holy Father.

The dawn of June 23 broke to the thunder of German artillery on the Russian front. The thieves had fallen out, and were now at each other's throats. Because of the Church's implacable opposition to Communism, Mussolini and Hitler believed that the Vatican could be persuaded or forced into proclaiming the Axis war against Russia a crusade and into summoning all Christian nations to their aid. The Italian ambassador to the Holy See suggested to Cardinal Maglione that the Pope address a letter to the bishops of the world, calling for the formation of volunteer legions to fight the Soviets. The answer, of course, was no.

If, as it was rumored, President Roosevelt asked Pius XII to declare a crusade against the Axis nations, the same answer was given. Ambassador Taylor, after leaving Vatican City in late 1940 because of illness, returned on September 9, 1941, with a message to the Pope from President Roosevelt. He was received in private audience on September 21, and departed the next day, bearing an autographed picture of the Pope to the President. The purpose of his visit and the contents of his message have not been officially divulged, and therefore it is idle to conjecture. Ambassador Taylor did make a personal gift to His Holiness of his magnificent villa, Schifanoia, near Florence, Italy. The villa has been assigned to Rosary College, Chicago, Illinois, as a house of studies for the Dominican sisters and their students.

While all Americans applauded the Holy Father's "no" to the Axis' request, some have criticized him because he refused to proclaim a crusade against the Nazis and Fascists. In this they forget that the Sovereign Pontiff must be politically neutral, while morally belligerent, in time of war. The common father of both the Russian and the Axis people, he is forbidden by justice and charity to become the ally of one and the enemy of the other. The Church is a spiritual institution, alien to and aloof from the political world save in its relations to the eternal salvation of mankind, and therefore she is neither permitted nor required by her character or purpose to make a choice in purely political matters. The course of the Church was drawn by her founder, when He said: "Render to Caesar the things that are Caesar's, and render to God the things that are God's." Political decisions belong to Caesar, spiritual decisions belong to God, whose Vicar on earth is the Bishop of Rome.

To protect and to foster the things of God in Spain, Archbishop Gaetano Cicognani, Nuncio to Madrid and brother of the Apostolic Delegate to the United States, and Señor Ramon Suñer, Minister of Foreign Affairs, executed an agreement on June 7, 1941. By it the Catholic Church was established as the official religion of Spain, her paramount interest in the education of youth was recognized, and her independence in the appointment and control of bishops and priests was conceded. The agreement does not constitute a concordat, which is still in the process of preparation. Much has been written and said in criticism of the Vatican's attitude toward Franco's Spain, the latest being the accusation of Harold Laski that the Holy See is plotting to restore the Spanish monarchy. It would be idle to refute each charge and lie, but we will discuss, briefly, the Vatican's policy toward Spain during World War II.

Pius XII had one wish and one prayer for Spain, peace. He counseled and exhorted the government and people of Spain to keep out of the holocaust, for the wounds of the revolution could not be reopened by war without death to the nation. Franco, who is neither the haloed saint of certain Catholic periodicals nor the incarnate devil of the so-called liberal press, obtained diplomatic recognition from the Vatican and nothing else. He does not have papal approval for the Fascistic evils and errors of his government, which have been condemned without specific reference by Pius XII and his predecessor on numerous occasions. Whether Franco's government remains in power or is replaced by another is immaterial to the Church, provided the successor respects her divine mission and the laws of God. The Vatican has neither the wish nor the duty to oppose or aid any particular form of government, but she must fight the spiritual evils of any government, be it a republic, monarchy, dictatorship, or oligarchy.

From America's so-called liberal press came the malicious accusation in 1941 that Pius XII supported the racial policy of Spain with respect to the nations of Central and South America. This was branded as a lie by *L'Osservatore Romano* and the Papal Secretariate of State. It is true that the Holy Father interested himself in South America during 1941. Peru and Ecuador were on the verge of war because of a boundary dispute. His Holiness wrote directly to the presidents of these nations and to the presidents of Argentina, Brazil, and the United States, pleading for a peaceful settlement. The dispute was submitted to arbitration and peace remained between Peru and Ecuador.

The privations of war did not bypass Vatican City. The "snack" bar, which in addition to pastries and liqueurs, served genuine coffee, so hard to find in blockaded Italy, closed in May. By summer supplies of meat, canned goods, spices, and clothing had fallen to the point where rationing became necessary. No ration stamps or coupons were issued, but a record of the purchases made by each family was kept. In October Marquis Carlo Pacelli, nephew of the Pope and general councilor of Vatican City, established an office in Lisbon, Portugal, for the purchase and routing of supplies from the United States and South America. Count Enrico Galeazzi, the economic advisor of Vatican City, flew to the United States in November to purchase large quantities of food, medicines, and other items. These went by ship to Lisbon and then by truck through France and Italy to Vatican City.

"Today the Axis has lost the war" was the general comment of Vatican circles on Sunday, December 7, 1941. That very morning Ambassador Taylor told the members of the Notre Dame Club of New York City: "In Pius XII we can have a supreme confidence founded not only on his holy office, but also on his embracing spirituality, his vision, and his very great talent. Within the historic walls of the Vatican are found, as in no other place among the war-torn nations, an atmosphere of tranquillity, of thoughtful analysis, of deliberate judgment, and of courageous and unchanging resolve." A few days later Harold J. Tittman, Jr., President Roosevelt's chargé d'affaires to Pius XII, installed himself within those walls in an apartment which had long been ready for him.

The fire had grown to a conflagration, and the entire world was at war. The tyranny of Nazism had crossed new frontiers, and all Europe was in slavery or fear. One voice alone was raised in praise of peace and in defense of mankind. On the eve of Christmas Pius XII spoke by radio to the world.

To the detriment of human dignity and personality as well as society the conception makes headway that it is might which creates right. . . . In some countries a political conception which is Godless and hostile to Christ has, through its many tentacles, achieved a complete absorption of the individual so that it can hardly be said that there is any longer any independence either in private or public life. . . . We direct our appeal to all that the day might be not delayed in which the Star of

Bethlehem will rouse all mankind to say with the angels: "Glory to God in the highest," and to proclaim as a gift restored at last by heaven upon the nations of the earth: "Peace to men of good will."

The new year of 1942 began with a papal gift of a million and a half francs for relief and reconstruction work in the war-torn dioceses of France. Later, the Holy Father gave the Nuncio at Berlin a half million francs with which to purchase food, clothing, and medicines for the French prisoners of war. When he was informed by the Apostolic Delegate at Athens of the starvation destroying Greece, His Holiness immediately sent huge quantities of food and medicines to the wretched victims of Axis cruelty. The papal Bureau of War Prisoners and Missing Persons, officially known as the Vatican Information Service, now extended its services to the Far East, and added our soldiers and civilians to its list. The Washington unit operated from the Apostolic Delegation under the guidance of His Excellency Archbishop Cicognani, and served as a transmission point for messages originating in and destined for the United States, Canada, Australia, and, to some extent, Central and South America.

From January, 1943, through December, 1945, the Apostolic Delegation sent 487,144 messages to the Vatican and received from it 241,653 messages. Outgoing messages were checked and sealed by the Office of Censorship and then sent to the Papal Nuncio at Lisbon, Portugal. He in turn forwarded them through his own facilities to the Papal Secretariate of State, where they were classified according to country and reforwarded to the respective apostolic nuncios and delegates for final delivery. Incoming messages were received from the Vatican through the nunciatures at Lisbon, Portugal, and Madrid, Spain, and, after being submitted to the censorship authorities, they were turned over to the Apostolic Delegation for further distribution. The Delegation forwarded the messages addressed to foreign countries to the respective papal representatives, and distributed those with American addresses through the chancery offices of the various dioceses or, in the case of prisoner of war camps, through the Office of Chaplain.

The messages were from and to families of prisoners of war in Axis and Allied camps, and of civilian refugees, internees, and slaves in enemy and occupied countries. Several actual incidents will illustrate the work of the Vatican Information Service. During the North African campaign a boatload of Allied wounded was brought to Italy for hospitalization and imprisonment. Immediately on arrival a Vatican representative boarded the boat and distributed message forms among our soldiers. After these were filled, signed, and addressed they were rushed to the Vatican and then sent by airmail to the United States. The families of our wounded soldiers had written word from them within less than six weeks after their capture by the enemy. An Episcopalian family in Washington, D. C., received through the Vatican the first word of their wounded son. He had until then been listed by the War Department as missing, because the Nazis had failed to report him to the International Red Cross as captured. The soldier was convalescing in a hospital in Italy, where a Vatican official found him and obtained his name and the family's address. A Baptist family in Kansas, as an expression of gratitude for news that their son was a war prisoner and not dead, sent the Holy Father their weekly tithe of twenty-two dollars.

A sad, yet consoling, work of the Vatican Information

Service, is that of furnishing families with information on the deaths of their soldiers. The following letter, which was sent and from which only the name is deleted, is an illustration of this work.

February 8, 1946

Mr. ——   ——

——————

——————

My Dear Mr. ——

With further reference to my letter of September 6, 1945, regarding the inquiry about Second Lt. ——, I beg to submit in summary a report which has come to me from the Apostolic Internuncio in Holland, under date of January 24, 1946:

Lt. ——, with a companion, was in a pursuit plane which was hit. His companion was able to make use of his parachute, but Lt. —— crashed with the plane. This was on Tuesday, January 11, 1944, at about 1:30 in the afternoon, halfway between Staphorst and Meppel, between the main highway and the railroad. On Friday, January 14, his remains were interred in the cemetery at Staphorst in the first row, grave number two on the east side. Early in December the bodies of Lt. —— and six of his fellow fliers were transferred from Staphorst to the military cemetery at Maastricht.

The Apostolic Internuncio writes further that, through the assistance of the pastor of the near-by parish, he has succeeded in obtaining the overseas cap of Lt. —— and the metal insignia which he wore on his uniform. The insignia was mounted on cardboard and signed with a dedication by the members of the Municipal Staff at Staphorst. He has also secured a photograph of the Lieutenant's resting-place at Staphorst, and is endeavoring to get a photo of the new grave at Maastricht. These articles are being turned over to the office of the American Ambassador at the Hague, who is to transmit them to me as promptly as possible. I shall then see to their forwarding to the family of Lt. ——. The priest at Hasselt sent a letter evidently intended for the family of Lt. ——, and I am enclosing it herewith, feeling that it may be a source of comfort to them to know how deeply the sacrifice of their valiant son was appreciated. Please assure them also of my own heartfelt sympathy, and of my prayers that God will give them the courage to carry their cross bravely in the spirit of their heroic son.

Sincerely yours in Christ,

Signed: AMLETO GIOVANNI CICOGNANI
Archbishop of Laodicea
Apostolic Delegate

In March, 1942, the Papal Secretariate of State announced that Japan had requested and had been granted diplomatic recognition by the Holy See. Ken Harada, a few days later, presented his credentials to the Holy Father as Japan's Minister, and Archbishop Paolo Marella, the Apostolic Delegate in Tokyo since 1937, was granted diplomatic privileges by the Japanese government. The Vatican-Japanese agreement, which had been discussed as far back as 1922, was criticized by many American and British newspapers. While such opposition is understandable, it failed to take into account certain important factors. Japan and Japanese-controlled lands contained 18,000,000 Catholics and held thousands of war prisoners and civilian internees. The establishment of a regular diplomatic channel to Tokyo facilitated the spiritual guidance of the former and the furnishing of material assistance to the latter. When the condition of the British war prisoners from Hongkong and Singapore became desperate in 1944, Great Britain asked the Vatican to act as its agent in the purchase and delivery of food and medicines. Later in 1942 China entered into diplomatic relations with the Holy See, and the fantastic rumor (promptly denied) was heard that Stalin also had asked the Pope to send a nuncio to Moscow.

The moral belligerency of Pius XII against the evils of Nazism and Fascism did not lack allies in the conquered countries and the Axis nations. The resistance of the Bel-

In one of the final ceremonies of the public consistory, the new Cardinals prostrate during the chanting of the Litany. — *Acme.*

Pius XII embraces the newly elevated Cardinal McGuigan, of Toronto. — *Acme.*

The Pope and former President Hoover discuss the problems of food relief in Europe. — *International News Photo.*

His Holiness, Pope Pius XII, "Keeper of the Keys." — *Chicago Tribune.*

gian Church to the Nazi invaders was led by Cardinal Van Roey, Archbishop of Malines, who proclaimed in Belgium's most abject captivity: "The Fatherland continues to exist and all its children owe it loyalty and service." The few Fifth Columnists and collaborationists among the Belgian people were publicly excommunicated, and the sacraments and Christian burial were denied Belgian Nazis. Archbishop De Jong (now Cardinal) of Utrecht, Holland, declared his belligerency against the Nazi persecutors in a pastoral read at all the Masses on Sunday, August 3, 1940. That morning the Gestapo chief, who had heard that the pastoral was being secretly printed and distributed, stormed into the Archbishop's office and demanded its suppression. The Archbishop cleverly put him off for several hours by pretending to consult with the other Dutch bishops, and after the last Mass blandly said: "I am sorry but I cannot comply with your request. The pastoral has already been read." In this pastoral Dutch Catholics were forbidden under pain of excommunication to assist the Nazis voluntarily in any way, and were warned that membership in any Nazi organization or active support of one would be punished by denial of the sacraments and Christian burial. Of course, the Nazis retaliated with imprisonment and execution, the concentration camps being the Golgotha of many priests and religious. But the Church in Belgium and Holland adhered steadfastly to the principles of Christ and His Vicar, and during the entire war never had to be ashamed of a clerical Quisling or collaborator, for there was none.

Unlike newspaper commentators and radio analysts an historian must write the truth even of those who were our enemies. It is a fact provable from the records and evidence introduced by the prosecution at the Nuremburg trials that many of the German people resisted Hitler and his evil, courageously and wholeheartedly. If this were not the truth, there would have been no necessity for nor explanation of a Gestapo numbering a million agents and concentration camps imprisoning hundreds of thousands of Germans. In the German bishops and priests and laity Pius XII found allies of "a courage no less exalted than that of the Christian martyrs in pagan Rome." One can write of German priests who tolled instead of rang the parish bells over the capture of Warsaw, of the Berlin monsignor whose public prayers for the Jews placed him in a concentration camp, of monks who sheltered war prisoners and foreign slaves, but it is more convincing to quote. On Passion Sunday, March 22, 1942, the pastoral of the German bishops, which had been written at Fulda the previous fall and had been distributed at great danger, was read at every Mass in every parish throughout the entire Reich. Declaring that the Nazi government was seeking to exterminate Christianity while the soldiers were at the front, the pastoral related and denounced the confiscation of Catholic schools and seminaries, the paganization of the children and youth, the persecution of the clergy and laity because of their religion, the suppression of the religious press and societies, the theft of church property and possessions, the campaign of calumniation and defamation against the clergy, the Holy See, and Christianity itself. Then with the bravery of martyrs, the German bishops declared: "We emphasize that before the authorities we stand for the human rights bestowed by God on mankind. We German bishops protest against every disregard of personal freedom. We demand juridical proof of all sentences and the release of all fellow citizens who have been deprived of their liberty without proof of an act punishable with imprisonment. With great horror the Christian Germans have learned that by order of the State insane persons were destroyed as so-called unproductive citizens. We German bishops shall not cease to protest against the killing of innocent persons." The American newspapers and government officials praised this courageous pastoral, but today it is forgotten and all Germans are branded equally guilty.

As testified by von Ribbentrop at the Nuremburg trials, the Holy See again and again protested to Germany against the inhumanities of the concentration camps and the brutal persecution of foreign slave workers and other non-Germans. The papal notes were ignored but the plea of Pius to the German bishops to comfort and assist the victims of Nazi oppression did not go unheeded. On November 18, 1942, His Holiness through Cardinal Maglione wrote to Cardinal Bertram, Archbishop of Breslau, a long letter in which he recommended to his charity the lot of the Polish workers and requested information on the concentration camps. Cardinal Bertram's letter, which was smuggled into the Vatican, is reproduced here in part.

It is greatly to be deplored that all priests are forbidden to instruct the children of Polish workers in the Catholic religion. On December 31, 1941, I petitioned the Ministry for Ecclesiastical Affairs in the name of all the Bishops of Germany that we might not be forbidden to prepare these children between the ages of eight and twelve years for their first Confession and Holy Communion. But such preparation of the children has been strictly forbidden. On August 17, 1941, I sent a solemn protest to the Ministry for Ecclesiastical Affairs against the Edict of the Governor of Upper Silesia dated June 24, 1941, and of other Government offices, by which it was most strictly forbidden for German priests under pain of being sent to a concentration camp, to extend their care of souls to Poles. There is the further grievance that we may not give to Poles any religious printed matter by way of instruction. For the use of Polish workers in the Archdiocese of Breslau a booklet of prayers and hymns was published in Polish under the title *Droga do Nieba* (The Way to Heaven). This booklet was officially passed by the Supreme Command of the German Army and 120,000 copies were distributed, with very good results, all over Germany. But on July 15, 1941, the use and the distribution of this booklet were forbidden.

Your Eminence is aware that, by Edict of the Ministry for Ecclesiastical Affairs of September 2, 1942, a most stringent prohibition on liturgical service for Poles has been imposed, so that they may be present at Mass only once a month, and all use of the Polish tongue is forbidden. For some years past from the Breslau curia we have published each month the text of a short discourse, which might be used for the sermon at the Sunday Mass. The text was printed in German, Polish, and French, and was freely used in various dioceses of Germany. Now the use of these sermons is forbidden because the Polish language may not be spoken.

Then there is this most deplorable of all grievances for individual souls, that one may not allow them to come singly to make oral confession of their sins in order to receive the sacrament of Penance. To give an example, an excellent parish priest of my diocese has incurred the penalty of being sent to a concentration camp for not having repulsed, while hearing Confessions in the parish church, a Polish workman who had taken his place in the line and come into the confessional. Now we are allowed to have a general Confession and general absolution only once a month, a practice which neither secures peace of soul nor certainty as to the validity of the absolution by reason of the lack of proper disposition.

This is an outline of the most urgent grievances. I have never omitted to send formal protests against the intolerable decrees mentioned here to the Ministry for Ecclesiastical Affairs, setting forth the reasons why each of the edicts is not only insupportable, but even harmful and ruinous to the common good of the whole nation. Along with me each of the other members of the Hierarchy, in whose dioceses these edicts were most odiously enforced, asked separately for a remedy. And in each case His Excellency Bishop Wienken, who lives in Berlin and has been deputed by the Fulda meetings to deal with the Ministries, supported our petitions and the reasons for them in a personal interview. But all was in vain. And

German priests who out of a sense of duty and charity must denounce all injustice and dispense to every Christian, without making national discriminations, the treasures of Christian doctrine, and must work to the best of their ability for the salvation of all souls, are looked upon, in consequence of this all-embracing charity of theirs — even though it is exercised for exclusively supernatural ends — with the greatest mistrust as if they were unlawfully in favor of the enemies of the present State, and their political aims.

We have been able, up to the moment, to learn little about the concentration camps, because we know scarcely anything of the reason why the individuals are sent there, of the treatment they receive, of their fate, their health, or their needs. Those who are put into the camps are compelled by threat of the severest penalties to maintain the strictest silence about all that happens in the camps; as a result they dare not say anything. All the Bishops feel the deepest sympathy and a keen sense of pity for those in concentration camps, especially as we are persuaded that the great majority of those held there are innocent. Many of the clergy of my diocese have died there — men whom I hold in special esteem and love for their upright life and conduct, known to the whole people.

At the request of the priests held in Dachau, I sent them on February 25, 1941, one hundred and twenty Roman Breviaries, and on June 27, 1942, a number of Mass vestments and a large ciborium for Holy Communion. On July 2, 1938, December 4, 1940, and June 3, 1942, I made an urgent appeal to the authorities of the concentration camps that the celebration of Mass should be allowed in other camps as in Dachau, and that spiritual ministry should be allowed especially among the sick and the dying. I also presented a petition that the bodies of those who die should not be indiscriminately burned, but should be given due burial whenever they had asked for it. These petitions were rejected.

Freedom of religion and of minorities was one of the American war objectives, which Ambassador Taylor discussed with Pius XII on September 19, 1942. The Ambassador flew to Rome from Lisbon, Portugal, and then traveled by automobile to Vatican City. The Lateran Treaty provided that foreign diplomats may travel through Italian territory to the Vatican, even when their countries are at war with Italy. Ambassador Taylor's visit was the first noteworthy test of this provision.* As usual, fantastic explanations for the Ambassador's visit appeared in the newspapers and were rumored in "official" circles. The Pope was to approach Italy with a separate peace! The Catholics of the United States were to be ordered to vote for the Democrats in the Congressional elections in the following November! Again there has been no official statement as to the purposes of Ambassador Taylor's visit; but it would seem quite probable that he informed the Holy Father of President Roosevelt's views on the war and of the United States' aims for the peace.

The Pope's thoughts on international problems and the Holy See's principles for an enduring peace were again told to the little-heeding world on Christmas Eve. In a radio broadcast Pius XII described the milestones which must be passed before "the Star of Peace, the Star of Bethlehem may shine out again over the whole of mankind." The absence of the Star from the international heavens today, though Italy, Germany, and Japan have surrendered unconditionally, must be blamed on the other principles which the nations have preferred to follow.

* Ciano's note for October 26, 1942, is interesting. Mussolini has asked him to let the Vatican know that "concordat or no concordat" Taylor would be jailed if he tried to return to Italy (cf. *op. cit.*, p. 534).

CHAPTER VIII

PIUS XII AND PEACE

WORLD WAR II, which he had tried hard to prevent and often to end, became a personal experience for Pope Pius XII on July 12, 1943, when the American Air Force bombed Rome. During the two-hour raid the Holy Father remained alone in his office, watching the bombers from his window and praying for their helpless victims. When the all-clear sounded, he hurried from the Vatican to console and comfort his terrified people. With aching grief he viewed the corpses of the dead, the bodies of the wounded, and the ruins of monuments to religion and culture. Tears mingled with prayers as the Pope stood before the Basilica of St. Lawrence, built in the sixth century by faith, and in the twentieth century destroyed by war.

In a letter to Cardinal Marchetti-Selvaggiani, the Vicar General of Rome, Pius XII deplored the raid and pleaded with the belligerents of both sides to spare the city further devastation. For this he was criticized by many American editors, who caustically asked: "Why didn't the Pope condemn the German raids on the cities of England?" Their memories were very short! The papal donation of $50,000 made in January, 1943, for the reconstruction of British churches, was accompanied by a letter deploring the air raids which had destroyed them. A cursory glance through the statements and writings of Pius XII would uncover numerous condemnations of the bombing of noncombatants and their institutions of faith and civilization. The morality of air raids on cities was argued throughout the war, with one's viewpoint depending in the main on whether he was bombing or being bombed. Once Prime Minister Churchill condemned the bombing of noncombatants as hideous and barbaric; but later, when it was "convenient and useful," ordered the saturation bombing of German cities. The Nazis, who added the word "coventrize" to our language, denounced the "immoral English" in their futile plea to Pius XII for intervention against the Allied raids. It was a crime when the Luftwaffe devastated Coventry, England, and it was equally a crime when the Royal Air Force slaughtered 40,000 civilians in a single raid on Hamburg, Germany. If the adolescent argument "They started it" is valid, the Allies ought to imprison 4,000,000 Germans in concentration camps and then kill them by starvation, gas, experiments, torture, and the other devices of the Nazis. "After all, they started it." Space does not permit a discussion of the atomic bombing of Hiroshima and Nagasaki, but its condemnation by Catholic and Protestant leaders was morally correct and basically American. Because there are in the United States many and varied interpretations of the moral law, it is rightful only to disagree with, but not to criticize, on moral grounds, the majority who approve the atomic bombing of civilian populations. On the other hand, is it not intellectual hypocrisy for the majority to have condemned (and correctly so) the robot bombing of London as immoral and degenerate, and then to approve the atomic bombing of Hiroshima as just and moral? Such mental flipflops are comparable to arguing on Tuesday that 2 plus 2 is four, and then on Thursday that the same 2 plus 2 is five.*

When Rome was bombed again on August 13, Marshal Badoglio, who had taken the reins of government after Mussolini's ouster, requested through the Holy See that Rome be recognized as an open city. The swift victories of the Allies in Sicily and their invasion of the Italian mainland swept the plea aside, because Italy surrendered on September 8 and the Germans seized Rome on September 10. There was considerable speculation at that time over the role which the Vatican was thought to have played in the surrender of Italy. The visit of Archbishop Spellman to the Holy See in February, the appointment of Count Ciano as Ambassador to the Vatican, and various conferences between Vatican and Italian and foreign diplomats the secular press had interpreted as moves of Pius XII to get Italy out of the war. However, so far as is actually known, the Holy Father did not mediate between the Allies and Italy nor did he take any direct action in the Italian surrender. He may have transmitted the views of either side, but, as yet, the official records remain closed.

With Rome in the hands of the Germans Pius XII became more the prisoner of the Vatican than any of his predecessors. Nazi paratroopers in battle dress took up positions at the boundary line between Rome and Vatican City, and Gestapo agents kept close watch on all visitors and residents. The Governor of Vatican City posted addi-

---

* This is not to accuse the members of the American Air Force who participated in the saturation bombing of Germany and the atomic bombing of Japan of personal guilt. They rightfully accepted the judgment of their superiors, who alone must answer for or justify air raids against noncombatants.

tional guards at each entrance and at the papal churches and institutions throughout the City, which were also marked with placards in German and Italian "Property of the Holy See. Extraterritorial Zone." For several months the Vatican had no contact, except by radio, with the outside world, because mail and telephone services were interrupted by the Nazi authorities. Fantastic stories began to spread throughout the world: the Nazis had invaded the Vatican, the cardinals were under arrest, the Pope would soon flee to South America, to Portugal, to Ireland, etc. The truth is that the Nazis at all times respected the sovereignty and the integrity of Vatican City as well as the officials and the activities of the Holy See. When the Pope protested the arrest of the Peruvian ambassador en route to Vatican City from Switzerland, the Germans released him at once and with apologies. The reason for their politeness to the Pope is not clear* because the Nazis were at the same time persecuting the Church in Germany and the occupied countries. In 1943 there were 3000 German priests and an unknown number of Polish priests in the concentration camps, most of whom starved to death. Perhaps the Nazis hoped that the Holy Father would protect them from the justice of the Allies, when they lost the war — a false hope, as this passage from the Pope's Christmas Message of 1944 proves: "No one certainly thinks of disarming justice in its relations to those who have exploited the war situation in order to commit real and proven crimes against the common law, and for

* Minutes of the German High Command introduced at the Nuremburg trials reveal that Hitler proposed that the Nazis break into the Vatican and seize the papal documents. Nothing came of this suggestion. Members of the staff of Justice Jackson, United States prosecutor at the trials, recently disclosed that there are some grounds for belief that at one time Hitler also planned to assassinate the Pope.

which supposed military necessity could at most have offered a pretext, but never a justification."

The most groundless rumor of the war in reference to Pius XII was the often repeated one that he would leave Rome. To a certain diplomat who had suggested such a move to him, His Holiness replied: "We have ordered all our bishops throughout the world to remain at their posts as good shepherds among their flocks in time of national distress. The Bishop of Rome does not wish to be the first to disobey that order, which he himself gave." The Holy Father is a man of great personal courage, one who places duty above safety and devotion above life itself. He might have left Rome, but only in a narrow box or at the point of a gun. In the latter event it is said that he had sent secret letters to foreign prelates who would then open them and be guided by the instructions given therein. When Napoleon deported Pius VII to Paris in 1811, the instructions given were that if the Pope could not act freely, the cardinals were to accept his resignation, already in the possession of one of them, and elect a new pope in some free country. By the providence of God neither in the case of Pius VII nor of Pius XII was it necessary to carry out the instructions.

Friday evening, November 5, toward eight o'clock, a low-flying plane dropped four fragmentation bombs on Vatican City in a diagonal line running from southeast to northwest. The first bomb fell near the residence of Cardinal Canali, blowing in the windows, the shutters, and the doors. The mosaic studio received a direct hit from the second bomb, which destroyed several mosaics and damaged numerous paintings. This blast also blew in many of the windows of the Basilica of St. Peter, even those of the lantern atop the dome, which are at a height of four hundred feet. The third bomb, which fell behind the Governor's palace, smashed the doors and windows, tore the plaster from the inner walls and ceilings, and broke up the furniture. The fourth bomb exploded between the Ethiopian College and the radio station, but did no harm except to the reservoir. The sole casualty was one Palatine Guard, who suffered minor cuts and bruises.

Soon after the raid, several German officers presented themselves at the Vatican and requested permission to conduct a thorough investigation. They were politely refused. The next day General Eisenhower from his headquarters in Africa announced that no allied plane had been in the vicinity of Rome or Vatican City at the time of the raid. On Christmas Eve Pius XII informed the Sacred College of Cardinals that the identity of the parties responsible for the criminal attack had been ascertained by Vatican authorities. Names have not been named, as yet, but the weight of evidence bears against the innocence of the Nazis. The plane flew low and circled slowly over Vatican City and then over Rome, yet was not fired on by the German antiaircraft batteries. It seems probable that the Nazis furnished Fascist anticlericals with a plane and, perhaps, British bombs, and permitted them to make the raid.

If the bombing of Vatican City, which was not repeated, was intended to intimidate Pius XII, it failed of its object, as later events proved. In September the German authorities threatened to shoot or to deport the Jews of Rome, unless they ransomed themselves with a million lire and fifty kilogrammes of gold. The Jews could not complete the ransom, and so the Chief Rabbi (who later became a Catholic) appealed to the Holy Father. The difference was made up out of the papal funds and treasures. Nevertheless, the Germans resumed their persecution of the Jews a few months later. Therefore, *L'Osservatore Romano,* the Pope's newspaper, published on December 3 and 4 sharp protests against the inhuman and immoral treatment being accorded the Jews. And, on many occasions, the Holy Father protested to the German ambassador and to the occupation authorities against the Nazi brutality, pleading that justice, if not charity, be granted the Jews. Certain of the Jews sought refuge in the Vatican, which resolutely refused to surrender them to the Gestapo.

The people of Rome and the opponents of Mussolini, whose puppet government the Holy See refused to recognize, also received aid and protection from the Holy Father. The plundering by the German troops left little food for the Romans, whom three years of war had made lean and hungry. For them Pius XII established relief agencies where one could obtain a bowl of soup, some bread, and a helping of macaroni or spaghetti. The anti-Fascists, who had come out of hiding with the fall of Mussolini, and the ex-Fascists who had helped to oust him, were the special objects of the Gestapo and Fascist manhunts. Many of these patriots, as well as Jews and fugitives from the German labor gangs, sought refuge in the religious houses and institutions which the Holy See owns in various sections of Rome. The Gestapo, when refused entrance to these buildings, invariably left; but the Fascists no longer had any reason to respect papal neutrality. The diary of Jane Schrivner, *Inside Rome with the Germans,* in the entry for December 22, 1943, notes that the Oriental Institute was searched and two of three Jews being sheltered by the Jesuits, were taken. As warrant

for searching this Pontifical property the Brother porter
was shown a revolver. The entry continues:

"Only three were caught at the Russicum [the College
for Russian Church students], but it was searched like
the other two houses. As he was going, the leader of
the gang turned to the rector and said: 'Why do
you hide these men?'

" 'For the same reason for which we shall probably be
hiding you before long,' said the rector."

On the nativity of the Prince of Peace, it was impossible
for His Vicar to celebrate midnight pontifical Mass in
St. Peter's. The curfew imposed by war barred the worshipers from honoring their newborn King. The sorrowful
shepherd of Christendom celebrated Mass alone in his
chapel; but unlike the rulers of the world his soul was
at peace. Since the previous Christmas he had given with
a generous and fatherly hand to the war prisoners and
wretched victims of every nation. Through his spokesmen
and his own statements he had denounced the Japanese
mistreatment of the missionaries and their charges, the
brutal labor policy of the Vichy government, the inhuman
persecution of the Polish and other peoples by their Nazi
conquerors, and every injustice and grief inflicted upon
the sons of God and the brothers of Christ. Like his
Master, Pius XII had been to the world the way, the truth,
and the light.

The new year of 1944 had come to Rome, but the
Romans had little cause for rejoicing. Food supplies had
dwindled to famine level: and the Nazis, well-fed on
stolen food, gave only empty promises to the starving
people. But Pius XII, whose Master had fed the multitudes on the shores of Capharnaum, organized a fleet of

trailer trucks to scour the countryside around Rome for flour and foodstuffs. What was found together with the supplies of the Vatican kept alive hundreds of thousands of Romans and refugees from the adjacent areas. On one trip the food fleet was joined by a number of German military trucks against the objections of the Vatican officials in charge. A squadron of Allied planes "spotted" the Germans and strafed the entire column, destroying two papal trucks and killing their drivers. Later, when food became even harder to find, the Pope arranged to import supplies from Spain and Portugal in ships flying the papal flag. The Allies consented, but the Germans would permit the ships to dock only if 70 per cent of the supplies was turned over to them. The Pope refused to pay tribute; and, by redoubling his other efforts, he saw to it that no Roman nor refugee died of starvation. In an interview following V-J Day Count Enrico Galeazzi, the Vatican's economic director, disclosed that one-third of the flour brought into Rome during the Nazi occupation was supplied by the Holy Father. "Pope Pius," the Count said, "also arranged to set up soup kitchens. We served hot soup to 200,000 people daily."

Unfeeling winter added its chill to the pain of hunger, for there was no coal whatever and wood was very scarce. The Holy Father ordered that the heat be turned off in his private apartments; and, when the Cardinals protested that the Vatican had coal and that the cold would endanger his health, he replied: "Do as you wish for yourselves. But in Our rooms there is to be no heat."

The Gestapo and Fascist manhunts continued to terrorize Rome. On the night of February 3 an abbey which is attached to the papal Basilica of St. Paul was forcibly entered by Fascist police under the command of Pietro Caruso,* and for ten hours was ransacked from cellar to roof. The brigands found what they sought — Jews, Italian officers, and youths who had refused to join the Nazi labor "gangs." Because the abbey is extraterritorial, Pius XII vigorously protested to the German authorities — to no avail. In April the Fascists executed Father Joseph Morosini, a young priest who had aided with food and comfort a group of Italian patriots. Before being blindfolded Father Morosini blessed his executioners and forgave the man who had betrayed him. A new name was added to the glorious list of those who died for love of man and devotion to Christ. Father Morosini had imitated the Pope, who was then giving refuge and assistance to hundreds of Jews and anti-Fascists in Vatican City.

The courageous example of Pius XII aroused the Romans to dare the dangers of hiding the hunted and of helping the persecuted. It was a dangerous game, with human lives as the stakes, but it saved from torture and murder thousands of innocent persons. Through the terror and sorrow of the German occupation the Romans walked unafraid, because the Bishop of Rome led the way. Had he not said to them: "All your suffering is Ours. Be assured that there is not a single one of your sorrows and anxieties, or physical and spiritual sufferings that does not pierce Our soul more deeply and more painfully than any personal suffering of Our own."

Meanwhile, the Allied armies were advancing on Rome through a series of grim battles at Anzio, Cassino, and elsewhere. In this advance certain unfortunate events occurred, which can be best explained and must be

* On the day of his execution by the Italian government, Caruso asked and received forgiveness of the Pope.

blamed on the chances of war. On February 11 the Allies bombed Castel Gandolfo, the papal summer residence, which Pius XII had opened to the homeless refugees from the theater of battle. Of the 15,000 people, mostly women and children, who crowded every room, hall, and nook of the papal villa, six hundred were killed and several thousand were injured. The property damage was extensive and costly, because Castel Gandolfo contains art treasures of many centuries. A few weeks later Castel Gandolfo was again bombed, even though the Holy See had denied an Allied statement that German soldiers had taken up positions there. The Pope then ordered the immediate evacuation of the refugees. In all likelihood the Allied bombers hit Castel Gandolfo while aiming at a German staff headquarters which was stationed a short distance away. When one learns that Castel Gandolfo, like all papal territory, is an island in an ocean of Italian territory, such an error is understandable. During the many raids on Rome that occurred in February through April, the papal colleges of Propaganda Fide and of the Augustinian Fathers received direct hits, and other bombs fell so close to Vatican City as to cause blast damage. The Holy See made no formal protest to either Great Britain or the United States, because, while the Pope disapproves of the bombing of cities, he knew that the Allied bombs did not intentionally fall on Vatican territory. Some writers have expressed the opinion that the Allies should compensate the Holy See for the extensive losses suffered in these raids. The United States did compensate Switzerland when American bombers accidentally damaged a Swiss city, but the Vatican has not asked for any compensation.

The advance of the Allied armies, while bringing to

Pius XII and the Romans the hope of deliverance, also increased their fear that Rome would be made a battlefield. The Holy Father on several occasions publicly pleaded with the belligerents of both sides to spare the lives of his flock, as well as the greatest treasures which the genius of man and the zeal of faith had ever fashioned. This would be possible only if Rome was bypassed or was accorded the status of an open city. Neither the Allies nor the Germans were willing to concede any advantage to the other, and, as the roar of artillery began to echo in Rome from the plains below, it seemed inevitable that the city would again lie in ruins. However, the American Fifth Army under General Mark Clark met only token resistance when they entered Rome the evening of June 4. Rome had been delivered 95 per cent intact. The next evening His Holiness spoke to an enormous crowd of American soldiers and Roman citizens in the Square of St. Peter's. "We have been troubled over the lot of the city. Today we rejoice because, thanks to God and to the will of both belligerents, Rome has been saved from the horrors of war. For this we must show gratitude to the Madonna for the salvation of the Roman people."

While remaining neutral in political matters, Pius XII welcomed the Allies to Rome and to Vatican City with joy and affection, in striking contrast to the cold and distant treatment which he had accorded the Nazis. German soldiers in uniform had been barred from the Vatican; but khaki-clad Americans by the thousands daily called upon the Pope. He conversed in English with each group and afterward distributed rosaries and conferred his apostolic blessing. Marshal Albert Kesselring, the Nazi Commander in Italy, and his staff had been received by the Holy Father once and at their specific request. During the early months of the Allied occupation, however, scarcely a day passed that failed to see the Pope and some prominent soldier or leader of the United Nations in cordial conversation. General Mark Clark, Prime Minister Churchill, General Alexander, Secretary of War Stimson, General William Donovan, were a few of the many.

Ambassador Myron C. Taylor returned to his post on June 19, and immediately began a series of conferences with Pius XII and Cardinal Maglione. Despite many rumors concerning the purpose of these conversations, the official records are silent. It has been claimed that the purpose of Ambassador Taylor's visit was to persuade the Pope not to oppose openly the crushing peace terms which the Allies proposed for Germany. The Pope on June 3 had quoted with approval these words of Cicero: "To conquer oneself, to curb anger, to spare the vanquished, to raise the fallen enemy — a man who does this I shall not compare with the greatest of men, but will deem as most like to a god." And the Pius XII who condemned the Nazi persecution of the Poles and the Belgians will not be silent, if the United Nations violate principles of justice and charity in their treatment of the conquered people. However, it would seem more likely that Ambassador Taylor only conveyed to the Holy Father the general views of the United States on peace, the European situation, and relief and rehabilitation.

Another rumor — one recurring semiweekly — was that the Holy See would act as an intermediary between the Allies and Germany. Pius XII on several occasions did suggest the possibility of ending the European War by some method short of complete victory and total defeat. He opposed, as did most reasonable men, the inflexible formula of "unconditional surrender," which the United

States wisely discarded when Japan asked for peace on the condition that the emperor might be retained. The present chaos proves that "unconditional surrender" is no magic sesame to enduring peace. However, the Pope took no direct steps toward bringing about a German surrender, and limited his discussions with foreign diplomats to an exchange of opinions.

It was no rumor that the Vatican and the Allied Military Commission in Italy soon were working in close co-operation. Starvation still preyed upon Rome and later upon the other cities which the Nazis in their retreat first looted and then abandoned. Therefore, papal relief continued, but now it was aided by the Allies who expedited in every possible way the movement of food supplies. When crime became rampant in Rome, the Holy Father spoke out against it and urged the people to be law abiding and co-operative. A pleasant example of the friendship between the Allies and the Vatican occurred at Christmas time. A group of American soldiers in Rome wished to sponsor a party for several thousand orphans. A large enough hall seemed unavailable, until the Pope offered the use of the Apostolic Chancery.

On Christmas Eve, 1944, Pius XII again spoke to the people of the world by radio, and the subject of his address is of vital importance to every person, regardless of religious or political belief. It is democracy and a lasting peace. The most false, and today the most repeated, lie about the Catholic Church is that she opposes democracy. One meets that slander in books, in newspapers, in magazines, and, of late, on radio programs. Recently a metropolitan newspaper began a new lie: "Pius XII is opposed to democracy." The words of the Holy Father himself are the best answer:

Beneath the sinister lightning of the war that encompasses them, in the blazing heat of the furnace that imprisons them, the peoples have, as it were, awakened from a long torpor. Taught by bitter experience, they are more aggressive in opposing the concentration of dictatorial power that cannot be censured or touched, and call for a system of government more in keeping with the dignity and liberty of the citizens. These multitudes are today firmly convinced that had there been the possibility of censuring and correcting the actions of public authority, the world would not have been dragged into the vortex of a disastrous war, and that to avoid for the future the repetition of such a catastrophe, we must vest efficient guarantees in the people itself.

In such a psychological atmosphere, is it to be wondered at if the tendency towards democracy is capturing the peoples and winning a large measure of consent and support from those who hope to play a more efficient part in the destinies of individuals and societies? It is scarcely necessary to recall that, according to the teaching of the Church, "it is not forbidden to prefer popular forms of government, without prejudice, however, to Catholic teaching on the origin and use of authority."

If we examine the forms by which democracy should be directed in order that it might be true, healthy, and capable of answering the needs of the moment, it is evident that the Church is interested not so much in the external structure and organization of democracy — which depend on the special aspirations of each people, but in the individual himself. Far from being the object and, as it were, a merely passive element of the social order, the individual is and must be, and must continue to be, its subject, its foundation, and its end.

Given that democracy, taken in the broad sense, admits of various forms, and can be realized in monarchies as well as in republics, two questions come up for our consideration: first, what characteristics should distinguish the men who live under democracy and a democratic regime? Second, what characteristics should distinguish the men who hold the reins of government in a democracy?

To express his own views of the duties and sacrifices that are imposed upon him; not compelled to obey without being heard — these are the two rights of the citizen which find in democracy, as its name implies, their expression. If, then, we consider the extent and nature of the sacrifices demanded of all the citizens, especially in our day when the activity of the State is so vast and decisive, the democratic form of government appears to many as a postulate of nature imposed by reason itself. When, however, people call for "democracy and better democracy," such a demand cannot have any other meaning than to place the citizen ever more in the position to hold his own personal opinion, to express it, and to make it prevail in a fashion conducive to the common good.

In a people worthy of the name, the citizen feels within him the consciousness of his personality, of his duties and rights, of his own freedom joined to respect for the freedom and dignity of others. In a people worthy of the name inequalities based not on whim but on the nature of things, inequalities of culture, possessions, social standing — without prejudice, of course, to justice and mutual charity — do not constitute any obstacle to the existence and the prevalence of a true spirit of union and brotherhood. On the contrary, far from impairing the civil equality in any way, they give it its true meaning; namely, that before the State, everyone has the right to live honorably his own personal life in the place and under the conditions in which the designs and dispositions of Providence have placed him.

Since the center of gravity of a democracy normally set up resides in the popular assembly from which the currents of political life radiate into every field of public life — for good or ill — the question of the high moral standards, practical ability, and intellectual capacity of parliamentary deputies is for every people living under a democratic regime a question of life and death, of prosperity and decadence, of soundness and perpetual unrest. To secure effective action, to win esteem and trust, every legislative body should gather within it a group of select men, spiritually eminent and of strong character, who shall look upon themselves as the representatives of the entire people and not the mandatories of a mob, whose interests are often unfortunately made to prevail over the true needs of the common good — a select group of men not restricted to any profession or social standing but reflecting every phase of the people's life; men chosen for their solid Christian convictions, straight and steady judgment, with a sense of the practical and equitable, true to themselves in all circumstances; men of clear and sound principles, with sound and clear-cut proposals to make; men above all capable, in virtue of the authority that emanates from their untarnished consciences and radiates widely from them, to be leaders and heads especially in times when the pressing needs of the moment excite the people's impressionability unduly, and render it more liable to be led astray and get lost: men who — in periods of transition, generally stormy and disturbed by passion, by divergent opinions and opposing programs — feel themselves doubly under the obligation to send circulating through the veins of the people and the State the spiritual antidote of clear views, kindly interest, a justice equally sympathetic to all, and a bias toward national unity and concord in a sincere spirit of brotherhood.

But where such men are lacking others come to take their places in order to make politics serve their ambition, and be a quick road to profit for themselves, their caste and their class, while the race after private interests makes them lose sight of completely and jeopardize the true common good.

If the future is to belong to democracy, an essential part in its achievement will have to belong to the religion of Christ and to the Church, for she teaches and defends supernatural truths and communicates the supernatural helps of grace in order to actuate the divinely established order of beings and ends which is the ultimate foundation and directive norm of every democracy.

Finally, after six years of hope and prayer, Pius XII received the joyful news on May 5 that the European War was over, and on August 14 that the Asiatic War was over. He rejoiced in thanksgiving to God whose Church and whose people he had served so well during the night of World War II. And the prayers of the Holy Father were followed by fervent petitions that the peace of the moment may prove the blessing of every tomorrow.

World War II, which had taken the lives of millions, the treasures of centuries, and the happiness of all mankind, was over. Victory had ended the threat of Nazism, Fascism, and Japanese imperialism to the liberty and security of mankind, and had destroyed the evil forces

which alone, our leaders said, prevented a peaceful tomorrow. Yet, today there is no peace, and there is little
hope for peace tomorrow. The victors speak of peace but
prepare for war. Russia has begun to build a larger navy,
the United States proposes to continue military conscription, Great Britain seeks military alliances, and the lesser
nations hurry and scurry for shelter against World War
III. Most tragic of all indications is the cynical despair of
the peoples of the world who will have to bleed, die, and
pay for the next war. They hope for peace, and surely
are entitled to it; but they are convinced that there will
be another war. Why is peace always to be sought, and
never had?

During his student days at St. John's University, College-
ville, Minnesota, the author attended a symposium (1938)
on the causes of war and the bases of peace. The first
speaker discussed war and peace in terms of economics,
arguing that nations quarrel principally over foreign trade,
natural resources, and other material advantages. The
political scientist explained war and peace in terms of
diplomacy and statecraft, and contended that peace could
be had only through force and power. Another speaker
found the causes of war in history, and would have peace
based on a rectification of historical errors. The educator
blamed war on ignorance, the journalist blamed war on
propaganda, and they would secure peace through im-
proved education and a free press. Another speaker probed
various systems of philosophy and sociology for the causes
of war, contending that a correct system of thought and
the improvement of social conditions would bring about
peace.

Then the Father Abbot, Alcuin C. Deutsch, O.S.B., a
man of wisdom and sanctity, arose, even though he was

not a scheduled speaker. Acknowledging the partial truths of the earlier statements, the Abbot summed up, fully and absolutely, the causes of war and the bases of peace. "The causes of war lie principally and ultimately in the effects of original sin on human nature. The bases of peace must be laid on an overcoming of these effects through the aid of God and His Church." These wise words were lost on the majority of the students, just as the statements of Pius XII on war and peace are little known and even less heeded by the world of today. But if the reader desires to understand the paragraphs that follow, he must remember the words of the Father Abbot, for their truth underlies and forms the nucleus of the papal peace plan.

Each Christmas Eve from the outbreak of the war until its close, Pius XII presented and explained to the world the papal peace plan. It is succinctly expressed in the motto of the Holy Father: "Peace is the work of justice," and in the warning of St. Paul: "Without charity no man is just." The core of the papal peace plan consists of twenty basic points which were given in the Christmas messages of 1939 through 1942, and were repeated by way of general commentary in the Christmas messages of 1943 and 1944. The body of the plan is to be found in the encyclicals and statements of Pope Leo XIII and his successors on international, social, economic, and religious problems. Sixteen of the twenty points (four being repetitions) will be stated below, and a commentary on each point will be drawn from a related point of the peace of the United Nations or from a related event of recent occurrence. A general discussion of peace, based on the encyclicals and the statements of Pope Leo XIII and his successors, will follow. Naturally the contrast drawn between, or comment made on, the papal peace plan and the peace of the United Nations and current events are exclusively this author's, and thus cannot constitute nor necessarily reflect the official views of the Catholic Church, the Holy See, or Pius XII.

1. "A fundamental postulate of any just and honorable peace is an assurance for all nations, great or small, powerful or weak, of their right to life and independence. The will of one nation to live must never mean the sentence of death passed upon another. When this equality of rights has been destroyed, attacked, or threatened, order demands that reparation shall be made, and the measure and extent of that reparation is determined not by the sword nor by arbitrary decision of self-interest, but by the rules of justice and reciprocal equity."

Esthonia, Latvia, Lithuania, which the United States for twenty years recognized as sovereign nations, have been forcibly incorporated into Soviet Russia. Albania, Finland, Poland, Hungary, Rumania, Bulgaria, and Yugoslavia enjoy only nominal independence, with Russia their actual and absolute master. If Great Britain and the United States were unable, because of the necessities of war, to prevent Russian aggression, is it necessary today to approve this injustice by silence or to camouflage it with propaganda as "a right to security"? Expediency is the first cousin of appeasement.

2. "The order of peace and security requires that the nations be delivered from the slavery imposed upon them by the race of armaments, and from the danger that material force, instead of serving to protect right, may become an overbearing and tyrannical master. Any peaceful settlement which fails to give fundamental importance to a mutually agreed, organic, and progressive disarmament . . . will sooner or later show itself to be lacking in coherence and vitality."

The state of international relations is so precarious to-day that it would be foolhardy for any nation to disarm, unless there is an universal disarmament. Therefore, prudence requires the United States to maintain an unparalleled navy, an adequate air force, and a large army (conscript, if necessary*). It is a strange fact, however, that up to this time (May, 1946) the major powers have not instituted even a discussion of disarmament. It bodes ill for tomorrow that in all the international conferences and in all the policy statements one can find scarce a word on disarmament. That force can preserve peace is an illusion which history has again and again dispelled, each time with a war more horrible than the preceding one. Many things can be done with bayonets, but one cannot sit on them nor for very long keep peace with them.

3. "In order that a peace may be honorably accepted and in order to avoid arbitrary breaches and unilateral interpretations of treaties, it is of the first importance to erect some juridical institution which shall guarantee the loyal and faithful fulfillment of the conditions agreed upon, and which shall, in case of recognized need, revise and correct them."

The United Nations Organization is intended to be such an institution, but the allotment of rights and powers under its charter makes it, at most, a military alliance among France, Great Britain, China, Russia, and the United States. They control the Security Council which exercises supreme authority over the Organization; and far worse, by their veto power they are above international

* The author admits that military conscription produces moral evils and that it is more an incentive to war than a guarantee of peace. However, the United States is not at peace but in an armistice, and ought to prepare for World War III which is unavoidable so long as the victors refuse to secure justice among themselves and toward the vanquished.

law and authority. Furthermore, the peace treaties which the Big Three or Five will, some day, dictate to the conquered peoples will be subject to the nominal approval only, not to the revision and correction, of the United Nations Organization. Nevertheless, we should support the United Nations Organization, while working to deprive the major powers of their veto and to give every nation a forceful voice and an effective vote in international matters. The philosophers' argument that it is better to be than not to be is indeed applicable to world organizations in the present era of chaos and confusion.

4. "If a better European settlement is to be reached, there is one point in particular which should receive special attention: it is the real needs and the just demands of nations and populations, and of racial minorities. It may be that, in consequence of existing treaties incompatible with them, these demands are unable to establish a strictly legal right. Even so, they demand to be examined in a friendly spirit with a view to meeting them by peaceful methods, and even, where it appears necessary, by means of an equitable and covenanted revision of the treaties themselves. If the balance between nations is thus adjusted, and the foundation of mutual confidence thus laid, many incentives to violent action will be removed."

The removal of the Jewish minority in Europe to a homeland in some suitable territory, e.g., Northern Rhodesia, is a humane and far-sighted solution of the anti-Semitic problem.* The same problem raises its ugly head

* The desire of the European Jews to seek refuge from persecution and cruelty in Palestine is understandable, but, as pointed out by prominent members of Jewry in the United States and England, it may not be advisable. The Arabs after seven hundred years residence in Palestine consider it their home and will oppose Jewish immigration and settlement with force and violence. A Jewish state in Palestine may be a case of jumping from the fire into the frying pan.

in the United States, as the malicious and the cunning prey upon the ignorant with lies and insinuations. Unless Americans act promptly to crush the contemptible snake of anti-Semitism, it will infect our nation with destructive hate and discord. Catholics, lay or clerical, who repeat "Kike" stories and talk against the Jews, forget that anti-Semitism is heresy against the Catholic religion and treason against the American Constitution.

The provisions of the Potsdam agreement concerning the German minorities in Poland, Czechoslovakia, and other countries outrage justice and charity. To compress more millions of people into a Germany deprived of a quarter of her land is a death sentence for the entire nation. The victors should take heed lest their hands be as red with the blood of our brethren as were the hands of the Nazis. While justice requires that Japan be stripped of her stolen empire, the Japanese people are entitled to a fair and equitable share of the world's resources even in the lands of other peoples. The right of every human being, regardless of race, creed, or nationality, to a decent livelihood is superior to the right of private property and of sovereign dominion.

5. "But even the best and most detailed regulations will be imperfect and foredoomed to failure unless the peoples and those who govern them submit willingly to the influence of that spirit which alone can give life, authority, and binding force to the dead letter of international agreements. They must develop that sense of deep and keen responsibility which measures and weighs human statutes according to the sacred and inviolable standards of the law of God; they must cultivate that hunger and thirst after justice which is proclaimed as a beatitude in the Sermon on the Mount and which supposes as its natural founda-

tion the moral virtue of justice; they must be guided by that universal love which is the compendium and most general expression of the Christian ideal, and which, therefore, may serve as a common ground also for those who have not the blessing of sharing the same faith with us."

The spirit which today guides international policy is too often that of materialism and expediency, the principles of Machiavelli substituting for the Sermon on the Mount. Vengeance masquerades as atonement, injustice as realism, and aggression as spheres of influence. In an imperfect world one may not expect perfection, but does this justify the cold indifference of the majority to the necessity of every man making himself worthy of peace and of every nation, conqueror and conquered, of re-establishing the principles of the divine law. "Who hath resisted God, and hath had peace?"

For a new order of peace and security certain premises are necessary.

6. "Victory over the hatred which divides the nations today and the disappearance of systems and actions which breed this hatred. As a matter of fact, in some countries an unbridled propaganda is to be seen; it does not recoil from methodical distortion of the truth in order to show the enemy nations in a falsified and vilifying light. He who, however, really wants the good of the people and wants to contribute to the future co-operation of nations and to preserve this co-operation from incalculable damage, will consider it as his sacred duty to uphold the natural ideals of truth, justice, and charity."

Some misguided writers and speakers in the United States consider hatred of the German and Japanese people a premise for a permanent peace, thus forgetting "Forgive us our trespasses as we forgive those who trespass against us." If God loves sinners, His enemies, can we do less, who stand so much in need of forgiveness for our national and personal sins? To the extent that we love the German and the Japanese people we shall gain them to democracy and international brotherhood. Our enemies are not as evil nor are we as holy as our propagandists and pseudo-historians claim. The majority of humanity is six of one kind and a half dozen of the same.

> For nought so vile that on the earth doth live,
> But to the earth some special good doth give:
> Nor aught so good, but, strained from that fair use,
> Revolts from true birth, stumbling on abuse:
> Virtue itself turns vice, being misapplied,
> And vice sometime's by action dignified.
> — *Romeo and Juliet*, Act II, Sc. 3.

The Holy Father is criticizing hatred not only between nations but also among the peoples of a nation. In the United States racial, national, and religious groups incite hate for one another by lies, distortions, and uncharitable and unjust actions. The arrogant condescension of the white people toward the colored people is not Christ's notion of fraternal love, nor is it Christlike for Americans of Anglo-Saxon and Celtic descent to sneer, "Hunky," "Pollack," "Dago," or "Greaser." The Rutherford publications and the *Protestant Digest*, because of their malicious slanders and vitriolic attacks against Catholics, are too frequently neither American nor Christian. The same criticism is applicable to certain Catholic periodicals, which in recent months have been "running down" without regard to charity or complete facts the founders and leaders of Protestantism. The editors and writers of these ought to imitate Pius XII who condemns false doctrines, rebukes un-Christian actions, and upholds the truth, the way, and the life without impairing Christian charity and fraternal love.

7. "Victory over distrust which exerts a paralyzing pressure on international law and makes all honest understanding impossible. Therefore, return to the principle of mutual trust. Return to the loyalty for treaties without which the secure co-operation of nations and especially, the living side by side of strong and weak nations, are inconceivable. The foundation of justice is loyalty, reliability, and truth of the pledged word, and of the understanding which has been reached."

With some cause Americans are distrustful of the European nations, yet in the interests of international harmony we ought to reserve judgment on British imperialism, French venality, and Russian aggression until we have facts rather than suspicions. Once obtained, the facts should be made known as they are and acted upon without prejudice — our government knows that both in Spain and in Yugoslavia the principles of democracy are flouted and the rights of man are violated, but the United States supports Tito and crusades against Franco. We ought to crusade against both or leave both alone. Every war violates some treaty, and hence peace depends to a great extent on the loyalty of nations to their freely pledged word (a treaty dictated to and forced upon the conquered by the conqueror is, of course, neither valid nor obligatory). Treaties between nations, like contracts between individuals, ought to provide penalties in the event of violations, which a world organization could enforce with whatever means necessary.

8. "Victory over the dismal principle that utility is the foundation and aim of law, and that might can create right. This principle is bound to upset all international

relations and is inacceptable to the weaker nations. Therefore, return to honest, serious, and moral international
relations. This conception does not exclude the desire for
the honorable improvement of conditions or the right to
defend oneself if peaceful life has been attacked, or to
repair the damaged sustained thereby."

The foreign policy of the United States, as stated by
President Truman in his Navy Day speech, October 27,
1945, places our country unreservedly on the side of right
and morality. If we follow the spirit as well as the letter
of our foreign policy, and correct certain injustices already
made because they were temporarily useful to us or to our
allies, there is every reason to expect that tomorrow will
know only peace.

9. "Victory over those potential conflicts arising out of
the unbalanced state of world economy. Therefore, a new
economic order has to be gradually evolved which gives
all nations the means to secure for their citizens an appro-
priate standard of life."

Unless the world eliminates gross inequalities among
the nations, it is idle to hope for peace. So long as some
nations feast while others starve, there will be wars, because empty stomachs do not listen to arguments, moral
or physical. Yet the Potsdam agreement, in the opinion of
foremost economists of Great Britain and the United
States, will reduce Germany to destitution by destroying
her industry, depriving her of foreign trade, and reducing
her arable land by 25 per cent. A similar fate is planned
for Japan, whose people must export or die. Among Hitler's earliest followers were the unemployed thousands
who saw in his false promises some hope from the despair
of years without work.

10. "Victory over the kind of egoism which, relying on

its own power, aims at impairing the honor and sovereignty of nations, as well as the sound, just, and ordered liberty of individuals. This egoism has to be replaced by a genuine Christian solidarity of a legal and economic character, and by a brotherly co-operation of the nations, the sovereignty of which has been duly secured."

Prudent internationalism is now the duty of every Christian and citizen, for peace will not be attained unless all nations co-operate in solving the problems of one another. The isolationism which would have the United States seclude itself in an armed tower is a negation of Christian brotherhood and a denial of reality. On the other hand, the internationalism which would have the United States become an international Mr. Anthony is a quagmire of tragedy and frustration. The first duty of the United States is to itself and its citizens, and then it has obligations to the world. And these obligations should be met in the spirit of an equal among equals, not of a master among inferiors nor of a father among children.

11. "Within the limits of a new order of peace and security founded on moral principles there is no place for the persecution of religion and of the Church."

On the first Christmas night the angels sang "Glory to God in the highest, and on earth peace to men of good will." Their hymn should warn the nations that God alone gives peace, and will take it away if His Church and religion are persecuted. Yet, another Calvary is in preparation for the Church and Catholics of Poland and Eastern Europe. The path of religious persecution leads to war.

12. "He who would have the star of peace shine out and stand over society should co-operate, for his part, in giving back to the human person the dignity given to it by God from the very beginning; should oppose the excessive herd-

ing of men, as if they were a mass without a soul; their economic, social, political, intellectual, and moral inconsistency; their dearth of solid principles and strong convictions, their surfeit of instinctive sensible excitement and their fickleness."

The fundamental error of Nazism, Fascism, and Communism is the denial of the dignity given to man by God. These systems echo the attitude of unbridled capitalism which for long treated man as a commodity rather than a personality, and of "modern" education which still considers man a filing cabinet rather than a thinking individual. The unhappy product is the average man who thinks as the propagandists do, lives as the advertisers wish, and considers the majority opinion as the acme of wisdom and culture. Until men think, live, and act as sons of God and brothers of Christ, the problems of the world which lead to war will never be solved.

13. "He who would have the star of peace shine out and stand over society should reject every form of materialism which sees in the people only a herd of individuals who, divided and without internal cohesion, are considered as a mass to be lorded over and treated arbitrarily. . . . He should defend the indissolubility of matrimony; he should give to the family space, light, and air so that it may attend to its mission of perpetuating new life, and of educating children in a spirit corresponding to its own true religious convictions."

Everybody agrees that international morality is a necessary premise for peace, and that the world is as moral or immoral as the majority of the nations. Yet, never before in history have the commandments of God and the teachings of Christ been violated so cynically and impenitently. Divorce, vice, irreligion, injustice, hate, pride have become

commonplace and universal, while the puerile world bab-
bles of peace through the brotherhood of man. Unless the
fatherhood of God is respected in thought, word, and deed
by each of us, World War III will come as just retribution.

14. "He who would have the star of peace shine out and
stand over society should give to work the place assigned
to it by God from the beginning. As an indispensable
means toward gaining over the world that mastery which
God wishes for His glory, all work has an inherent dignity
and at the same time a close connection with the perfection
of the person; this is the noble dignity and privilege of
work which is not in any way cheapened by the fatigue
and the burden, which have to be borne as the effect of
original sin, in obedience and submission to the Will of
God."

The statement that another world depression of long
duration will lead to another war needs no elaboration —
it proves itself. Yet, we are told to expect an atomic and
plastic tomorrow free of work and full of joy, provided
the government, or capital, or labor, or science has its way.
This school of economy and sociology, which daily gains
in ascendancy, is driving the world post-haste to complete
collapse. It ignores the incontrovertible fact that our world
is a vale of tears and toil, so has it been and so will it ever
be. Prosperity can be secured only through the honest
work and intelligent enterprise of every person, who may
just as well quit expecting paradise in this world and
begin making himself worthy of it in the next. Therefore,
mankind must again recognize the noble dignity of work
and the unending need of sacrifice and hardship, while
striving to improve the lot of all.

15. "He who would have the star of peace shine out and
stand over the social life should collaborate toward a com-

plete rehabilitation of the juridical order. . . . The relations of man to man, of the individual to society, to authority, to civil duties; the relations of society and authority to the individual should be placed on a firm juridic footing and be guarded, when the need arises, by the authority of the courts."

The Holy Father has in mind the need of improving the judicial systems in many nations and of establishing an international court which can settle disputes among the nations. The judicial systems of Italy and Germany were corrupt tools for the enforcement of the wishes and objectives of the Fascists and the Nazis; and that of Russia and her satellites quite often follows the dictates of the State rather than the precepts of justice. In the democratic nations political and economic considerations at times influence the decisions of the courts, and too many of the judges lack the necessary qualifications of intellect and soul. The international court, which the charter of the United Nations Organization establishes, does not possess sufficient and independent powers, because the Security Council influences to a great extent what cases may be heard by it. Moreover, the court does not have jurisdiction apart from the consent of the parties to the dispute and lacks effective means of enforcing its decisions. Regardless of the integrity and competency of the courts, national and international, justice will not prevail in the world until the nations and the peoples value her more highly than their own desires and ambitions.

16. "He who would have the star of peace shine out and stand over human society should co-operate toward the setting up of a State conception and practice founded on reasonable discipline, exalted kindliness, and a responsible Christian spirit. He should help to restore the State and

its power to the service of human society, to the full recognition of the respect due to the human person and his efforts to attain his eternal destiny. He should apply and devote himself to dispelling the errors which aim at causing the State and its authority to deviate from the path of morality, at severing them from the eminently ethical bond which links them to individual and social life, and at making them deny or in practice ignore their essential dependence on the Will of the Creator. He should work for the recognition and diffusion of the truth which teaches, even in matters of this world, that the deepest meaning, the ultimate moral basis and the universal validity of reigning lies in serving."

If every nation enjoyed the American philosophy of government, the Holy Father would not have written these words. But certain countries in South America and Europe still follow the totalitarian philosophy that the citizen is a slave and the State the master, depriving him at their whim of inherent rights to life, liberty, and the pursuit of happiness. Other nations, democratic to their own citizens, are totalitarian toward the subjects of their colonial empires. The excuse that the colonial peoples are not ready for independence merely underscores the incompetence and selfishness of their masters. The colonial powers — Great Britain, Holland, France, and Belgium — have failed miserably, and should be replaced by international trustees whose sole duty will be to the Africans and the Asiatics.

It will be noticed that the principle common to these sixteen points is the spiritual change which the political, social, educational, economic, and personal life of mankind must undergo before peace can become an enduring reality. Therefore, the teachings of Leo XIII on labor and

capital, of Pius X on spirituality, and of Pius XI on education and marriage are as necessary for the preservation
of peace as are the specific proposals of Benedict XV and
Pius XII. Sin in any aspect of human life undermines the
dominion of peace, just as an infected tooth endangers the
health of the whole body. Yet today's world, like yesterday's, seeks peace apart from God preferring the fantasies
of false prophets to the hard wisdom of the sovereign
pontiffs. These blind leading the blind Pius XII identified
in his Christmas Message of 1943 as "the disillusioned
souls who placed all their faith in a world expansion of
economic life"; as "the deluded ones who placed happiness
and prosperity exclusively in a form of science and culture
which was adverse to recognizing the creator of the universe"; and as "the unfortunate ones who placed their hope
of happiness in the enjoyment of this passing earthly life
alone."

When today we read that peace will be enduring because of the atomic bomb, or the United Nations Organization, or the armed might of the democracies; that prosperity will be secure because of atomic energy, electronic
discoveries, or the supremacy of the common man; and
that complete happiness will be universal because of tech-
nological advancements, world democracy, or common
brotherhood, the story of Nineveh comes to mind.

"And the word of the Lord came to Jonas the second
time, saying: Arise, and go to Nineveh the great city; and
preach in it the preaching that I bid thee. And Jonas arose,
and went to Nineveh according to the word of the Lord.
Now Nineveh was a great city of three days' journey. And
Jonas began to enter into the city one day's journey; and
he cried, and said: Yet forty days, and Nineveh shall be

destroyed. And the men of Nineveh believed in God; and they proclaimed a fast, and put on sackcloth from the greatest to the least.

"And the word came to the king of Nineveh; and he arose up out of his throne, and cast away his robe from him, and was clothed with sackcloth, and sat in ashes. And he caused it to be proclaimed and published in Nineveh from the mouth of the king and of his princes, saying: Let neither men nor beasts, oxen nor sheep, taste anything; let them not feed, nor drink water. And let the men and beasts be covered with sackcloth, and cry to the Lord with all their strength, and let them turn every one from his evil way, and from the iniquity that is in their hands. Who can tell if God will turn, and forgive; and will turn away from his fierce anger, and we shall not perish?

"And God saw their works, that they were turned from their evil way; and God had mercy with regard to the evil which he had said that he would do to them, and he did it not" — (Book of Jonas, Chap. 3).

Pius XII and his predecessors have given the world a plan which can ensure peace and security for all the peoples of the world. There seems to be no reason, however, for hoping that the victor powers will follow the papal plan, because already they have rejected it in the Yalta and Moscow conferences, the Potsdam agreement, and the peace treaties now under consideration. There is no likelihood that Pius XII will be represented at any peace conference, because the policies and the principles of the victor powers would find his presence embarrassing. God Himself is not likely to be remembered when the nations sit down to make their plans. Yet, all this can be changed, and the future gained for peace, if the peoples of the world would return to God, the sole giver of peace. An unjust and unkind member destroys the peace of a family, quarreling and wicked families corrupt the harmony of the State, and disorderly and grasping States bring war to the world. Let each individual then renew his own life in accordance with the teachings of Pius XII and his predecessors, and God will reward the world with peace, bringing to naught the wickedness of some leaders and the ignorance of others. Catholics especially have the duty of learning and teaching the papal peace plan, so that all might guide their steps toward peace by the sure light of truth.

CHAPTER IX

PIUS XII AND THE POSTWAR WORLD

A FOREIGN correspondent of the American press recently declared: "Pope Pius XII is a cautious but persistent innovator. He has a wider perspective than most secular rulers on the changes the war has wrought, and is more alive to the necessity of adapting old institutions to new conditions." This is indeed fortunate for the Church, because she faces greater dangers and difficulties than ever before in her long, tumultuous history. The comparison may be challenged; one may point to early Roman persecutions, or the epidemic heresy of Arianism, or the corrosive disunity of the Western schism, or the foundation-shaking revolt of Protestantism. These perils, however, were limited in scope and purpose, whereas today not only *some* doctrines but the whole creed and culture of Christianity, not only Catholics but the entire family of mankind, and not only the Vicar but the King and His earthly and heavenly kingdoms are the objective.

The enemy today is multiple in form but single in purpose. Red Fascism, also known as Communism, seeks to enslave man's soul by imprisoning his body in a reformatory State which admits no rights and allows no freedoms. International Fascism, also known as imperialism and power politics, strives to perpetuate hate, greed, injustice, and violence by reducing the conquered peoples to serfdom and by retaining the colonial peoples in bondage. National Fascism, in the form of white supremacy, unbridled capitalism, arrogant and unreasonable unionism, and racial superiority, furthers the evil by refusing to see in every human being a child of God with equal rights and duties. Educational and social Fascism, whose slogans are "Keep religion out of the schools" and "Don't be old fashioned," work with the enemy in luring men away from God and Christianity. And the wake of World War II with its famine, devastation, immorality, irreligion, and economic and social chaos is the enemy's chosen battleground. Let us discuss the fronts and chronicle the efforts of the enemy's wise and courageous opponent, Pope Pius XII.

In January of 1945 France under General De Gaulle renewed diplomatic relations with the Holy See, sending as ambassador Jacques Maritain, the famed Catholic philosopher, and accepting as nuncio Archbishop Angelo Roncali. Because Bishop Henri Dutoit of Arras, France, and Bishop Francois Auvity of Mende had failed to prove themselves exemplary patriots during the Nazi occupation, Pius XII requested and received their resignations. Bishop Auvity had advised the youth of his diocese that they ought to accept forced labor in Germany, and Bishop Dutoit had published in a diocesan bulletin articles critical of the Allies and the resistance movement. They might better have chosen to follow the Archbishop of Toulouse, Cardinal Saliège, who openly and defiantly denounced the Nazis and their cruelties, and the other French bishops and priests who so clearly demonstrated that Catholicism obliges its members to be loyal and patriotic citizens.

The recent success of the Mouvement Republicaine Populaire, a political party guided by Christian principles, in the French national elections augurs well for the future of France and the Church. Likewise, the cordial discussions between the government and the Church on matters of education, religious training, and ecclesiastical properties indicate peace and concord. However, things may not be as they seem. Present difficulties centered on the adoption of the new constitution indicate that France's troubles are not yet past. "In no other nation of northwestern Europe are there such distrust and loathing between classes and groups as in France today," reports one writer in *The American Mercury* of April, 1946. "I personally witnessed the Communist terror which reigned in southern France after the defeat of the Nazi armies; . . . the seeds of today's explosive hates were sowed in that terror and fed by the blood of its victims. Officers of the Securite Militaire have told me that they estimate the number of these victims at fifty thousand. Most of them were executed by the Communists. All this is known. One aspect of their operations, however, deserves special attention — their resort to anti-Semitism. In the summer of 1945 the French Communists adopted a Jew-baiting policy as an integral part of the 'Party Line.' Such is the fuel under the bubbling cauldron that is France today."

On September 12, 1945, the puppet government of Poland unilaterally denounced the Concordat which had been in force with the Holy See since 1925. The explanation of the Polish government was that in 1940 the Vatican through its Nuncio to Berlin had handed over to the German bishops the administration of several Polish dioceses. *L'Osservatore Romano* countered with an account of Polish bishops and priests being imprisoned, of contact with the Pope being barred by the secret police, and of subsidies to Church schools and students being illegally stopped. It also demolished with the truth the maliciously false explanation of the Polish government.

The bishop of Chelmo, Poland, was forced into hiding by the Nazis, and his auxiliary was totally incapacitated by illness. The Archbishop of Poznan-Gniezno, Cardinal Hlond, was an exile in France and his auxiliary was in prison or in hiding. And the German government would not recognize the appointment of Polish bishops. Therefore, His Holiness, to safeguard the spiritual welfare of the Polish people, appointed the German bishop of Danzig as administrator of the Diocese of Chelmo and two German prelates as administrators of the Archdiocese of Poznan-Gniezno. These appointees were directly responsible to the Pope and were completely independent of the German hierarchy. Moreover, when the Nazis did demand that all Polish dioceses be filled with German bishops, the Pope's reply was an unqualified no.

In a world broadcast June 2, 1945, Pope Pius XII expressed the hope that "Germany can rise to new dignity and a new life, once it has laid the satanic specter raised by National Socialism and the guilty have expiated the crimes they have committed." He reaffirmed this hope in a letter written last October to Cardinal Faulhaber of Munich, but events and policies tend to place the Pope's wish beyond present realization. In his own letter he had to commiserate with the German people "in Berlin and Eastern Germany over the unhappy events occurring there" and to lament "above all the violence perpetrated against German women and girls." The Potsdam pact and the Allied policy — and lack of policy — for Germany are causing anarchic unemployment, are keeping the standard of living at bare or below subsistence, and are inflicting needless cruelties on people who, like ourselves, "are endowed by their Creator with certain inalienable rights, among these are life, liberty, and the pursuit of happiness." Since an economic slum and a slave compound foster neither Christianity nor democracy, every democrat and Christian ought to demand that the United Nations, while exacting justice of the German people, give them justice and charity.

The future of relations between Italy and the Holy See depends to a great extent on who will obtain political control after the Allies have withdrawn. The interim government of Italy shares its power with several Communists, who publicly favor the Church but who, necessarily, plot against her in secret. When certain Catholics some months ago formed the Italian Catholic Communist Party, the Holy Father in blunt and direct terms reminded them that Catholicism and Communism are unalterably opposed to one another. Recent studies of the Italian situation indicate that the Communists may eventually prevail, and then it is only reasonable to predict that the Holy See and the Church of Italy will know evil days.

The rise of Tito in Yugoslavia has brought persecution and sorrow to the Catholic Church of that misguided country. Like Hitler, Tito is a totalitarian dictator, and, therefore, he must work to destroy religion and the Church. In October, 1945, the Catholic bishops of Yugoslavia issued a pastoral which told of priests murdered or imprisoned, of religious schools and institutions confiscated, and of both brutal and subtle opposition to the mission of the Church. Tito termed the pastoral a lie, but in December he ordered the hanging of four priests on false charges of collaboration with the Nazis. Bishop Hurley of St. Augustine, Florida, has been appointed Regent of the

Nunciature at Belgrade, and it is hoped that he will be able to ease the lot of the Church of Yugoslavia.

When Czechoslovakia handed the province of Ruthenia to Soviet Russia at the end of the war, the right of the Ruthenian Catholics to religious freedom was ended. The Catholics of Ruthenia in general belong to the Greek rite, which differs from the Latin rite in matters of ceremonies and customs, but not in faith and morals and spiritual allegiance to the Pope. Last fall Patriarch Alexei, Metropolitan of Moscow, urged the Ruthenian Catholics to abandon their true shepherd and return to the schismatic Orthodox Church, which their fathers had renounced in the sixteenth century. In March the Soviet press announced that the Catholic Church of Ruthenia had done so by vote of its synod meeting at Lwow.

The story of the Church of Ruthenia since the Russian annexation shows how invalid and crooked is the return to schism. Last December 19 the Vatican radio in a special broadcast denounced the imprisonment of the Ruthenian bishops, the mass deportation of the Ruthenian priests, and the campaign of annihilation being waged by the Russians against the Church of Ruthenia. In January Pius XII wrote an encyclical (*Orientales Omnes Ecclesias* — All Eastern Churches) to the Church of Ruthenia in which he declared: "These men (Russian agents) are doing their utmost to force the Ruthenians to join a group of schismatics against their will and their conscience. All bishops and priests are prohibited from exercising the rites of their Church under blanket orders recently issued throughout the region." The alleged synod contained no bishops and only excommunicated priests, and hence it could not legally act for the Church of Ruthenia. When the

Ruthenian bishops were asked to submit to the Orthodox Church, all refused and were then imprisoned at Kiev. Some have died and the others are in concentration camps. When the 2700 Ruthenian priests were ordered to abjure Christ, only forty-two apostatized and the others are living martyrs in the slave camps of Russia. The truth is that the Soviet government made the break with the Holy See for the Church of Ruthenia, and will now enforce the schism with firing squads and concentration camps.

The cross of the Church in Eastern and Southeastern Europe is the Russian occupation and supremacy, because the Reds must uproot Christianity, if they are to advance their ideology of totalitarianism and achieve their goal of revolution. After the Yalta Conference Edward J. Flynn, former chairman of the Democratic Party, visited both the Vatican and the Kremlin. Rumor had it that the purpose of his visits was to establish diplomatic relations between the Holy See and Soviet Russia. Pius XII would negotiate with Stalin, if the welfare of the Catholics under Red rule could be promoted thereby without compromising with Communism. It was Pius XI who, in discussing his negotiations with Mussolini, remarked that he would negotiate with Satan himself in the interest of mankind's salvation. However, there is no likelihood that the Vicar of Christ and the Dictator of Communism will get together, because theirs is the unchanging and uncompromising struggle between good and evil.

The union of all Christians and non-Christians under the Shepherd of Rome would be a most effective weapon against the enemy and his evil. In a letter to Archbishop Carlo de Ferrari of Trent, Italy, commemorating the four hundredth anniversary of the first session of the Council of Trent, December 13, 1545, the Holy Father, expressed the hope that "When those outside the Catholic Church observe that it remains firm in faith, powerful in works, enriching all men without distinction of race, creed, or color, they will seek that necessary union with Peter and his successors." Until then Catholics should daily say the prayer which closed the final session of the Council: "Vouchsafe, O Lord, our God, what thou hast promised would one day occur, may come to pass, namely that there be but one flock and one shepherd."

The enemy's greatest victory would be the writing of an unjust peace by the United Nations, because another war would then be an inevitability. To ward off such a tragedy, Pope Pius has again discussed the characteristics of a just peace and has criticized actions and events which, though the work of the victors, are yet totalitarian and fascistic in spirit and letter. Addressing the Sacred College of Cardinals, December 24, 1945, His Holiness asked: "Peace on earth? True peace? No: only 'the postwar world,' to use a sad but meaningful term. Today, men but faintly realize how much wisdom and foresight, how much rectitude and good will must go into the task of bringing the world back from physical and spiritual devastation and ruin to law, order, and peace." The Pope then presented three necessary conditions for the writing of a just peace.

"1) The present hour calls imperiously for co-operation, good will, reciprocal confidence among all peoples. Motives of hate, vengeance, rivalry, antagonism, unfair and dishonest competition must be excluded from economic and political affairs. (2) Men must everywhere forego the artificial creation, through the power of wealth, arbitrary censorship, and false propaganda, of a mass opinion that sways the minds and the wills of the people like reeds shaking in the wind. (3) An end must be made to totalitarianism which reduces man to the status of a mere pawn in political affairs and a mere cipher in economic calculations."

Referring to the war trials the Pope declared: "He who in justice punishes criminals for their misdeeds ought to take care not to do himself what he denounces in others." On the vexatious question of reparations His Holiness advised: "He who seeks reparations ought to base his claim on moral principles and on respect for those inalienable natural rights, which remain valid even for those who have surrendered unconditionally to the victors."

Criticizing the recent political agreements Pius XII stated: "With the stroke of the pen totalitarianism changes the frontiers of a State, by a peremptory decision it deprives a people's economy of its natural outlets, and with ill-concealed cruelty it drives millions of men, hundreds of thousands of families, from their homes and lands and tears them away from a civilization and culture, which they had striven for generations to develop." Rebuking the Dachau treatment which certain nations have accorded their prisoners of war, the Holy Father lamented: "We cannot conceal the pain we felt when, in addition to the sufferings inevitably occurring from the war, others were inflicted on prisoners of war. Their captivity was prolonged without reasonable cause, their yoke of imprisonment, of itself oppressive, was aggravated by hard and unjustified labor. In unconscionable disregard for standards erected by international convention and by the still more sacred standards of Christian and civil conscience, they were refused in an inhuman way the treatment due to the vanquished."

In his struggle with the enemy Pius XII relies especially on the members of the Sacred College of Cardinals, whose membership had fallen during the war years to thirty-eight. On Sunday, December 23, *L'Osservatore Romano* published a special edition announcing that His Holiness on February 18 would elevate thirty-two prelates to the Sacred College of Cardinals and presenting a biographical sketch of each cardinal-designate. In his allocution, the following morning, to the Sacred College, the Pope pointed out that the creation of thirty-two cardinals would be the largest in the history of the Church, for the previous record was thirty-one created by Popes Leo X and Pius VII. For the first time since the eighteenth century the Sacred College of Cardinals would be filled, but in this wish the Pope was to be denied, because Cardinal Boetto of Genoa died before the consistory and Cardinals Glennon of St. Louis, Von Galen of Muenster, and Gasparri of Vatican City shortly after. (It is possible that Pius XII will create new cardinals again this year, for in his allocution he recalled that Pope Clement XI created twenty cardinals on May 17, 1706, to fill the College, and then created one cardinal on June 7 to replace Cardinal Filipucci who had resigned.)

The appointment of thirty-two cardinals representing twenty countries and the five continents, Pius termed eloquent proof of the supranational character of the Catholic Church. "She is the mother of all nations and all peoples no less than of all men individually. She does not and cannot belong to this or that people, nor more to one than to others but equally to all." The new cardinals are from Argentina, Austria, Brazil, Canada, Chile, China, Cuba, England, France, Germany, Holland, Hungary, Italy, Lebanon, Peru, Poland, Portuguese East Africa, Spain, and the United States. They include the semiparalyzed Jules Saliège, Archbishop of Toulouse, who during the occupation of France publicly condemned the Nazi persecution of the Jews, the tall Antonio Caggiano, Bishop of Rosario, who is the builder of Argentina's Catholic Action movement, and the red-turbaned Gregory Agagianian, Patriarch of Cilicia, who is the second cardinal from the Greek rite since 1472. Among the new cardinals are also Thomas Tien, Bishop of Tsingtao, China's first cardinal, Teodosio de Gouveia, Archbishop of Lourenco Marques, Africa's first modern cardinal, and Edward Mooney, Archbishop of Detroit, who was the first American to hold the post of Apostolic Delegate (to India and to Japan).

The ceremonies of elevation began Monday morning, February 18, when His Holiness announced the names of the cardinals-designate to the twenty-seven old cardinals gathered in secret consistory. Meanwhile, six papal messengers had set out from the Secretariate of State with the official notifications or *biglietti* for the new cardinals. The four cardinals-designate from the United States, Archbishops Glennon, Mooney, Spellman, and Stritch, were awaiting their messenger, Monsignor Martin Gilligan, at the Apostolic Chancery, which is across the street from the Vatican. Monsignor Gilligan handed a *biglietto* to Archbishop Glennon, who opened it with a silver knife and handed it to his secretary to be read aloud. "His Holiness, in secret consistory this morning, deigned to elevate to the dignity of cardinal His Excellency the Most Reverend Archbishop Glennon. This gracious act of sovereign consideration on the part of the Holy Father is conveyed to John Glennon in recognition of his enlightened zeal. Signed: Giovanni Montini, Substitute Secretary of State." After the other *biglietti* had been read, a papal master of ceremonies announced to the new cardinals: "The Holy

Father will be pleased in his graciousness to confer the biretta upon you at five o'clock Wednesday afternoon." Among the first to congratulate the new cardinals was Franklin Gowen, the American diplomat in charge of Ambassador Taylor's mission to the Holy See during the latter's absence.

Wednesday afternoon the new cardinals moved singly through the Hall of Benedictions, where 3000 prelates, diplomats, and friends were gathered, and knelt before the papal throne. The Holy Father placed a scarlet skullcap and biretta on the head of each cardinal and exchanged with him the kiss of peace. Afterward the cardinals seated themselves in a semicircle before the throne, and the Pope made a brief address. Among other things he sharply criticized the agreement of the United Nations that refugees in Western Europe from Russia and Russian-dominated countries be forcibly returned, even though their return meant enslavement or execution.

Thursday morning at 9:27 loud-speakers announced to the thousands crowding the Basilica of St. Peter: "Attention. The new cardinals are now taking the oath in the Chapel of the Holy Trinity." Each cardinal swore to defend the Church and to obey all laws regulating the papal election and the Sacred College of Cardinals. Pius XII, robed in a miter of gold cloth and a cope of red brocade, was carried on the *sedia gestatoria* down the main aisle to the papal throne, as the cheering crowds acclaimed him with shouts of "Long live the Pope" and the waving of hands and handkerchiefs. With their purple *cappa magnas* (great capes) fully extended behind, the cardinals approached the papal throne singly, paid homage by kissing the slipper, knee, and hand of the Holy Father, and received from him the "red hat" symbolic of the cardinalate.

Actually the new cardinals obtained their own "red hats," which are circular with wide brims, high crowns, and fifteen tassels, that afternoon by messenger, since one "red hat" was used for all in the investiture ceremony.

Friday morning the Pope and the cardinals met again in secret consistory. At the beginning His Holiness opened the mouths of the new cardinals to symbolize that they are to give him advice and wise counsel, and at the end he closed the mouths of the new cardinals to symbolize that they are to keep the secrets of their office. Then a sapphire ring engraved on the inner side with the Pope's coat of arms and the "title," the name of the church of which he will be the nominal pastor and after which he will be called, were given each cardinal. His Holiness gave Cardinal Spellman the title of Cardinal Priest of SS. John and Paul, which was his own when he was cardinal.

Two of the new cardinals, Archbishop Jules Saliège of Toulouse, France, and Archbishop John de Jong of Utrecht, Holland, were unable because of illness to come to Rome for the ceremonies of elevation. While it has not been done, the Pope could send them the scarlet biretta and skullcap by a papal guard or a distinguished prelate. Or, in the case of Cardinal Saliège, the President of France, by a custom centuries old, could present him the scarlet biretta and skullcap. The late Cardinal Maglione, while Papal Nuncio to France, received his biretta and skullcap from President Lebrun at the executive palace in the presence of the cabinet and representatives of the Church and diplomatic corps. If either practice were followed, these cardinals would still have to come to Rome within a year for the further ceremonies described above, or they would forfeit their right to speak in the consistory and to vote in the papal election.

The new cardinals were honored with receptions held throughout Rome at the foreign embassies, national colleges, and large hotels. Prince Humbert, Lieutenant-General of Italy, held a reception at which the Russian ambassador was present. Perhaps, Cardinal Sapieha of Poland, whom the puppet government had threatened, and Cardinal Mindszenthy of Hungary, whose passport the Soviets had delayed, recalled a remark of Henry VIII of England. When John Fisher was named cardinal, King Henry snapped "Well, the Pope can give him a hat, but I won't leave him a head to wear it." And Cardinal Fisher was beheaded before the "red hat" arrived. On February 25 at an evening reception in the Consistorial Hall for the Cardinals and the diplomatic corps, Pius XII declared, among other things: "We have refrained, despite certain tendentious influences, from expressing either by word or by pen a single indication of approval or encouragement in favor of the war started against Russia in 1941. However, our silence cannot be counted on, when the faith or the foundations of Christian civilization are at stake." The receptions and other entertainments for the new cardinals were kept at a minimum upon the express request of the Pope.

That forty per cent of the new cardinals are from North and South America is a signal indication of the importance with which Pius XII views our hemisphere. Nowhere else has the Church such freedom and assistance in fulfilling her divine mission to teach and to save. It is the conviction of the Holy Father, often expressed, that, if mankind is to surmount the present crisis of hunger, devastation, and conflict, the Americas must provide the world with material and political strength and with moral and democratic leadership. Because of our industrial might and our financial power the Holy Father is looking to the United States especially for the guidance and the help which the world needs to emerge from the postwar confusion and chaos. The reappointment, on May 3, of Myron C. Taylor as President Truman's personal representative to the Pope makes possible a continuation of the "parallel efforts for peace and the alleviation of suffering," which the late President Roosevelt sought in appointing Ambassador Taylor. One may be confident that the mutual work of the United States and the Holy See for mankind will be blessed by Mother Cabrini, whom Pius XII, on July 7, proclaimed a saint. St. Frances Xavier Cabrini is the first American citizen to be canonized.

To end the biography of a living person is difficult, because the author must look forward instead of back. The state of today's world foretells that the tomorrows of Pius XII will know critical problems and sorrowful anxieties. Of these the most terrifying is the threat of another war. Addressing the Sacred College of Cardinals on June 1, the Pope declared: "One gathers the impression that true peace is moving away, and rather than gaining strength and reality, it tends almost to fade away and vanish. The more the cards heap up on the international conference tables, the greater become the difficulties and obstacles to the achievement of solutions that are morally justifiable." No less crucial is the mounting conflict between Christianity and communism, between the civilization of the individual man and the civilization of the serf, between democracy and totalitarianism. Because of his wisdom and character Pius XII can provide moral headship and guidance in the struggle to secure peace and to preserve our heritage, but for victory he must have the zealous and intelligent co-operation of all Christians.

Although the present is disillusioning and the future is frightening, "there is no reason," as the Holy Father recently stressed, "why we should become dejected or downhearted. We are many, we are strong, we are stronger than our enemies, because our inner convictions (it is they that count the most) are true, sincere, fundamental, founded on eternal principles and not on false ideas, or erroneous systems, on fallacious doctrines, on materialistic philosophy or on opportunism. God is with us."

INDEX